Becoming Baba

Becoming Baba

Fatherhood, Faith, and
Finding Meaning in America

Aymann Ismail

Doubleday
New York

Published by Doubleday, a division of Penguin Random House LLC,
1745 Broadway, New York, NY 10019.

DOUBLEDAY and the portrayal of an anchor with a dolphin are registered
trademarks of Penguin Random House LLC.

This is a work of nonfiction. Some names have been changed
to protect the privacy of the individuals involved.

Book design by Betty Lew
"In the name of God": Arabic lettering by TumizMK / Adobe Stock.

All images were taken by the author or are part of the author's family's archive.

Library of Congress Cataloging-in-Publication Data
Names: Ismail, Aymann, 1989– author.
Title: Becoming Baba : fatherhood, faith, and finding meaning in America /
Aymann Ismail.
Description: First edition. | New York : Doubleday, [2025]
Identifiers: LCCN 2024054745 (print) | LCCN 2024054746 (ebook) |
ISBN 9780385549615 (hardcover) | ISBN 9780385549622 (ebook)
Subjects: LCSH: Ismail, Aymann, 1989– | Muslims—United States—Biography |
Egyptian Americans—Biography | Journalists—United States—Biography |
Fatherhood—Religious aspects—Islam | Islam—United States |
LCGFT: Autobiographies.
Classification: LCC E184.M88 I85 2025 (print) | LCC E184.M88 (ebook) |
DDC 297.092—dc23/eng/20250501
LC record available at https://lccn.loc.gov/2024054745
LC ebook record available at https://lccn.loc.gov/2024054746

penguinrandomhouse.com | doubleday.com

Printed in the United States of America
1st Printing

The authorized representative in the EU for product safety and compliance
is Penguin Random House Ireland, Morrison Chambers, 32 Nassau Street,
Dublin DO2 YH68, Ireland, https://eu-contact.penguin.ie.

For Mama,
who certainly did not *fail her children.*

بِسْمِ ٱللَّهِ ٱلرَّحْمَٰنِ ٱلرَّحِيمِ

In the name of God,
the most gracious, the most merciful.

هَلْ جَزَآءُ ٱلْإِحْسَٰنِ إِلَّا ٱلْإِحْسَٰنُ (٦٠)

Is there any reward for goodness
except goodness?

QURAN: 55:60

Becoming Baba

Mama, Hebah, and Mohamed gathered around the kitchen table
in our Newark, New Jersey, apartment, 1994.

Tying the Camel

IT WAS MOVING DAY. BUT BEFORE WE COULD BRING ANYTHING INTO our new apartment in South Brunswick, New Jersey, Mama needed to complete her inspection.

Mama opened one of the kitchen drawers and, after making a satisfied grunt, slammed it shut, as though she was crash-testing it.

I examined the new space. The kitchen and bathroom sinks were running at full blast. "Aymann, put your hand here. Tell me if you think it's hot enough," Mama said. She leaned forward and held her hand flat above the steam rising from the sink basin.

"Hot enough for what?"

"It should be hotter," she said.

I shrugged. "It's fine."

She squinted at the kitchen fixtures suspiciously, then turned the spigot off. She hated being taken for a sucker, and she carried suspicion everywhere. She referred to it as "tying her camel," a nod to an Islamic oral tradition that urged followers of the Prophet to do their due diligence rather than relying entirely on God to ensure a certain outcome—to tie one's camel to a post so it wouldn't wander off, for instance.

I knew Mama would never be entirely satisfied with the apartment. She clocked every fault, no matter how minor. The cheap linoleum countertops, the cupboard doors that didn't close flush, the weird hum emanating from the fridge—these all felt like deal breakers the way Mama pointed them out. But we had already packed up our entire lives, and Mama had orchestrated everything, dragging me, her sixteen-year-old son, kicking and screaming behind her. She made it clear from the start that there was no going back.

Mama was nearly a foot shorter than me, but her presence was forceful. She usually wore an abaya, a long gown with loose flowing sleeves; her head was covered by a hijab that draped over her shoulders. Whenever she left the house, only her hands and face were exposed. If you asked her what it meant to be in hijab, she would describe it as a sacred covenant between her and God. Being a covered woman was her identity, and if this invited confusion or anger from non-Muslim neighbors, she believed that made veiling more rewarding. To Mama, each judgmental stare was an opportunity to express her devotion, a small yet profound way to keep carrying out God's will.

Regardless of her coverings, Mama was anything but invisible. Her laugh boomed; her eyes pierced.

MAMA WANTED ME TO BE EXCITED ABOUT THE MOVE, BUT IT WAS AN impossible ask. I would have hated any place that wasn't Newark. The only consolation was that I only had two years left of high school—as soon as I turned eighteen, I would be on my way.

As she continued her inspection, marching from room to room, Mama waved me over to her side. Her deputy. I was a moody teenager. I listened to the kind of music that encouraged thrashing, not dance, like NOFX and The Fall of Troy; I wore only dark colors and boot-cut jeans, but my ability to express myself in rebellious fashion was undercut by the fact that Mama bought it all for me. I had convinced her that I needed my large black wristbands for basketball; I promised her that the CD player I kept stuffed in my pocket would be used for Quran recitations.

As I followed Mama in her walk-through, my steel wallet-chain (stolen from my older brother's at-home gym) rattled loudly against my leg. "It will be quiet up here," Mama said. She walked over to the small balcony protruding from the living room, which faced a dark, densely shrouded forest.

"Sure," I said. I missed the sounds from our last apartment—triggered car alarms going off, the burping of engines. I didn't care for the silence of the suburbs.

While Mama settled in, imagining her new existence, my mind busied itself with all the ways in which my life was completely over. The new apartment felt more like a broken-down trailer in the middle of the woods than a home. And it was *too* quiet. There weren't any signs of movement in the parking lot below.

Mama did get excited about the in-unit washer and dryer, an upgrade from our previous basement laundry, which had required a roll of quarters, but I was too upset to be any shade of supportive. She had kept me in the dark as to why we were leaving Newark, so I was left to speculate. Was it because our landlord had suddenly raised the rent? Was it that Mama had reached her limit with the criminal activities at our doorstep? Or was it something else entirely? So there I was, stranded in the unbearable isolation of the suburbs, as though stowed away on a beat-up dinghy in the middle of the ocean.

The only place I had ever lived was Newark, in the populous, migrant-filled section lovingly called the Ironbound. I had the entire neighborhood mapped in my mind, and every detail was a marker—from the cracks in the sidewalks caused by overgrown plane-tree roots to the small local discount stores and eateries with misspelled signs in their windows, to the elderly Portuguese men sitting at their usual corners on plastic chairs. The park was filthy, littered with used needles and empty drug baggies, but my friends and I didn't care. (I couldn't walk one block without having someone I knew scream out *YERRRR!*) And when Newark felt too small, we knew how to get to New York City without paying the train fare.

What was I going to do in the suburbs? All I knew was what I'd seen through the car window. This was an in-between place. It felt lonely. To me, moving to the suburbs would be a daily punishment; I longed for the freedoms and customs I had been forced to leave behind.

BEFORE THE MOVE, MIKE MOLINA, MY BEST FRIEND, WARNED ME TO watch my back. He reminded me of the time a group of friends from school and I rode our janky hand-me-down bikes out a little too far from Newark and panicked when we realized all the houses looked the same. We were too afraid to approach people to ask for directions. "These the type of white people to call the cops," Mike cautioned.

Newark, as rough as it was, felt safe in many ways. There was a certain kinship in the shared struggle of newly arrived communities to America. Everyone was constantly teasing others for their countries of origin, often expressed through the lens of soccer rivalries, but we understood that no one group could claim to be more American than another. I wondered whether I would lose that cover in the suburbs, especially as someone whose family was from the Middle East.

But more than anything, I was mourning the loss of the only home I'd ever known. It wasn't a particularly decadent apartment. I shared a bunk bed with my big sister, Hebah; my two big brothers, Mohamed and Ahmad, had split another room; my parents had the biggest room, situated in the back of the apartment. Theirs had its own bathroom, but it was never *just* theirs, no matter how much they tried to enact that rule. Now, even before the move, with my older siblings off to college, our home didn't hum like it once did.

I was the only one who missed Newark. For my siblings, Newark was a nasty shithole overrun with gangs and drugs. But they weren't as rooted to the place as I was. Before my birth, my family had relocated to several different apartments, and my parents hadn't even grown up on this side of the planet. I was the only one who had never lived anywhere else. And though my parents had at least *some* agency in their exodus, I felt the choice was forced on me: I wasn't a traveler, just the luggage they carted along with them.

————————

ON MOVE-IN DAY, AFTER MAMA COMPLETED HER ASSESSMENT, SHE rolled up her sleeves and got to work sanitizing every conceivable surface. To my eyes, the apartment was spotless, but Mama needed to take a pass using her own blend, which was loaded with vinegar.

To escape the smell—and to avoid recruitment into the cleaning effort—I joined Baba and my oldest brother, Mohamed, outside, and waited for Mama's green light to begin unloading our belongings. Mohamed, in his dark sunglasses, stood off to the side, gazing into the woods as he blew clouds of cigarette smoke into the air, while Baba took a power nap in the driver's seat of the idling U-Haul. Its exhaust mingled with Mohamed's cigarette smoke.

My brother was twenty-three years old, handsome and well built. He stands roughly five foot eight, though he claims that he would have been taller had he waited until after he hit puberty to lift weights and drink coffee. He was on the wrestling team in high school, and read Arnold Schwarzenegger's bodybuilding book again and again, until he could recite passages from it more readily than from the Quran.

He could be showy, too, giving the appearance that he was a genius surrounded by idiots. He had posters of expensive cars taped up in his bedroom—to cover up the massive holes he and Ahmad made when they roughhoused. But his ambitions were matched by his smarts and sensitivity; I begrudgingly admit that he often had the answer to everyone's problems. In those years, however, I avoided him, because our interactions frequently devolved into arguments.

In comparison to Mohamed, I was lanky—spaghetti-armed, as Mohamed said. My most distinctive feature was my big, crooked nose, which never quite healed after a football had crashed into my face, years before. I didn't work out, and spent my free time playing video games, browsing the internet, and messaging friends on AIM like, "He's SOOO annoying!!11!! brb bro's yelling at me :P ttyl!!"

At the time my family moved to South Brunswick, the seven-year age gap between Mohamed and me felt like a century. He hadn't grown up with the internet quite like I had. As soon as Mohamed came of age, he was plotting to find work and make money. I, however, was only interested in exploring unrestricted chat rooms and pirating software to mess around on Photoshop and Macromedia Flash. But, despite our frequent clashes, Mohamed thought of himself as responsible for me. When he noticed my computer obsession, he bought me brand-new computer parts and encouraged me to take the family PC apart and upgrade it. Mohamed also took me with him when he went to the internet café in Fort Lee, a thirty-minute drive away, to play *StarCraft* or *Counter-Strike* with him.

But these instances of brotherhood were still overshadowed by the times when we were at each other's throats, committed to our mutual aversion.

AT THE TIME OF THE MOVE, MOHAMED HAD ALREADY GRADUATED from college, started his own website design company, and landed a high-paying computer-science job in Princeton, New Jersey. When he told me he was moving back home to save money ("cake," as he called it), I was further convinced of his brilliance, though I'd never have told him that. In any case, we both understood that the move gave us an opportunity to leave our beef back in Newark, at least for a little while.

I stood near Mohamed in silence as he chain-smoked.

"Who are you mean-mugging?" he said.

"Nobody," I answered.

"You don't have to be watching your back out here. You're not in Newark anymore," Mohamed said.

I twisted my expression into a crooked, bogus smile.

Mohamed nodded his head; he understood. "They're doing this for *you*, you know?" he said.

"For *me*? I have two years of high school left."

He took another long drag from his cigarette, turning his head so he wouldn't blow smoke in my direction. "Exactly," he said. "You've spent too much time in Newark already. Look at you. You're dressed like a punk."

When he had his head turned away from me, I took a quick glance at my outfit, from my wallet-chain to the seasoned shoes barely holding on. Mohamed, on the other hand, wore a royal-blue polo with the collar popped, crisp khaki shorts, and brand-new tennis shoes.

"What's wrong with what I'm wearing?" I asked.

"The fact that you don't see it *is* what's wrong. Where did you get that chain, anyways? Some ditch?" he asked.

"No. I ripped it off your gym, the one you kept in Mama's room," I said. There was an edge to my voice. Despite my best intentions, I couldn't help baiting him.

"Exactly," Mohamed said. "They should have pulled you out of Newark years ago."

To be fair, the tension between me and Mohamed came from his having been shaped by a different version of our parents, parents who had been far less forgiving. He took most of the heat from our parents, who held him accountable whenever any of us acted up. My other siblings often told me that before I was born our parents were *different*—more involved and much stricter. By the time I came along, they were burned out. Since they didn't keep such a tight grip on me, Mohamed naturally stepped into the role of a third parent, bearing down on me with all the frustrations and expectations our parents might have expressed.

MOHAMED MOVED TOWARD THE FRONT DOOR OF THE APARTMENT building just as Mama opened it, as though they had choreographed the move. I grunted when Mohamed dumped a heavy box into my arms. The box was marked "مطبخ"—kitchen. I ran upstairs with it, eager to show off my agility, and dropped it squarely in the center of the kitchen floor.

In the few minutes it took me to run up that single box, Mohamed had emptied half the truck, and the entrance to the apartment building was crowded with our belongings. Our family's entire life was laid out before us. It didn't look like much.

Mama grabbed some smaller things and made her way back

upstairs in a hurry. Baba was now awake, but he stayed reclining in his seat, shouting into his phone on speakerphone like it owed him money. He wasn't angry. That's just how he took his phone calls—I could hear him rattling off instructions to his younger brother and business partner, my uncle Mustafa (everyone called him Harby, meaning "warrior," because he was born during the Egyptian uprising that kicked out the British occupation). Uncle Harby, the youngest of Baba's four siblings, was enormous—six foot four, and something like 250 pounds—with a big round face and bald head, and a kind, gentle demeanor. He was in Newark, handling their co-owned business—a tow-truck company—while Baba focused on the move that day.

The tow-truck company was a dream for Baba. The idea had come about during the early 2000s, when Uncle Harby and Baba both worked as drivers for hire in New York. One night, Uncle Harby lost control of his cab and swerved into a muddy ditch off the highway. He was charged two hundred dollars for towing, and during the drive home, Baba contemplated the money that had just been paid for a job that seemed relatively easy. Within a few months, he had convinced Uncle Harby it was a good idea for them to max out their credit cards and buy their own truck. Uncle Harby still drove his cab in New York, but the truck became Baba's primary means of earning money.

Baba ran the whole business in his head. He could recite full credit card numbers, bank account numbers, and license plate numbers directly from memory over the phone. I'd heard him rattle off several numbers belonging to the dozen or so mechanics or auto shops nearby; his brain was a perpetually spinning Rolodex. But without set prices, a receptionist, or a dispatcher, Baba was always tethered to his phone. He had to be at work constantly, even when his brother was in Newark driving the truck.

Of all his kids, I looked the most like Baba. He was tall, lean, with soft, droopy brown eyes that matched the hue of his dark-olive complexion. His narrow, lightly hooked nose looked elegant on his slender face.

Curiously, he didn't have a single hair on his body below his neckline. When I asked him about this he told me it was because there was a tradition in his ancestral rural village for parents to bathe their firstborn son in milk. I believed him, and whenever it came up, I would repeat the tale, until, one day, he dismissed the notion as idiotic and denied the story completely: "You think we'd waste milk that way?"

That lack of consistency was one of Baba's signature traits in my experience. It was never clear whether he was giving a serious answer or messing around. He often seemed to be committed to conserving himself, neither wasting his energy on small talk nor wasting the soup at the bottom of his dish.

AFTER HIS LOUD PHONE CALL, BABA LEANED BACK IN HIS SEAT IN THE idling truck, dangling his arm out the window. I wondered if, like me, he was bringing to the suburbs his own city baggage, and felt he needed to keep watch of the truck to make sure no one would steal it. Newark, after all, was the car-theft capital of the country. Mohamed's car had been stolen and stripped down twice. I couldn't imagine that happening in South Brunswick, a suburban town so dull that it was named for being south of another town.

Mohamed gave me a nod through dark sunglasses and gestured back to the cardboard boxes. "Ready, Spaghetti Arms?" He stacked box after box in my arms, the weight of the pile digging into my hands, until I could no longer see over the boxes; I followed him blindly as he marched up the stairs.

By the time we got upstairs, Mama had somehow already unpacked the entire kitchen—all her favorite pans, oils, and seasonings were lined up on the counter. When I saw her smile, it dawned on me that she held a new sense of pride in finally pulling herself and her family out of Newark.

I had given her a hard time about the move, but in that moment, I tried to remind myself that what was good for her and what was good for me weren't always the same thing.

———

ONCE MAMA HAD HER TWO FRIDGES STOCKED, THE KITCHEN WAS officially open. Mohamed stepped outside to smoke another cigarette, but I stayed to witness the apartment coming alive, with bright sizzles and the tinny ringing of pans.

I quietly wondered what Mama was making, but I craved it all: the sautéed garlic in her molokheya, the earthy spices in her bamya, the aromatic medley of koshari. Everything she cooked was extraordinary, even by Egyptian mama standards.

Whenever Mama wasn't cooking, she was working. And when she wasn't working, she was cooking, elaborate Egyptian breakfasts before we left for work or school, even larger Egyptian dinners. This constant cycle planted her in the kitchen all day.

MOHAMED WENT BACK DOWNSTAIRS TO HAVE ANOTHER CIGARETTE, and I lay on one of the couches we had just carried inside, taking in the fragrant smells of Mama's cooking.

She was making kofta: for the sake of the uninitiated—and the miserably deprived—a cigar-shaped log of cooked ground meat that's popular in North Africa, the Balkans, the Middle East, and South Asia. (Kofta doesn't require sauce, which says it all.) Mama almost always has a pre-seasoned Ziploc bag defrosting in the sink.

She begins with halal ground beef (ground lamb when we have guests). Using her bare hands, she stirs and tosses it with freshly minced onion, garlic, parsley, red and green peppers, cumin, coriander, paprika, sumac, salt, and black pepper, all held together with a fist-sized scoop of breadcrumbs. This gives the meat enough fortitude to hold its shape around the handle of a wooden spoon after being squeezed around it, lending the kofta its hollow cylindrical shape.

Mama makes kofta the same way her mama made it, who made it the same way her mama made it. She started learning to cook before she was tall enough to see over the stove, she told me, first helping with the prep by chopping, mincing, and observing the colors, textures, and feelings associated with each step, dish by dish, portion by portion.

I didn't grow up in the kitchen the way my mama did. Neither did either of my two older brothers. But my sister, Hebah, did. She was often confined to tradition in ways my brothers and I weren't, required to fulfill a role that had been passed down through generations, and that she would be expected to pass along in the future. For us boys? Well, the expectation was that we'd eventually get married and have wives to handle women's work.

Mama kept Hebah close, to teach her to take on someday for a family of her own the role she played in our family. But Baba was often too consumed with work really to prepare his sons to become babas ourselves. I guess we were expected to figure out how to do that on our own, as had my baba and, presumably, all the babas in our ancestry.

Mama and Baba with a friend's playful wife, 1980.

Chapter 1

A New Life

MAMA'S FIRST BIG MOVE HAPPENED WHEN SHE WAS A BABY. SHE WAS born in Ismailia, a prosperous city in the Nile Delta, established in connection with the construction of the Suez Canal, where her baba, my maternal giddo—a regional supervisor for the government-run rail network—was stationed.

I don't know much about Giddo. Apparently, he was charming, sharp, and principled to a fault. (In Ismailia, while Mama was still a newborn baby, he allowed Egyptian national revolutionaries to hide out in their government-owned home, and turned away British occupation forces when they tracked the fugitives to it.) But Mama wouldn't have any memory of that place. Soon after that, Giddo was recalled to their native Alexandria: a gorgeous port city on the Mediterranean coast.

Mama's family lived modestly. She had eleven siblings—seven sisters and four brothers. Mama's eldest sister had *kids* her age. Mama grew up in a three-bedroom corner unit on the second floor of an apartment building where the boys shared one room and the girls shared another.

Three bedrooms for a family of fourteen sounds impossible, but they managed. Kids grew up and moved out before their younger siblings were born, so it never got too cramped.

WHEN SHE WAS A YOUNG GIRL, SHE WATCHED FROM THE BALCONY AS her baba came home from work carrying something unusual—a live lamb. Every year, for Eid al-Adha, the Feast of Sacrifice, Muslims celebrate by sharing a whole lamb with their extended family and the needy. The local butcher usually transforms the shop into a hub for community giving, coordinating donations and distributions like a charity drive, but this year, Giddo brought home what Mama thought was a new friend to play with the kids.

She remembers the lamb chasing her around the balcony. When she got tired of running, the lamb would catch her and bump its head into her legs. Her older siblings thought this was too funny to intervene. Mama didn't mind, either; she'd made friends with the silly lamb. Her baba may have cautioned her that the next time she'd meet her new pet would be on a plate, but she recalls that memory fondly anyway.

Mama didn't have any hobbies or play any sports. She would go to school, then come straight back home. The first time she left Alexandria was on a school trip to visit the Pyramids in Giza. Until then, she'd only seen pictures of the ancient structures in textbooks, and she was awestruck at their sheer size.

Her baba was protective of his family, and especially careful of his many daughters. He kept them close to protect them from the perceived dangers of the outside world, but he must have known that he couldn't contain them forever. He had a rule—every one of his daughters had to go to college. A degree would serve them well when he was no longer present, because an educated woman would be much harder to take advantage of. Some of his daughters earned master's degrees. Three of them earned doctorates.

As her older siblings grew up and moved out, Mama spoke with them on the phone about what their new lives were like, her vivid imagination contributing to her idea of life away from Alexandria. One of her sisters, who had moved to a newly expanded part of Cairo, invited her to come see it for herself (and also help with her kids). Mama couldn't contain her excitement.

Her baba secured her a ticket from his employer, the government rail company. Mama had never traveled alone and had no idea what to expect. She packed light and made her own way to the train station and marched inside.

She had just settled in on the train when a body shifted into the seat next to hers. It was her baba. "I didn't expect to see him *that* soon," she quips each time she retells the story.

He had booked the seat next to hers when he booked her ticket for her, and rode the train with her all the way to Cairo, to hand-deliver her to her older sister at her apartment. Mama recalls it as a grand gesture of love.

Not long after that, Mama made another journey, this one infinitely more consequential. Her trip to the United States wasn't planned—not by her, anyway.

Mama had an older sister who had married an Egyptian man in New Jersey. One day, my maternal nana received a cassette that petrified her. Her daughter was pregnant, homesick, afraid, and pleading for help. Traditionally, birth was a family affair, in which sisters, cousins, neighbors, and other women would chip in with cooking, cleaning, babysitting—anything to help the new mama. Nana was terrified to learn that this was not the practice in America.

Nana considered making the trip to America herself, but she had gotten quite old, and worried that she'd only add to her daughter's burden. Instead, she sent word that she would be sending Mama, who had just graduated from college and was unmarried and unemployed. Though she was excited to get her own life started, Nana assured her that the stay would be temporary.

THIS TIME, GIDDO HADN'T BOOKED THE SEAT NEXT TO HER. SHE'D never left Egypt or flown in an airplane before, and it was much harder for her to swallow her fear. Still, she whispered a prayer and shut her eyes.

As the plane took off, she thought about all that she was leaving behind. She loved Egypt. She didn't know exactly what was in her future, but she had never imagined it would involve leaving home. Even before the wheels lifted off, she was homesick. She's been burdened by a deep fear of flying ever since.

When she arrived, she was taken aback by how different Jersey City was from the America she'd seen in films. Mama couldn't understand why her sister would leave beautiful Alexandria for Northern New Jersey, where the factories that marred the skyline made the nickname "Garden State" feel like a cruel joke.

Mama's life there was miserable, she recalls. She took on all the household chores, cooking, cleaning, taking out the trash, all of the childcare—she felt like a servant. She never once complained, just looked forward to the day when she could go back home to the warmth of her native Egypt and begin her journey into adulthood, the day when her older sister no longer needed her help.

But as the months crawled by and turned to years, Mama's sister got pregnant twice more, and Mama fought hard to silence her creeping resentment. She felt trapped, and things only got worse when Mama found out that her big sister had sent several letters back home complaining about Mama's lack of enthusiasm. Still, she remained loyal and bit her tongue.

ONE DAY, AN EGYPTIAN MAN IN TOWN HAD BEEN ENCOURAGED BY HIS best friend's wife to settle down and start a family, and had turned to a local lawyer to ask if he knew any Egyptian women who might be suitable. The lawyer mentioned his Egyptian law clerk—Mama's sister—and suggested she might know someone. The lawyer passed along the number, and when the man called, it was Mama who answered.

Mama connected him with another Egyptian woman, but this woman called her afterward to complain that she had been stood up. A little while later, the man called back. Mama was certain the other woman was no longer interested, but was surprised when he asked *her* to marry him instead. After a pause, a spontaneous "okay" escaped her mouth. For now, her plan to go back home would have to be put on hold.

———

THE MAN ON THE PHONE, MOHAMED ISMAIL, WOULD BECOME THE man I'd call Baba, and he, too, expected his stay in the States would be temporary.

I'VE ALWAYS KNOWN BABA TO BE A GUARDED MAN. HE DIDN'T EASILY give up details about what he was doing, his future plans, or stories about his past. Perhaps his reserve added to my admiration for him. The few details I did know, I had picked up through anecdotes from his relatives on my occasional visits to Egypt.

Our family has deep roots in the outskirts of Al Maragha, a small village in Sohag Province in Upper Egypt. Recently, in passing, Baba casually revealed that we belonged to an old Arabian tribe—the Juhayna tribe. When I pressed him for more details, Baba shrugged and said, *"Our* tribe is Islam."

BABA OFTEN REFERRED TO HIMSELF AS SAʿIDI—SOMEONE FROM THE Saʿid, the southern rural farming communities along the Nile, often called "Upper Egypt." But he was born in Ismailia, like Mama, where the fertile Nile Delta meets the edge of the vast and empty Sinai Desert, where his baba, Abouzid, a military police officer, was temporarily stationed to help secure the British-occupied Suez Canal.

Still, Baba enjoyed much of the clout that comes with introducing himself as Saʿidi, whom urban Egyptians respect for having true grit and unimpeachable morals. The Saʿid embodies thousands upon thousands of years of culture, going back to Egypt's pharaonic period. To this day, Saʿidis farm along the Nile using rudimentary tools and techniques similar to those depicted in ancient hieroglyphs. They are a people connected to the land in a way that perhaps no one else on Earth is.

But there's also an entire genre of jokes at their expense. My mama's favorite one goes something like this: There was once a Saʿidi man who used his head to hammer nails into the wall. He was so good at it, it took only one strike. One day, the nail wouldn't go through. So he checked to see what was on the other side, and he found another Sa'idi leaning against it.

My siblings and I went looking for other Sa'idi jokes on our own. My personal favorite was: A Sa'idi once complained to his wife that every time he drank tea his eyes hurt. So she told him to take the spoon out of the cup.

WHEN BABA WAS ABOUT FIVE YEARS OLD, HIS BABA GOT A JOB AT THE Cairo International Airport, at a time when international flights were new and exciting. Though Abouzid intended to plant family roots in Cairo, Baba wasn't to stay long. Afraid that growing up with the many privileges of city life would soften his son, Abouzid sent him to live with his uncle in Al Maragha.

He worked his mother's family farm, helping grow everything from sugarcane and onions to olives and tomatoes, alongside dozens of his cousins. A family member once remarked that if I were to ever visit that village I'd find extended family hidden beneath every stone.

Baba lived in Al Maragha until his final year in high school, which he completed in Giza, and then went to study electrical engineering in college. But Egypt was slow to become industrialized and struggling to keep up with the world economically, and he never had an opportunity to make use of his degree in Egypt. Instead, he relied on his knowledge of Sa'idi farming techniques and took seasonal gigs as a farmhand across Southern France, harvesting oranges, tomatoes, and wine grapes.

During one of these trips to Europe, Baba overheard another Egyptian imagining a new life in New York, a life that didn't require backbreaking labor in the hot sun. Baba had never been to America before, but the thought of sending American dollars home to his family in Upper Egypt was irresistible. So he joined a handful of other Egyptians he knew and arrived at JFK Airport in Queens, New York, in the late 1970s.

———

BABA AND HIS CREW OF EGYPTIANS MADE THEIR WAY TO A RECENTLY established mosque in New Jersey. Here they were able to sleep a few nights, and got connected with steady work, mostly back-of-house in various New York City restaurants. He and his friends moved into a small one-bedroom apartment in Astoria, Queens; eight of them lived there. The bedroom accommodated two bunk beds, so they alternated their work schedules between day and night shifts, to take turns sleeping. After splitting the rent evenly, they had plenty of expendable income left over, to send back home, but also to do some sightseeing. Fortunately, one of them had a camera. Baba still denies ever having an Afro, but the photographs of him and his friends wearing bellbottoms and swank French jackets as they explore New York City are irrefutable.

FOR BABA, EACH OPPORTUNITY IN NEW YORK SEEMED TO LEAD TO A new one. One night, a roommate told the group about an opportunity to drive a taxi. Baba knew of other Egyptians driving cabs, and after one trip to a Manhattan taxi dispatcher to scope it out, he had a new job.

Baba recalls that as a cabbie he learned to navigate New York City better than the people born in it. Best of all, he managed his own schedule and could pull over and pray the five daily ritual prayers right on the sidewalk whenever he wanted.

Still, riders would jump out of the cab and sprint away to evade fare and, on at least one occasion, mug him. This was, after all, New York City in the late 1970s. But as a Sa'idi man, Baba was proud and fancied himself unaffected. He carries that grit with him to this day.

WITHIN JUST A FEW YEARS, BABA HAD UPGRADED HIS TAXI FOR A higher-earning black Lincoln Town Car, which he drove for an expensive limousine service. He still drove the night shift, but now was driving news anchors, actors, and Wall Street hotshots all over Manhattan, and making more money: good enough so he could finally get his own place and find a wife.

Though he had continued to want to send his earnings back home, he saw many of his roommates beginning to grow out of the bachelor lifestyle—getting married and starting families. Baba might have felt that it was his turn to follow suit.

THINGS MOVED QUICKLY BETWEEN THEM. WITHIN FOUR MONTHS OF meeting, they were married. They had a small wedding in a Jersey City mosque, and a reception with cake at Mama's sister's place. That same night, while Baba was still in his tuxedo and Mama was all dressed up, he invited her out to "a nice Italian restaurant" in New York City. She rode in the passenger side of Baba's taxi and he brought her to Joe's Pizza, a New York slice spot in the West Village. That was their fancy dinner. Mama doesn't remember this story, so I have no idea whether she was delighted or disappointed, but Baba would grin every time he suggested that it was, hands down, the best eatery in all of New York, and that he was a gentleman the entire night.

IN 1981, CHASING AN OPPORTUNITY TO USE HIS ELECTRICAL-engineering degree, Baba moved them to Rhode Island and to Massachusetts. They had a son—my oldest brother, Mohamed. But when that job abruptly laid him off, they moved back to Jersey City, where Baba returned to work as a taxi driver in New York.

In a last-ditch effort to return home, Mama intended to bring her newborn son back to Egypt and have Baba send her dollars to sustain them. But her mother didn't approve, telling her she had a religious duty not to break up her family. Mama's last hope to go back home was gone.

A YEAR AND A HALF AFTER MOHAMED WAS BORN, IN JUNE, ANOTHER boy was born: Ahmad. This time, the birth was less ceremonious. Baba fell asleep in the car as he waited for Mama, who gave birth in the apartment, with only the company of a neighbor who rushed over after hearing awful screams through the wall. Mama still holds that against Baba; she cannot understand how he could have slept through it all, even after the ambulance, the police, and the fire department all arrived.

Another year and a half later, in January, came my sister, Hebah, and just shy of five years after Hebah, in September, they had me. By the time I was born, my family had already lived in five apartments.

Baba and Mama had a traditional arrangement—he'd work his ass off, and she'd stay with the kids. But money was always an issue. Baba continued to send earnings to his family in Egypt and donated generously to Islamic charity organizations, and Mama felt she needed to move heaven and earth to afford family necessities. Things didn't change after they decided to send their kids to an expensive private Islamic school.

It sounds crazy to consider a private school while they were just scraping by financially, but, for both of my parents, sheltering their kids from the harsh realities of Jersey City in the 1980s (and tethering them to Islam in a non-Muslim country) was a top priority. Mama wanted us to be surrounded by other Muslim kids and not to feel like outsiders in a country in which she had felt like a stranger. Baba wanted his kids to have the entirety of the Quran memorized by heart, as they sometimes do in Egyptian schools.

To make it all work, Mama did what she didn't want to do and took a job as a teacher's aide at the Islamic school. She hoped that working at the school we attended meant she could still be close to us. Plus, the discounted tuition made the prospect more practical.

BABA'S LIMOUSINE NIGHT SHIFT PUT HIM ON AN OPPOSITE SCHEDULE from the rest of the family, and it fell to Mama to teach her sons to be men. I see now that she imparted my ideals of manhood to me. And to that end, she instilled in me ideals about womanhood. She's stoic, satisfying her family's needs without ever stopping to consider her own. She's generous, and puts on a happy face as she expends energy she doesn't have tightening loose buttons and sewing patches into our clothes.

What made Mama special to us children was her generosity. She gave everything she had away, keeping nothing for herself. The only flaw in this effort was the infallibility of her self-presentation. Baba would tap out when he was tired, and it was never an issue, but Mama would never have allowed us to see her in a weakened state. Because she always seemed unfazed, her children often made the mistake of believing she was invincible, and so we treated her as such. She endured this without complaining.

Chapter 2

A Dollar for the Bazaar

WHEN I WAS GROWING UP, THE VERY AIR IN OUR HOME HELD A hushed reverence around the Quran. It was a living presence—as if the inked pages and bindings themselves had a soul. We carried those books the way you might carefully raise a steaming kettle brimming with boiling tea, mindful of its weight and substance.

Mama kept a collection of them on the highest shelf of the bookcase in our living room. Those shelves were only for her most valuable books, all of them to do with Islamic tradition and scholarly research. The spines of all these books were decorated with intricate calligraphy and swirling geometric patterns, but the Qurans held a different air, one of pure sanctity. No art or family portraits hung on the walls in our home. The books, and the ink inside, were Mama's Van Goghs.

Each night, in the warm glow of lamps in the living room, Mama did her best to teach her kids to love the Quran the way she loved it, reciting verses in a soothing melody of old Arabic. As a child, I felt the words wash over me like waves. But when my siblings and I grew older, those warm feelings wavered, as teenage defiance took root. The strictures of faith became synonymous with constriction.

WE MADE CHEAP EXCUSES TO AVOID JOINING MAMA ON THE COUCH. My oldest brother, Mohamed, had schoolwork to finish after he came home from work. Ahmad was still hungry and eating alone in the kitchen. Hebah was in the middle of a fantasy novel. I, the youngest

Students in communal prayer, Al-Ghazaly Elementary School, 1995.

sibling, needed the bathroom, where I'd quietly play with my hidden cache of toys. Eventually, Mama's persistence waned, and she stopped trying.

Still, she had managed to teach us all the ritual practices, even the minor ones. If I dropped a Quran by accident, without thinking, I'd instinctively kiss the book and tap it to my forehead. Even as a kid, I was sure there was some spiritual reason for this, and wondered what the most devout of Muslims might say if they were to see me rushing and nearly hitting myself in the head with the book.

MUSLIM RITUALS ARE STILL IMPLANTED INTO MY MUSCLE MEMORY, and there seemed to be a Muslim tradition for pretty much everything. Getting in the car? There's a Muslim way to do it. Wiping your butt? There's a Muslim way. Falling asleep? Waking up? Eating breakfast? There's even a special Muslim way to greet someone after they've groomed: Na'eeman. I didn't know what it translated to in English; I said it because that's what you say.

I see Islam now like a spiritual piggy bank: the more you commit to it, the more you get out of it. But little kids aren't asking such big questions. I wanted to know how to get out of doing homework, not how to make sense of the universe. What happens when you're trying to guide someone down a path that they didn't seek out for themselves?

FROM THE TIME I WAS THREE OR FOUR YEARS OLD, I JOINED BABA AND my brothers in the men's section of the mosque, and while the adults lined up to perform the congregational ritual prayer, I would seize my temporary freedom and use Baba as my personal jungle gym, clinging to his back while he focused on not flinching.

One day, after the prayer, the men and women dispersed, leaving behind a vast carpeted expanse, and the mosque was transformed into something of a sports arena. One of the boys closer to my brothers' age retrieved a football from the imam's office, and Mohamed and Ahmad, with their mischievous grins, dashed off to play.

THE BOYS PLAYED A STRIPPED-DOWN VERSION OF TACKLE FOOTBALL, called Kill the Man with the Ball. Imagine rugby but no rules, no points, and no goals—a primal game of chase that made the empty mosque reverberate with squeals of laughter and anguish. It was usually enough fun for me to watch from a safe distance, off to the side, but one time I took off after them, a mere four-year-old in pursuit of a pack of kids between eleven and fourteen.

I threw myself into the mix, tugging at my brothers' arms and legs as they disappeared into the dog pile, but they were too absorbed in the game even to notice me. I ran around attempting to pick up speed by waving my arms like a windmill, though I never got close to the ball.

When Ahmad finally spotted me, he burst into laughter. "Look who's joining in!" he called out. Suddenly the game paused. All eyes turned to the little kid weaving through the chaos. There was no malice, but I couldn't shake the feeling of being out of place, like I was the butt of some joke; I pouted and retreated to Baba's side.

He was busy, deep in conversation with another dad, both making light conversation while waiting for their sons to exhaust themselves. I tugged at Baba's pants, craving his attention.

"What is it?" he asked me gently in Arabic, his eyes still on his friend.

"Can we go home now?" I pleaded, putting on my best sad-boy voice. He flashed me a smile, then turned back to his conversation.

Lingering at his side, I glanced over at the other kids just as one of them yelled, "Get him!" and sent another boy crashing to the carpet.

"Baba, can we leave?" I insisted, tugging at his pants again.

He looked down at me, still smiling, and nodded, but he didn't turn away.

"Baba?" I persisted.

Finally, he relented, and stooped to my level, "إِنَّ ٱللَّهَ مَعَ ٱلصَّٰبِرِينَ" Innallaha maʿa as-sabireen, he reassured me, quoting a verse from the

Quran that means, "Allah is truly with those who are patient." Satisfied, he resumed his conversation as if he'd solved all my problems.

"Can I have a dollar, then?" I asked eagerly. I was young, but I'd already learned to ask Baba for candy money whenever he was with his peers at the mosque. It worked every time.

He dug into his wallet, pulled out a giant fold of dollar bills, and handed me one. My mind was already on the shop inside the mosque. But before I could dash off, Baba grabbed my hand and held it firmly, imparting yet another lesson.

"Aymann, the Prophet, peace be upon him, once said that a person who doesn't thank others isn't truly thankful to Allah."

"Shukran!" I said, thanking him in Arabic, before darting off to satisfy my craving for Airheads.

I admired Baba for being a walking Islamic encyclopedia, but as I got older, his attachment to Islamic lessons often made me feel I was being parented by an action figure with a pull-tab on its back.

ON THE BOTTOM FLOOR OF THAT MOSQUE WAS THE ISLAMIC SCHOOL, Al-Ghazaly Elementary, named for the most influential jurist from Islam's eleventh-century golden age, and the beating heart for the Muslim community in that area of New Jersey, particularly for my family. It was among the first K–12 Islamic schools and community centers in the state, established by the first wave of Egyptian migrants to come to the United States, mostly highly educated doctors and scientists. The school became a magnet for Egyptian Muslim families like ours.

I CAN STILL REMEMBER SUBTLE DETAILS FROM THE MORNING OF MY first day of school.

Mama rushed my siblings but took her time dressing me in the school's uniform: a white shirt with a collar, and navy pants. I was excited to be finally wearing that uniform, to be like my older siblings (I'm pretty sure it belonged to one or both brothers before it became mine; Hebah required a pristine white hijab as part of hers).

"Ya salam! Ya gameel!" Oh harmony/peace. You beautiful. Mama exclaimed. I remember feeling extra warm as Mama pressed her pursed lips against my cheek.

It was all excitement until Mama turned her head to check the wall clock by the front door. Suddenly her tone flipped.

"Have you eaten?" she asked me. There were only crumbs left from the fuul-and-falafel breakfast on the kitchen table; my older brothers had made quick work of it. "Khalas"—Enough—Mama assured me. "I'll get you food from the school," she said in Arabic.

Mama was dressed in a pristine, freshly ironed abaya, adorned with beautiful buttons and embroidered patterns, a traditional Arab gown that she had prepared for a special occasion. It was her first day at school, too.

Just as everyone was ready, Baba arrived home from a long night's driving in New York. He looked exhausted, though he stopped to give me a pat on the back before shutting the door to the bedroom behind him—just enough attention to give me a surge of confidence.

Ready as ever, I followed my brothers out the front door. Twenty minutes later, past two drawbridges and into one of the most neglected sections of Jersey City, we arrived at school.

Hebah put her arm around me and led me to the rear of the building, where students entered. Mama walked right behind us, but peeled away to report to the principal.

I always saw Hebah as an adult. She was sensitive and didn't shy away from responsibility, which gave her an acute awareness of when I needed an open hand to hold, and when I needed a nudge to be okay on my own.

She walked me over to the kindergarten class, brushed my clothes to remove any lint or crumbs, and rubbed her thumbs over my messy eyebrows. If she felt I would be okay, I knew I would be, too.

A few other new kindergartners were scattered around the miniature desks inside the classroom. I sat myself down next to a boy who was sitting alone and confidently offered my name.

"I'm Aymann," I said.

"I'm Ahmed," he answered.

AHMED STOOD OUT NEXT TO THE OTHER ARAB KIDS, WHO LOOKED
more like me, with brown skin and black hair. He had light skin, wavy
blond hair, and bright-blue eyes. He looked American to me, but he
was Egyptian, too. *I didn't know we could look like that,* I thought.

He opened his lunchbox to show me what was inside. "My mama
told me to wait until everyone else was eating before I eat mine," he
said, pulling out all the contents.

And just as I was about to say something, I slipped out of my chair
and fell onto the ground. My arm holding my plastic lunchbox flung
out behind me, and the box hit the ground and popped open.

Ahmed, seeing the snacks sprawled out behind me and the look of
utter defeat on my face, couldn't contain himself. He laughed so hard
that it made all the other kindergartners laugh, too. Even I couldn't
keep myself from giggling. The teacher ran over and helped me back
into my seat. Ahmed and I became inseparable after that.

OUR FRIENDSHIP CARRIED OVER INTO FIRST GRADE. IN ONE CLASS,
while we were supposed to be sitting quietly tracing letters on a work-
sheet, I teased him with a story about how I kept a pet tiger at home.

"Sometimes it sneaks into my lunchbox and eats my snacks. Actually, I think I can hear it in there right now," I said, holding the lunchbox up to my ear, doing my best to keep the ruse going.

The teacher took notice. "Aymann, come here," she said from the
front of the classroom.

I put the lunchbox down and walked slowly toward the teacher,
taking the smallest steps possible.

"Today, Aymann," the teacher said with a sigh. "Do you want me
to call your mom in here?" she threatened. I straightened up and came
right away after that. Teachers were quick to invoke my mama as a
way to coax me into good behavior during the school day.

By third grade, Ahmed and I had expanded our clique to include all the boys in our class. Almost all of us were children of Arab migrants, mostly Egyptians and Palestinians. I wasn't even the only Aymann in our class (except the other one spelled it "Ayman," which was a big deal between the two of us).

Older classes were gender-segregated, but in the younger classes we were good friends with the girls. During lunch period, after we had finished eating, one girl wanted to play a game none of us had ever heard of. She had with her a sheet of paper and a big blue Crayola marker.

"My older sister taught me how to do it," she explained. "It's called MASH."

SHE WROTE "MASH" IN BIG LETTERS AT THE TOP OF THE PAGE, AND picked one of the boys to start. "Ahmed," she said, smiling, as she jotted down some categories on the sheet: "Wife," "Kids," "Job," "Car," "House," "City." "Who do we think Ahmed will marry?" she asked the group. The boys jumped in, shouting names of girls in our class as the girl quickly jotted them down.

"And how many kids will they have?" she asked. We eagerly threw out absurd numbers—five, seventy, ten thousand. We went through all the categories.

When everything was filled out, she turned her attention to Ahmed and began drawing loops in the shape of a spiral on a blank part of the page.

"Okay. Tell me when to stop," she said.

Ahmed didn't wait. "Stop!"

She counted the number of loops she had just drawn. "Okay. So . . . your number is six. And so now I'm going to cross out every sixth thing, until there's only one left in each category."

We watched as she went down the list, crossing answers out as she did so. When she was finished, she held the paper up.

"Ahmed. You're going to marry . . . Maryam!" she announced with authority. Ahmed blushed, and Maryam nervously laughed. She continued, shouting over everyone's laughter.

"You're going to have . . . seventy kids!!

"You're going to work as . . . a butler!!

"You're going to drive a . . . garbage truck!!

"You're going to live in a . . . mansion!

"That will be in . . . Poopville!"

We lost our minds, laughing so hard that other kids came over to see what we were up to. We played the game a few more times. I don't remember what my future was, although I remember that I was going to marry Michael Jackson.

The game was innocent enough, until a grown-up got involved. A teacher must have overheard us making jokes about one of us being married to another, and it snowballed into a scandal.

"AYMANN ISMAIL, COME STRAIGHT TO THE PRINCIPAL'S OFFICE," a booming voice said over the intercom. Specific kids weren't usually called up like that.

My third-grade teacher opened the door to her classroom, inviting me to leave. The classroom was quiet as I got up.

The principal was terrifying. I felt like a bug that could be squashed out of existence at any second.

"Are you going to tell me the truth?" the principal began.

"About what?" I genuinely had no idea what this was about.

"Do you want me to call your mom over here? I can call her over the intercom if you like," she threatened. I slumped in my seat. *This threat again,* I thought.

"But I didn't do anything!" I protested.

"Somebody told me you're playing boyfriend and girlfriend," she said.

I was in shock.

She popped open the drawer in her desk and reached in. "We're Muslims. We don't have boyfriends and girlfriends. It's *haram,*" she said.

The principal exposed a pair of scissors—not the blunted kind we used in third grade, but the sharp metal ones for adults to use. My eyes immediately fixed on the sharp ends of the scissors.

"Did you know that words hurt?" she asked menacingly. "Do you want to hurt people? Because, as Muslims, you shouldn't. You need to be careful with your tongue. And you need to prove to me that you can use your tongue responsibly. Or I'll cut it out. Got it?"

I was petrified. I don't think I could have said anything even if I'd tried. She snapped the scissors in between her fingers. I stared forward, using all my focus on showing her I was impervious to her little lesson.

"Got it? Now go back to class," the principal instructed. Without saying a word, I stood up and left, feeling like I had just taken a jab to the gut, feeling betrayed. The people in charge had revealed themselves to be even more childish than the students.

I did immediately stop any talk about boyfriends and girlfriends. Some other kids kept the game going, but I stayed quiet and isolated myself during lunch periods. I was scared.

THE FOLLOWING YEAR, IN FOURTH GRADE, CLASSES WERE SEPARATED by gender. The math teacher liked to mock us boys, saying things like "The girls' class is already on the next lesson; why are we having such a hard time with this one?" So did the English teacher: "Why can't you all sit quietly and pay attention, like the girls?"

An unspoken rivalry developed between the sexes. We still shared lunch periods with the girls, sitting in the same general multipurpose area, but there was a new air of resentment on the boys' side. Girls we'd played MASH with during lunches just a year before became targets for ridicule.

"Are you even allowed to wear that?" one boy teased a girl who wore tights beneath her skirt.

"When we're praying, can you smell our farts?" another boy jeered—boys had to bend all the way over in front of the girls to pray.

This resentment stuck, and only got worse. The school facilitated more girls-versus-boys activities under the guise of encouraging us through competition. The girls seemed to get better grades, maintain better attendance, and collect more money during fund-raising drives. Because the boys couldn't stand losing so regularly, we made it less cool among ourselves to be smart and punctual, and winning those competitions became a thing only losers cared about. This helped us cope, but it screwed up our friendships with the girls forever.

As a result, the boys became averse to school and religious rules, and I, too, considered myself one of the bad boys. It came out in silly ways. In gym, I huddled with a bunch of the boys in the back of the room and dared them to prove they were cool by saying a curse word. The boys giggled with excitement over the prospect of doing something naughty.

"Go ahead, say a curse. Any curse." One by one, the boys gave it a try.

"Fuck."

"Ass."

"Fart."

We laughed extra-hard at that last one.

"That's not a real curse!" I challenged, "You have to say a *real* one." The boy who'd said it looked timid and afraid. He took a breath, glanced upward like he was aware he was about to disappoint God, and then whispered in his quietest voice: "Bitch."

We went nuts—we'd just hit a home run—and chanted "Bitch" in unison. Ripping ourselves away from trying to be perfect together, we could now revel in the freedom that came with being bad.

IT BECAME INCREASINGLY DIFFICULT FOR ME TO TAKE RELIGION seriously. During afternoon prayers at school, we'd all line up in the multipurpose room—where we also had assemblies and lunch—and the principal would inspect every detail of our prayer posture and correct us. When he walked past my row, I'd brace myself, expecting the swift touch of his hairy knuckles.

I focused on appearing deeply absorbed in prayer, trying to embody the trancelike state expected of us. But it wasn't enough. The principal stopped in front of me, grabbed my arms, and repositioned them, placing my right over my left with a satisfied grunt, before moving on to the next student. Just a brief gesture, but the public correction made me hate prayer.

At home, Mama seemed busier than ever, and as I grew more independent, her involvement in our daily lives dwindled. Mohamed was fixated on getting stronger, pouring the money he earned lifeguarding into a home gym he set up in our parents' room. Ahmad, meanwhile, was growing taller and sharper, often trolling Mohamed by blasting heavy metal from a stereo they'd smuggled into their shared room professing he couldn't sleep without the noise. Their fights were frequent and brutal, but when they weren't at each other's throats, they were scheming together.

One day, they secretly brought home a Nintendo 64, swearing me to secrecy since Mama would've deemed it un-Islamic. Unable to resist the urge to brag, I sneaked out a few game cartridges to impress my friends. Encouraged by the attention, I later took Mohamed's prized possession—a Michael Jordan rookie card—but lost it when a friend borrowed it and never returned it. Mohamed's fury was terrifying, and while Ahmad found the whole thing hilariously entertaining, it destroyed what little trust Mohamed had in me. To him, I was nothing more than a thief; our already tenuous relationship crumbled.

BY THE TIME I'D REACHED FIFTH GRADE, MY FAITH WAS HANGING ON by a thread. I went through the motions, performing the bare minimum for the adults, and never caring about what any of it meant.

This attitude reached a breaking point one day before Quran class. The boys were waiting in the hallway while the girls collected their things and exited the classroom.

As I took my seat, I noticed a lunchbox left behind on one of the desks. I grabbed it and stepped back into the hallway. "Hey! Did someone leave this behind?" I called out toward the group of girls.

One of them, shy and quiet, came back to retrieve it.

"Thanks," she murmured, then went to rejoin her classmates. But as I turned to head back to my seat, I was intercepted by our Quran teacher.

"What was that?" he asked, his tone heavy with suspicion.

"Nothing," I replied, already bracing myself.

"Don't sit down. Come here," he commanded.

"Here we go," I muttered under my breath, just loud enough for the other boys to catch it. I turned to face him, squaring my shoulders. "What is it?" I asked, unable to hide the edge in my voice.

"Go stand in the corner with your arms up," he ordered. This was his signature punishment. At first, it didn't seem like much, but after a few minutes, one's arms felt like lead, and the tingling in the fingers would turn to a dull, aching throb.

I'd had enough.

"No. I didn't do anything!" I shot back, my voice rising. "I was being nice. So fucking what!" It was a line I'd picked up from a Metallica song my brother Ahmad liked. A collective gasp emerged from the boys behind me.

In a flash, the Quran teacher grabbed my collar, yanking me off balance, and shoved me toward the door. The doorknob jabbed hard into my stomach, like a punch, knocking the wind out of me, forming a bruise. I staggered back. Even though it hurt, I didn't resist—I knew I'd crossed a line. Swearing in front of an Islamic scholar was unforgivable, and I'd paid the price.

That outburst was enough to earn me a day's suspension and an expulsion from his class. But that wasn't the worst of it. When Mama found out, I tried to explain what had happened—that I was only punished because I returned a girl's lunchbox, and that the teacher had left a bruise on my stomach. I lifted my shirt, showing her the mark, hoping for some kind of support.

But Mama waved it off. "I know him. He would never hurt you," she said dismissively. In hindsight, I understand why she didn't push it further. In our tight-knit community, just one incident would be enough to spark a cascade of consequences. With most of the teachers being new arrivals from abroad, the school already struggled to staff roles with qualified science, English, and math instructors. This Quran teacher, educated at Al-Azhar University—one of the most prestigious Islamic learning institutions in the world—was considered a cornerstone of this school. If my allegation had been proven true and the Quran teacher fired, he would have left a void that no one was prepared to fill. For Mama, it may have felt like a lose-lose situation, forcing her to prioritize keeping the fragile threads that held our small world together from unraveling.

But I didn't see it that way. I felt betrayed. From that point on, I gave up trying to be the "good kid." I saw no point in following rules that only led to more punishment. I lost the remainder of my faith that day.

IN THE FOLLOWING YEARS, IT BECAME MY TURN TO ENGAGE IN CHAOS on the mosque carpet after prayers. We play-fought, and played contact sports as if we were in an arena. On occasion, my friends and I would venture outside to the Crown Fried Chicken two blocks away. It was a dangerous time in that area of Jersey City, but we felt safe in packs.

One summer day, after Friday prayer was over, I asked Mama for a dollar to buy a soda, but she refused: she had a bad feeling she couldn't explain, and urged me to stay inside the mosque. I joined my friends anyway.

She was right to worry. We were ambushed inside the shop by local kids, and a huge fight spilled out onto the parking lot of the chicken joint. With the kids chasing us, we ran back to the mosque and shut the door behind us, just in time. I told Mama what happened, and she told the school. Soon after that, we were enrolled in "Islamic Karate" classes.

KARATE CLASS IN THE MOSQUE FELT SILLY. IT WAS ONCE A WEEK WITH an instructor who asked us to call him "Sensei Mohamed," and at the end of the course, the teacher organized a county-wide karate tournament at a mosque in North Bergen. I was surprised to see Baba take on the responsibility of taking me to it. On the way there, I confessed to him that I was afraid to go, that the last time I had been to that mosque I had gotten jumped by some local kids.

"Why didn't you tell me?" he asked. I just shrugged. Baba didn't say anything, either, which I took as his way of approving that I had stayed silent about it.

At the tournament, Baba hugged me tightly and said, "As Muslims, we do our best, no matter what." My heart pounded.

In the ring, though I knew little karate (I was a yellow belt, only one step up from beginner), I won bouts by fighting handily like a boxer, punching hard and keeping my distance. That technique kept working until I made it to the final round.

Baba came over and told me to stick with what I was doing. He gave me a kiss on the cheek and then a rough punch into the padding, and with that, I turned around to face my opponent.

Before the final fight began, Baba looked so corny to me, showing his excitement. It was odd to see a man who rarely let his emotions surface so animated and bubbly, but I also felt encouraged to have brought it out of him with my successes in these bouts. I myself got giddy, wondering if he had more time away from work, we could do things like this more often.

When the final fight began, my opponent kicked me in the gut, just beneath my padding. Without thinking, I jump-kicked him square in the head.

As the judges paused the fight to adjust his gear, I glanced at Baba, who was grinning with pride. I won the fight, and Baba pushed to the front with his disposable camera to take a photo during the awards ceremony. That photo of me, trophy in hand, was the real prize that night. It's the only photo I have of me taken by Baba.

Hebah with her lollipop, as Mohamed teases her
from his perch in a tree above, 1991.

Chapter 3

Early Dismissal

EVERYONE ELSE IN OUR FAMILY SEEMED HYPERCRITICAL AND HAR-ried, but Hebah was patient, empathetic, and considerate.

Although we grew up together, Hebah's entire life had been dictated by gender roles. Mama didn't usually allow her to play outside, especially not with her brothers and their friends. Keeping the genders separate was always more important to Mama than giving Hebah space to be a kid.

Eventually, Hebah stopped asking to go outside. She spent endless hours in her room, immersing herself in fantasy novel series like *Lord of the Rings* and *Animorphs,* accumulating a giant library in our room. Though I teased her for going hours without moving a muscle, I was amazed by her focus.

HEBAH STARTED WEARING HIJAB WHEN SHE WAS FIVE YEARS OLD, whereas most girls aren't mandated to begin veiling until puberty, even in more conservative circles. She was inspired by Mama and all the other adult women around her who wore hijab, which became a pillar in her identity—she couldn't imagine herself without it.

This could be why she felt more different from the Americans in our neighborhood or on TV than the rest of us did. Hebah was expected to be the standard-bearer, to embody the virtues and values of our family, a role with little room for deviation.

But, despite the obvious constraints on her activities, veiling could also be the reason she had the strongest will. She got straight A's at every stage in school and used her near-perfect SAT scores to go from Newark to Harvard University, Harvard Law, and NYU's medical school, before settling into her job as an obstetric anesthesiologist. But perhaps even more impressive was when she went vegetarian in middle school and foreswore many of Mama's meat-based Egyptian dishes. She was always the smartest person in any room she entered.

EVEN THOUGH I TORMENTED HER, WE BECAME CLOSE FRIENDS. HEBAH was assiduous to a degree that none of her brothers were, and sometimes she seemed to me the only person who wouldn't give up on me.

"It's because you're smart," she said once, when I was in one of my moods.

I looked at her, confused, so she explained: "Think of the average person. Would you say the average person is smart? Or dumb?"

"Dumb," I answered reflexively.

"Okay. So, if the average person is dumb, that means half of all people are even dumber," she said jokingly.

"Oh my God. We're surrounded by idiots." She got me laughing.

"Now think of our family. Is anyone in our family dumb?" she asked.

"No," I answered.

"See? That's why we're hard on you. It's because we know you're smart, and we hate to see you acting dumb." She patted me on the back.

IN SEVENTH GRADE, I TRANSITIONED FROM THE ELEMENTARY ISLAMIC school to the joint middle and high school in Teaneck, New Jersey. I would have been in the same building as my big sister, Hebah, but two years earlier, all my siblings had transferred to the local Newark public high school. At this point, Mohamed was at the New Jersey Institute of Technology in Newark, and Ahmad had just departed for the University of Virginia. Hebah was a senior at the local high school, East Side, where she mostly socialized with the teachers and ignored the other students.

During my first week in seventh grade, a few of the teachers and older students immediately clocked me for being an Ismail. My brothers, Mohamed and Ahmad, had already left their mark on the school. They had a knack for landing in the principal's office to answer for frequent antics. Among Mohamed's most notorious exploits was selling illegal fireworks and smoke bombs—contraband from their secret trips to Chinatown in Manhattan. By the time I arrived, the Ismail name was something I felt expected to contend with. But later that week, before we had even been assigned any homework, things took an unexpected turn. It was the fall of 2001.

OVER THE INTERCOM, THE PRINCIPAL MADE AN ANNOUNCEMENT. "All students and teachers, report to the multipurpose room for an emergency assembly." There was no explanation. I was in my first-period math class, and the teacher looked as confused as the students. He called for quiet, but as we made our way out of the classroom, I could hear the other students' chatter:

"I think we're going to be let out early today!" one kid said.

"I heard we were all going on a field trip," said another.

I sat down next to my friend Ahmed as the principal tapped the microphone.

"The school is going to be closing early," he announced. "Your parents have already been notified."

A free day sounded too good to be true, though we still didn't know the reason. Nobody was eager to go back to class.

The plan was for all the students to sit and wait until their rides arrived, but almost immediately everyone got up and started going their own ways. Most students went straight to their lockers to grab their things. I watched as teachers tried to use their bodies to close off the exits, to no avail.

Ahmed and I roamed the hallway with several other kids in our class. One of us opened every classroom door, just to peek in. When he opened one door, he noticed what sounded like a sharp snap against the window, like a rock had bounced off it.

He went inside and pressed his face against the window. "There're people outside!" he warned the rest of us.

We all ran up to see for ourselves. I expected to see Muslim students hanging around, but instead there was a small group of kids in uniform from a different high school.

And a few adults were standing around, watching these students toss rocks at our building.

"Hell, no!" one of us yelled out the window. The kids outside noticed us, but they didn't look startled or scared. They stared up at us blankly. I wondered if they were the reason we were being evacuated.

We talked ourselves into the plan to make our way outside and confront them.

"Come on. This way," I said, leading the group to the girls' half of the school, which was normally off-limits to boys. We let ourselves out through the back entrance, and were surprised to see a bus there, and some adults waiting for us. One of Baba's friends spotted me and grabbed me by the arm.

"Yalla," he ordered. "Get in. I'm taking you to the Jersey City school." I shuffled in with some other students. I'd already forgotten about those strange kids throwing stones.

ON THE HIGHWAY BACK TO JERSEY CITY, I WAS STUNNED TO SEE WHAT looked like a volcano eruption in Lower Manhattan. A gigantic pillar of gray smoke plumed where the Twin Towers would have been. I had always used those towers as a kind of lighthouse, a point that told me which way was east. I knew that Baba worked nearby, driving Wall Street traders and bankers. Now the towers were obscured.

IT REEKED LIKE A CAMPFIRE. THE COLOR OF THE SKY CHANGED TO gray, filling the bus with gloom. The student sitting next to me stared blankly out the window and muttered, "My baba works in New York . . ."

"Mine, too," I said to him.

One kid, in the back, was giddy with excitement.

"I don't think we're going to be going to school tomorrow, either!" he said. I rolled my eyes.

TRAFFIC WAS SO CONGESTED THAT THE TRIP BETWEEN SCHOOLS THAT would otherwise have taken twenty minutes took close to two hours. When the bus finally came to a stop, I could see Mama standing outside waiting for me.

"Habibi!" she called out, before I could even get out of the van, and then hugged me tightly.

"Where is Baba?" I asked. I wasn't sure if he was in the city or at home resting. Mama didn't answer. She grabbed me by my backpack and pulled me toward our red minivan. "He's still at work," she said in Arabic.

MY BROTHERS WERE AT COLLEGE, AND HEBAH WAS HOME ALONE after walking herself back from the high school, just a few blocks from our home, and was as worried about Baba as Mama was. She was glued to the TV, watching images of the towers coming down, on repeat. Hebah and I obsessively scanned the faces of every person in the crowds running from the debris onscreen, hoping to catch a glimpse of Baba, but we never spotted him.

We zoned out as broadcast-news journalists alluded over and over to Muslim terrorists. They showed footage of Osama Bin Laden, and kept saying the word "jihad." They weren't even pronouncing it right, I thought to myself.

MAMA WAS GLUED TO THE PHONE, PACING BACK AND FORTH IN THE kitchen, slinking the cord behind her. She called Baba's car phone, Baba's brother Uncle Harby, and the mosque, but no one was picking up. It was no use. The first hours were exhausting, and as day gave way to night, I could see that Mama was utterly depleted.

Hebah looked nervous. She was obviously beginning to assume the worst. Mama picked up on that, too.

"Hebah," she called out from the kitchen, "take your brother. We need dinner," she said in Arabic.

"Hadir," Hebah responded—a formal way of saying yes, typically reserved for addressing an authority figure.

Hebah quietly retreated to her room to veil properly and grabbed some money from Mama's purse; we both made our way out the door and down the stoop.

Here we paused for a moment. The street that was usually busy with kids and cars felt eerily silent. The air tasted toxic and reeked of smoke. The mood was hazy and surreal.

"Whatcha want to eat?" Hebah asked me, breaking the silence in a forced joyful tone, like she was trying to shelter me from the disconsolate atmosphere. She was vegetarian and didn't eat fast food, but I had a craving.

"KFC?"

"Sure!" she answered.

The KFC was just three blocks away, but when we turned the first corner and I lost sight of our apartment, I felt a slow tingle take over me. It wasn't sadness or worry for my baba. It was apprehension for Hebah, who I thought now appeared like an easy target with her white hijab: a walking representation of Islam, one of the professed attackers TV broadcasters had been generalizing about all day.

I had my fight face on. I told myself defending Hebah was my duty, and though I was only eleven years old, I needed to be ready.

Just outside the KFC, I spotted a group of five kids just a little bit bigger than me playing wallball in the parking lot. I kept my eye on them, waiting for them to notice Hebah's hijab. They didn't.

The paranoia never left me, even after we had picked up our food and returned home.

Without Baba, we didn't pray as a family that night. Instead, we watched the news on TV. When we couldn't stay awake any longer, we went to sleep.

———

THE NEXT MORNING, HEBAH AND I WOKE UP AND FOUND MAMA STILL on the phone in the kitchen. Suddenly our attention shot toward the front door as it creaked open.

Baba shuffled through the door with an exhausted look in his eyes. He had some dust in his hair, and his black shoes had turned a dark gray, but otherwise he looked fine.

"What took you so long?" Mama demanded.

"I'm tired," he replied. He brushed past us and let himself into the bedroom, kicking his dirty clothes off mid-stride. Then he shut the door behind him. That was all.

He didn't come out to tell us what had happened.

OVER THE YEARS, MY SIBLINGS AND I SHARED NOTES, AND WE EVENTU-ally worked out that Baba was somewhere in Midtown when the attack occurred, but he picked up a reporter who paid him to take her downtown. When the towers collapsed, Baba was less than a mile away, and the cloud of debris eclipsed him in his car. He was able to drive back uptown, but the tunnel was shut down, so he just parked and waited for it to reopen. His car was his livelihood; he couldn't leave it in New York and evacuate without it. He waited.

It's impossible to know for sure what happened, or if there was more to the story. To this day, if we ask Baba what happened he just shrugs, or responds with a lesson on the Prophet's struggles in pre-Islamic Mecca.

After the attack, the Islamic school didn't immediately reopen. Mama had intended to keep me in there longer, like my siblings, but— perhaps wondering if it was safe to continue going there—she asked me if I was ready for public school.

"Yes!" I answered enthusiastically.

Mock-hajj at Al-Ghazaly Elementary School, 1995.

Chapter 4

Ironbound

THE HALLWAY SMELLED A BIT LIKE THE INSIDE OF AN OLD SODA CAN.
Mama sat me down in a small chair in the administrative office
while she argued with the school staff. They told her they couldn't
accept new students after the school year had started, but she took an
aggressive posture, leaning forward in her hijab and abaya.

"I'm a teacher. I know he already missed a lot, but he's a smart boy.
He will catch up," she asserted.

After a bit of back-and-forth, the principal relented, smiling at
me, and assured me that someone was coming to take me to the
classroom. I felt immediately and keenly the change from the Islamic
school principals I had known! Mama nodded, but her eyes stayed
sharp.

The student who came downstairs was a girl. I hadn't been in the
same class with girls in years, let alone one without hijab. My eyes
were immediately drawn to her straight brown hair tied up into a
ponytail. She wore a sleeveless low-cut shirt. It all seemed so exotic
to me.

"You the new kid? Follow me," she said briskly.

I felt giddy with excitement, like I was finally joining the *real* world,
escaping the enclosed, sanitized bubble in which I'd grown up.

"You're in that class," she said, pointing at a door in the hall. Before
I could say thank you, she turned away—so quickly that I felt the wind
from her ponytail on my face.

I approached the door, took a deep breath, put my hand on the knob, twisted it slowly, then burst it open to present myself.

Except that the room was entirely empty, just rows of small desks, with the lights turned off. I took my seat at the desk closest to the door and waited quietly in the dark.

A short while later, the school bell rang. In an instant, a flood of students came rushing in. Though someone flicked the light on, only one or two kids noticed that I was there.

A BOY SLID INTO THE SEAT DIRECTLY BEHIND ME AND TAPPED ME ON the shoulder. He had the same skin tone as me, dark eyes, and some facial hair which at age eleven seemed impressive. His loose-fitting T-shirt and perfectly worn jeans gave him an air of effortless cool, like he was the kind of kid who knew he had nothing to prove. He looked curious, but also concerned. Then he spoke, his voice startlingly deep like a grown man's, rapidly in fluent Spanish. But I couldn't understand anything, and my heart sank. As much as he seemed friendly, I began to worry that I would be stuck in a classroom with kids I couldn't even talk to.

"Um . . . English?" I responded hesitantly. "No hablo. Sorry."

He smiled. "Oh! My bad, dawg. I'm Mike. You're new?" he asked, seemingly also relieved. His voice was even deeper in English.

"Yeah. It's my first day. Like, first minute," I answered.

"Cool. What's your name?" he asked.

"Aymann," I said hesitantly.

"Word? Amen? Like . . . praying? That's cool."

"Something like that. It's Arabic. I'm Egyptian."

"Oh, snap! You speak English pretty good for someone who just got here," he said, laughing.

"Where are you from?" I asked him.

"Ecuador," he said. "You play basketball?"

I nodded.

"Word. When it's gym, you're on my team. Cool?" he asked.

"Cool," I responded.

Before I knew it, Mike and I were surrounded by what felt like the whole class, who all repeated the same questions as Mike.

"Egypt? Like Aladdin?" one girl asked.

"Phew. Thank God you said Aladdin and not Bin Laden!" I replied with a smirk.

"So—what?—you live in, like, a pyramid?" a different girl asked.

"Yeah, you know the one off Broad and Market? My mom dropped me off on our camel," I joked.

"Yo, can you give me a ride on your camel?" one boy asked.

"He's kidding! You're so dumb!" the girl answered.

MOST OF THE KIDS IN THE CLASS HAD KNOWN ONE ANOTHER SINCE they were babies, but there was nothing cliquey about them. They were genuinely excited about having a new kid around, and everyone wanted their turn to make the others laugh. I felt I had been part of their gigantic friend group from the beginning.

IT SEEMED LIKE EVERYONE IN THE SCHOOL WAS BILINGUAL, INCLUD- ing the teachers, who were surprisingly upbeat, gentle, and encouraging—the opposite of what I was accustomed to in Al-Ghazaly.

But not everyone was so friendly. When it was time for recess after lunch, kids were free to roam a blacktop lot, which felt like an upgrade from the Islamic school, because there were no cars to avoid. There was even a basketball hoop. Everything seemed to be going great until someone's arms reached around my neck and slammed me down on the pavement.

In a flash, I was on my back looking up at two boys I didn't know.

"Welcome to Newark, bitch," one said, and they both stormed off, laughing. I looked over to Mike, who was also chuckling.

"It's a rite of passage," he assured me. I smiled back. This was con- fusing, but something about Mike's casual reaction stifled any desire I might have had for retribution.

"A rite of passage? I've been living here my whole life!" I protested.

"Yeah, but now you're with us," he answered. I was put at ease when I saw the boys who pulled me to the ground do the same to another kid, who also got up from the ground laughing.

IT FELT STRANGE, AN OUT-OF-BODY EXPERIENCE, GETTING TO KNOW the girls in my class. It was normal for girls and boys to give one another tight hugs and kisses each time they said hello and good-bye. They were very comfortable in their own bodies, and with one another's. I became disoriented when a girl casually planted her lips on my face while Mike and I were sitting at the lunch table.

Mike noticed that I had a hard time making eye contact with girls and responded in monosyllables whenever a conversation began.

"I'm not even supposed to shake their hands, bro," I said to him, trying to explain myself. Even saying it out loud made me wince.

"But why?!" he demanded.

I genuinely didn't know why. "I'm Muslim! That's just the rules!"

"Who made these rules!?" he asked, exasperated.

"God did!" I practically shouted. We could barely hold in our laughter.

MIKE TOOK IT ON AS A CHALLENGE, AND MADE IT HIS MISSION TO "fix" me. He called over a girl in our class, Andrea, and explained to her that she needed to shake my hand. She was predictably confused.

"You still believe in cooties? You *wish* you'd get *my* cooties," she teased. Mike demonstrated shaking her hand to mock me. It drove me nuts. I jolted my hand out for a shake, but, just as I went for it, she pulled away.

"You wish!" she called out. Mike keeled over with laughter. I couldn't help smirking as Andrea walked away, with a wide smile on her face.

I chased after her, and after more torture, she shook my hand. Mike's excitement was contagious. It all felt silly and harmless, but it was a major break in my attachment to following Islamic rules at school.

————

THAT WINTER, JUST A FEW MONTHS LATER, I COULDN'T EVEN RECOG-
nize myself—kissing girls on the cheek, exchanging dirty jokes, any
pretense about shying away from girls gone.

Still, I wasn't on the same level as Mike, or the other boys. A few of
them had girlfriends, with whom they would make out throughout
the day. One of them was having sex. We weren't even teenagers yet.
I wasn't interested in crossing that line, but the thought that a girl
might be interested in me that way was irresistible.

THEN THERE WAS SARA, THE SMARTEST GIRL IN OUR CLASS, WHO MIKE
swore had a crush on me—just to see my reaction. She was the only
person in our class who consistently bested me on tests. She was Bra-
zilian, with crazy bright-green eyes that shone on her olive-tan skin,
freckles on her rosy cheeks, and a thick, seductive lisp. When I finally
worked up the nerve to ask her if we could do homework together,
it felt life-changing.

It was innocent at first. But that spring, right before summer break,
she kissed me.

It happened suddenly, after school, on the stoop in front of her
apartment. She stood there frozen, like she had been paused with a
remote control, slowly slid a piece of chewing gum into her mouth.
Then, in one quick motion, she reached forward with both of her
hands, grabbed me hard by my ears, and squeezed and twisted them,
using them like reins to pull my face to hers.

It lasted all of a half-second, and as soon as it was over, she turned
and ran up the stairs and into the apartment building. I felt dizzy with
excitement. My ears were throbbing. Rather than going home, I went
to brag to the boys playing basketball at the school. They went nuts,
jumping up and down, pulling me to the ground, suffocating me at
the bottom of a dog pile. I nearly died of happiness.

ON MY WAY HOME, AS I CONTEMPLATED HOW MY LIFE WAS FOREVER
changed, the giddiness gave way to bubbling guilt. Even at eleven
years old, I knew Muslim boys weren't supposed to have romantic

relationships with girls. It wasn't just that I had gone against my mama's rules; I was going against *God's* rules. It was haram. And as a middle-schooler, I needed to reconcile that with the fact that I'd really, really, *really* enjoyed that kiss, and that I was fanatical about wanting to do it again.

Sara and I met up after school all the time after that, saying sweet things to each other and kissing nonstop. I was constantly on the lookout, hoping to avoid being caught by Mama.

"My family wouldn't get it," I told Sara, explaining why I needed her to walk five paces behind me on our way to our favorite make-out spot: the Blockbuster video-rental store. At that point, I saw myself as protecting my parents from the devastation of catching me in the act. I had gotten good at maintaining the illusion of being faithful at home, and I hoped to keep it that way.

Mike and Sara couldn't possibly have understood how they were catalysts for my internal rebellion. They represented a clash between the identity I was expected to uphold and the one I was beginning to explore on my own. And, as I think she had predicted before my first day at public school, Mama and I began to grow apart.

BY THE NEXT YEAR, 2002, I'D ALREADY COME TO SEE MYSELF AS JUST one of many kids in Newark—each of us different in our own way. Exactly one year after September 11, I learned that it was possible for someone to *refuse* to see my family and me as anything other than Muslims in America.

Hebah had just left for her first year at Harvard University, and I was excited to have my own room. Mohamed was in the next room; his first semester at NJIT hadn't started yet. One night, I awoke to the bright beam of a flashlight pointing into my room from the doorway. The light got closer, as if from some kind of alien spaceship. I thought it was Mohamed playing a prank until the light shifted its focus and I saw who was carrying it: an extremely large man dressed head to toe in black, wearing a bulky bulletproof vest and holding a long rifle. He didn't say a word, just went through our things, opening our drawers, shifting the construction paper I had left on top, and kicking around the boxes of toys on the floor, then exited, leaving behind the mess he'd made.

I immediately shot out of bed and followed him out of the room, to see several men with flashlights and guns searching the apartment. It was only then that I saw what was written on their bulletproof vests: "FBI" in big white letters.

One man stood by the door with Mama, who was in her isdal, an oversized hijab she kept handy for performing her daily prayers at home. Mohamed stayed by her, trying to calm her down, as she fielded the armed FBI agents' many questions. With everything going on, I remember feeling violated most of all by the fact that they had their shoes on, a big faux pas in any Muslim household.

Mama jolted when she saw me emerge from my room. "They're here to help," Mama frantically explained to me in Arabic. But the men with their rifles didn't seem friendly.

"How can you do this?" Mama asked one man as he shuffled out. I'll never forget what he said, with a sly smile:

"Ma'am, you're the one who invited us in."

MOHAMED GAVE MAMA A TIGHT EMBRACE, BUT SHE SEEMED MORE embarrassed than anything else.

"They asked if they could come in, and I said okay, because we have nothing to hide," Mama explained, her breath still labored. I distinctly remember overhearing them questioning Mama about someone named Mohamed, and her urging them to be more specific.

After that incident, I had a sharp disdain for all the law enforcement I encountered. On my way to school soon after that, a crossing guard—not a cop, just a crossing guard—stopped me in the middle of the street and demanded to search my shoebox diorama, decorated with little painted Styrofoam balls representing planets and moons. When she tried to snatch my science project out of my hand, I recoiled and gave her the finger.

"Fuck off. Dumb bitch," I shouted.

My aggression only grew from there. Each day after school, without fail, I played basketball with Mike and other boys from our class until the early evening. We'd venture across the Ironbound, and play intense pickup games anywhere there was a hoop.

AT RIVERBANK PARK, WE JOINED A PACK OF BOYS OUR AGE WHO WENT to a different school. I had just enjoyed a growth spurt and towered over many of the other boys at an even six foot one, and was surging with confidence. The tallest kid from the other school naturally faced off against me. After I blocked his shots three times in a row, he squared up to fight me.

He threw his body at me. It felt like someone had thrown a heavy backpack square into my chest. I flinched and put my arms up to try to protect myself. But before I had even caught my bearings, my friends jumped in, without hesitation. Mike yanked the boy so hard he was lifted off the ground and fell backward. Before things could escalate, the other boys made their escape.

Though my friends and I laughed it off, I struggled to swallow my terror. My friends were more comfortable with danger; a few of them were in gangs and kept weapons in their backpacks—mostly knives, but sometimes guns. One of the boys who jumped in to defend me was nicknamed Homeless, because his parents refused to take him back after his stint in juvenile detention. I could only imagine what other kids in the neighborhood were dealing with.

Newark was a fun place to grow up, but only because we learned to live alongside the danger. The instinct to scan every room, every street, every face never faded. I was having fun, but my body was memorizing fear. And once learned, it never let go.

JUST BEFORE HIGH SCHOOL, I WENT THROUGH MY FIRST BREAKUP.

"Honestly, I just thought it was cool you were Egyptian," Sara instant-messaged me online. I'd thought there was more to our relationship, and it was gutting, but Mike helped me get over it, assuring me it was better to be a "free agent" at the start of high school.

He and I both attended Science High, which made the transition easy. Each morning, we met up at the local bakery on Ferry Street, Teixeira's, to decide whether to ride the city bus to school, or instead walk and sell our school-issued bus tickets for a profit.

To get to school, we needed to walk past Newark Penn Station, the last railroad stop before New York City. Mike had figured out that the conductors didn't ask for tickets between those stations, so, whenever we wanted, we'd hop aboard, skip school, and spend the day exploring the city. Mike took a job at Walgreens to help his parents with the bills, but he always had enough left over to buy us fruit from street vendors.

Science High was downtown, in a crumbling old building that had once been a brewery, when Newark was a wealthy manufacturing hub. The classrooms were oppressively small—one was literally a narrow closet, with just enough space for two desks side by side, the others lined up behind.

One of the quirks of the school was having gym class at the YMCA across the street. This meant leaving the school building and crossing the street every day. That might not sound like much, but it was Newark. Even in packs, moving around outside felt risky, so we always stuck together.

One day, one of our friends, Paul Braswell, lagged behind after gym. Handsome, with clear dark skin and perfect white teeth, he was adored by all the girls in his orbit. He loved wearing expensive basketball jerseys, and it seemed he wore a new one every day. But just one time, because he took a little bit longer to change out of his gym clothes and clean up than everyone else, he came back to the school missing both his jersey and his sneakers.

"Some crackhead robbed me," he said, hanging his head in shame. Our pack of friends found it hilarious—we laughed so hard even Paul couldn't help smiling.

Our freshman class got along great, mostly. A few students kept to themselves. One girl was particularly shy. My only impression of her was that I thought she was something of a class pet, eagerly engaging in Spanish class and answering all of the questions—of course, she was fluent and spoke Spanish at home. Sometimes, Mike and I played chess or cards in the back of the class instead. The teacher didn't seem to mind.

It was a lot of fun to explore high school with Mike, but near the end of my freshman year, Mama decided that I was going to switch high schools. She dropped the news on me at dinner one evening.

"I already called the principal at East Side," said Mama.

I nearly spat out my food. I couldn't believe what she was saying.

Science High was the magnet school, and the more desirable choice in every way. I'd had to take an exam to get accepted.

"East Side is where your siblings went. I know the teachers there. They will take good care of you," Mama said.

I had no choice but to accept my fate and finish my freshman year at East Side. This school had a reputation for being dangerous: even the security guards looked more like prison correctional officers. A demented part of me was drawn to the opportunity to develop street cred with Mike and other friends I had made at Science High.

THAT QUIET GIRL WHO I ONLY SAW COME ALIVE IN SPANISH CLASS turned out to be pretty cool—and she had great taste in music. After I left, she began dating one of the guys and seamlessly blended into the friend group I still saw often. Her name was Jessica Valladolid, but I called her JV, and soon everyone else did, too. We swapped AIM screen names and chatted online like we'd known each other our whole lives.

JV was Ecuadorian American, like Mike. She had long black hair, with bangs that framed her round eyes. She carried a little backpack instead of a purse, so we teased her by calling her Dora the Explorer. She turned out to be hands down the funniest kid in Newark, creatively tying themes together, and joking in a shy, nervous tone that somehow made everything she said even funnier. She brought a new level of joy to our group.

She fit in with the guys perfectly, but when we made crude jokes or talked about girls in a certain way, she'd check us. "You can't just 'steal' someone's girl, you know? She's got her own mind and choices," she'd say.

At first, I appreciated her corrections because I thought she'd help us seem more mature around other girls. But she soon became the conscience of our group, checking our language with a blend of seriousness and humor that never felt judgmental. We started coming to her with questions about the way other girls at school acted. It was like having a liaison who could translate between genders.

Of course, we'd still make jokes that were objectifying and rude, and sometimes we'd tease her for trying to "fix" us. But her presence was quietly helping us grow, even if we didn't realize it at the time.

I WAS FINE AT EAST SIDE, AND I KNEW A HANDFUL OF MY NEW CLASS-mates already, from Wilson Avenue School. The art teacher, Andrew Teheran, or Mr. T, spotted me in the hallway on my first day and called me over. "You're Hebah's brother, right?" he asked. "She was the brightest student I ever had. If you're anything like her, we'll get along great."

East Side High was a place where most teachers had given up and students were often left to fend for themselves. After all the doors were locked and attendance had been taken in first period, many students would wander the halls or find ways to leave the school building entirely. Even teachers cut class. It was chaotic, but I quickly found a place that sparked something in me—Mr. T's art class.

In my first class with him, while he was giving the students his spiel about the value of problem-solving skills, he was interrupted by the school intercom. Without hesitation, he slid a desk over to where the intercom was, stood on it, and then jabbed a pencil into the speaker. We giggled as he climbed down as if nothing had happened.

I spent nearly the entire school day in his classroom, on a Mac desktop computer he kept locked up in the back closet. This was my first experience with video-editing software.

"Do you know how to use this stuff?" I asked Mr. T during one of his free periods.

"Nope. We can learn to use it together," he suggested.

He printed out a list of keyboard shortcuts that he had found online and handed it to me. I went through them one by one, experimenting with each tool and figuring out what it did. Within a month, I was editing using only the keyboard. I developed a rhythm, too. My fingers moved rapidly from one shortcut to the next, cutting, slipping, and layering clips with a fluidity that felt musical. Each key press became part of a combo, a choreography of motions that turned editing into reflexive dance for my fingers on the keyboard like I was playing the piano.

THOUGH I WAS GETTING ALONG WELL WITH THE FRIENDS I'D MADE in Mr. T's classroom—mostly kids who painted graffiti, watched anime, and played Dungeons and Dragons—I did still get reminders that I was quite sheltered compared to other students at East Side High. Kids bused in from across Newark, and I was told the doors were locked to keep dangerous people out.

Mama had done her best to shield us from the hardships around us, but certain differences became obvious when I tried joining sports teams. Though I considered myself one of the best basketball players in the Ironbound, I quit after the first East Side practice, intimidated when students pulled off windmill slam dunks and alley-oops for fun. I turned to football, where the team took literally anyone, and it was on that team that I met Jamal. He was a junior—strong, intense, and tougher than anyone I'd known. Though he wasn't particularly social, he was the first to show up at the weight room, and the first to appear when a fight seemed imminent.

Jamal heard from another player that I was selling bootleg CDs. Using the Mac in Mr. T's classroom, I made albums and sold them for five bucks apiece, saving up for trips to New York with Mike and my friends from Science High. Jamal had a special request: his favorite artist, the Canadian pop-punk sensation Avril Lavigne. I was surprised, but he shrugged and said he liked what he liked and didn't have anything to prove. We became friends after that.

I asked him once how he got so confident, and he told me he was supposed to be dead.

He had joined a gang, the Bloods, because his older brother was a member. When he tried to leave the gang, they said it was fine—then shot him nearly a dozen times, right as he turned to walk away. These were people he had considered family. Miraculously, he survived. He showed me his scars, explaining which of his friends he believed had shot him where. We cried together as he shared horrifying details of his recovery.

That season, we scored only one touchdown, and the season's end marked the close of my friendship with Jamal. I quit the team, and for the rest of the year, I spent my time almost exclusively in Mr. T's room.

EVEN THOUGH I'D ALWAYS BEEN VAGUELY AWARE OF HOW ROUGH things could get outside, the incredible job Mama had done shielding us from the worst of it meant that we got to feel like kids. We'd run around on the mosque carpet, ignorant of the harsh realities faced by kids our age who didn't have that safe space. Now, coming face-to-face with some of those realities at East Side, I felt more grateful than ever for Mama's protection.

HALFWAY THROUGH THE YEAR, MR. T PROPOSED WE MAKE A FILM FOR a local festival, about an East Side High graduate who had died in the Iraq War. We spent weeks piecing together footage, recording voiceovers, and perfecting the edit. The final product was extremely polished, and even Mr. T was surprised by how well it had turned out. It won the festival prize.

This project became a tangible confirmation of the new identity I was carving out for myself outside of Islamic school and away from home. At home, I battled anger, confusion, and rebellion, struggling with the sense that I had strayed too far from the religious path ever to make anything of myself. Winning this prize helped me feel I had options.

Students posing in front of a graffiti-covered wall at the
Wilson Avenue Elementary School during recess, 2002.

But, as quickly as I discovered this new passion, I felt ripped away from it. That summer, Mama told me we were leaving Newark and moving to the suburbs. Without warning, I was pulled out of East Side and Mr. T's classroom, and enrolled in yet another high school. The rug had been pulled out from under me just as I was starting to find my footing.

Chapter 5

The Sandal

ON MY FIRST DAY AT SCHOOL IN SOUTH BRUNSWICK, BEGINNING MY junior year at my third high school in three years, I walked into my first class, English, about fifteen minutes after the last bell rang. At East Side, it always took a while for class to settle, but here, walking in late disrupted the lesson. The sound of the door opening drew all eyes to me, and the stunned students stared as I stood there awkwardly. The English teacher, though, seemed cool. "Don't worry, you haven't missed anything," he assured me with a wave, but I didn't have it in me to return the kindness with a smile.

I sat in the corner. All the students took turns standing up and introducing themselves. When it was my turn, I approached the front of the room slowly.

"I'm Aymann. I just moved here from Newark."

A white girl in the back let out a barely audible "Oh, shit!" I rolled my eyes.

The teacher asked the class if they had any questions for me. A different white girl asked, "Have you ever been shot?"

The question pissed me off. "Not me. Have you? On one of those hunting trips with Pappy?" I joked, mimicking a bad Southern accent. A few kids laughed, but the girl who asked didn't. *Good,* I thought.

I dragged myself back to my seat. Another girl sitting behind me, Divya, had the same skin tone as me—caramel with olive undertones. She tapped me on the shoulder to get my attention. "Hey, where are you from?"

"Egypt. You?"

"Half Desi, half Caribbean," she replied, her tone easy and self-assured.

"I want to have dinner at your house. I bet that food is banging," I told her, flirting openly. Divya gave me a half-smile and turned her attention back to the teacher.

She was cute. She wore these low-rise jeans and kept her long, straight black hair up in a messy bun, and she had some bite in her attitude. Five minutes in at a new school, and already I had a crush.

WE CLICKED INSTANTLY. I WAS NEW, AND DIVYA, HAVING RECENTLY moved as well, understood what it felt like to be out of place. In me, it seemed, she had found a comrade. She offered to show me around and make sure I'd make it to classes on time, and in those first few days, we became inseparable. She confided in me the intimate and guarded details of her stressful home life, being raised by a single mom. I admired how she carried herself with a cool, almost practiced nonchalance. It wasn't that she was completely secure in herself, but she had a way of masking her vulnerability with humor and a swagger.

Before long, we were holding hands in the hallways and passing notes in class—the classic high school romance, the kind you see in movies. I felt like an entirely different person from the one I'd been in Islamic school. Divya and I spent every moment outside of class together.

As my relationship with Divya deepened, so did my internal conflict. I needed to keep her hidden from my family, and I resented myself for how this made her feel like a dirty secret. The fear that I was betraying my family, my faith, and the identity I had been raised to uphold haunted me.

By the end of senior year, just as our relationship was starting to feel like true love, I invited her back to my family's apartment when I was sure nobody was home.

"Just promise to ignore the giant shrine to you in my closet, okay?" I joked.

"Did you remember to blow out the candles after last night's ritual sacrifice?" she said, playing along.

She took off her sandals at the door, and had fun looking through my belongings, including the family photo album with my baby pictures.

"I love this," she told me as we lay on my bed and kissed.

Then I heard a faint rattling in the background, and it intensified, and I realized that someone was at the door.

A shadow slowly took over my body, from my feet through my torso to the tips of my fingers. I couldn't move.

"What's wrong?" she asked. I didn't answer. Then she heard it, too.

Divya sprang up in a panic and asked if she should jump out of the window. I told her she was better off hiding in the closet. She tucked herself behind the hung clothes and pulled them over herself like a curtain.

I tiptoed over to the front door. Mama had opened the door and pushed her arm all the way through the gap. She was swinging her arm up and down wildly, trying to unhook the chain herself. The loose sleeves of her abaya flung violently up and down. It looked like a scene out of a Muslim zombie apocalypse.

I unhooked the chain, but before I could turn the knob to let her in, the door shot open from the other side.

"What is this?" Mama asked in Arabic. She brushed right past me to investigate what I was hiding from her.

"Whose sandals are these?"

I felt a paralyzing knot take over my entire body. I had forgotten about the sandals.

Mama presented one of the pair to me, but I could hardly breathe, let alone try to make up an excuse.

"Where is she?" Mama asked in Arabic. It was over for me. I'd gotten into trouble with Mama before, many times. She might raise her voice, sometimes crying out a du'a, a supplication, for Allah to give her patience and mercy. Once in a while, she'd chuck a slipper or cooking utensil at me. But this time she did nothing, and it felt worse than anything before.

"In my room," I fessed up. I had no choice but to beg for mercy. Mama turned and rushed into my bedroom. I followed her in. "Mama, I'm sorry," I begged in Arabic.

Mama went straight for the closet door. Before she could finish twisting the knob, the door flung open. Divya spilled out, tripping on shoe boxes. She made eye contact with Mama, in a moment that lasted just half a second but remains seared in my brain. Divya darted toward the door with her head down, ashamed of what had just happened. I held my head down, too.

Mama chased her out, waving Divya's own sandal at her.

This was a side of Mama I wish I had never seen.

Divya somehow managed to grab her purse on the way out but left her sandals behind. The door shut quietly behind her, as if it, too, was embarrassed by what had just happened.

Mama's vacant stare told me she finally saw who I was, much worse than if she'd yelled at me.

"Tell me the truth," she said calmly.

"She was here to work on a school project. We do homework together . . . She's really smart and a good influence. She's the reason why I'm getting good grades," I lied.

I braced for follow-up questions, and started to rehearse in my head for an interrogation, but Mama opted not to pursue it. "Mashi," she said in Arabic—Fine. For a moment, we let my lies hang in the air. Mama sat like she was in sujood, prostrated for praying. She looked sad. Like me, she, too, was operating on assumptions, and a fundamental lack of faith in being able to communicate.

"I'm supposed to be at work right now," Mama finally said. "I had a feeling that something was wrong. SubhanAllah. This feeling told me to leave everything and go home right away."

Her supernatural senses only heightened my fear that I had broken not just one of Mama's biggest rules, but one of God's.

"When we ask Rabbinah for strength, he doesn't just give us strength. He gives us tests and struggles to help us grow stronger. SubhanAllah," she said with pain in her voice. "But Allah never gives us more than each of us can handle. It's why the tests for the prophets were so intense, because Rabbinah knew they'd need that strength to spread his message. Don't tell your baba about this. He won't be as understanding as me." She dropped the sandal where she'd found it and retreated to her room.

I didn't feel relief. I didn't know Mama was capable of such a measured response, but I doubted she'd be able to shake the memory. It makes sense to me, now that I'm old enough to consider what she was up against. She was raising Muslim kids in a non-Muslim country, and had to substitute her own learned wisdom and experience for the wisdom in the Quran, and the sunnah, the anecdotal life experiences of the Prophet Muhammad and customs based on them. She held those stories closer to her heart than her own life experiences. The Quran helped us be more knowledgeable about religion, but her faith also constructed between us an unsurmountable wall.

DIVYA AND I DIDN'T BREAK UP RIGHT AWAY—THE ENCOUNTER SEEMED to thrill her. When we talked about it the next day, at my locker, she treated it like a joke.

"Oh my God, you have no idea how weird it was for me, trying to get home barefoot!" she recalled. Her excitement irked me; I felt my life was falling apart. We'd gotten into the same college and had planned on staying together, but now I was having second thoughts.

I wasn't honest with Divya about how deeply that experience had changed me, leaving me more aware than ever that, deep inside, I still wanted to be a good Muslim. Someday, I thought.

IN THE MONTHS THAT FOLLOWED, I TRIED TO LIVE MY LIFE AS IF IT were a boring scripted Muslim rom-com. I tried to behave like I had learned some important lesson. As I prepared to move away from home and into my new dorm on campus, I asked Mama for a prayer mat and a Quran to take with me, but Divya and I would continue to date on and off. I oscillated between guilt and regret, breaking it off with her each time I began to worry that my identity as a Muslim hung in the balance, then, always, coming back to her. I was compelled by the excitement and promise of that relationship, yet bitterly shadowed by the knowledge that I was hurting Divya.

Sometimes, I'd try to rationalize it to my non-Muslim friends on AIM. Mike Molina dismissed my guilt: I was too hard on myself, he said, and it was my mother's fault for wanting a perfect son. But JV wasn't so easy on me. She called me out directly, saying I was emotionally abusive toward Divya for not being honest with her.

"omg u got 1 foot out tha door already that's srsly messed up. smh :/," she wrote.

When I was finally ready to leave for college, Mama took it harder than I expected. She couldn't understand why I'd want to live in a dorm just twenty minutes from home. The only way I managed to get her to accept my decision was by fabricating a story about how Rutgers required students to live in the dorm their first year. She bought it, but not before making me sign a written contract in which I promised to pray and eat three meals every day, and come home every weekend. I agreed, though I negotiated weekends down to Sunday visits.

ON MOVING DAY, MAMA HELPED ME UNPACK MY SINGLE SUITCASE AND placed my clothes in the dorm dresser. She looked around, unimpressed.

"Where's the closet?" she asked.

I brushed off her concerns. She took her time, asking endless questions about my setup and the people I'd be living with. Finally, she gave me a quick hug and left; watching her car disappear, I felt an incredible rush of freedom.

Once Mama was gone, Rutgers revealed itself as an endless sea of

opportunities to explore life as I had imagined it. But then I went to a
dorm potluck where everyone brought dishes they made from their
culture. Someone brought jollof rice, another brought empanadas. I
brought Oreos.

I couldn't bring something Egyptian because I'd never cooked anything in my life. Only then did I realize how much I took for granted,
not just in Mama's cooking, but in her role as my connection to my
Arab and Islamic heritage. Feeling how distant I was from my Egyptian identity on my own, I became eager to reconnect. When I went
home that weekend, I asked if I could help her in the kitchen and
learn to cook for myself.

She was skeptical at first. "When you get married, bring your wife.
I'll teach her," she said with a cunning smile.

"Did your mama write recipes down or something? How do you
remember how to make all these different dishes?" I asked.

Mama chuckled. "We learned by watching," she explained. She
palmed an onion and diced it right in her hand. My eyes widened.
This was exactly what I was after.

Mama was big on tradition, often enforcing it like a set of rigid
rules with high stakes. But seeing her excitement as she shared her
cooking traditions with me was exhilarating, as if I was in the same
kitchen where *she* had learned to cook. For the first time, I felt I could
see my grandma in her. I marveled at how she cooked by feel, measuring spices with her palm, relying on scent and color to know when
something was done.

In my dorm room, I decided I'd try cooking on my own. Mama
had done me a favor and packed some pre-seasoned kofta, so I invited
some friends over and proudly set up to make it. Among them was
Mike Molina, my childhood friend from Newark, who was just as
eager as I to reconnect in the limitless excitement of college life. Mike
continued to push me to be more like him—confident, brash, and
ready to treat every girl on campus as a potential hookup prospect.
Though he drank and I didn't, he still dragged me to every house
party to "show me how it's done," reveling in the attention of girls

who threw themselves at him. But this time, I wanted to impress him
with something of my own.

All I had to do was defrost the minced meat and squeeze it onto
a wooden spoon to shape it into oblong patties and cook them in a
pan with a little bit of oil. I'd watched Mama's technique, but my first
attempt was clumsy. The meat stuck to the pan, and I misjudged the
timing.

"That doesn't look right," Mike said, smirking.

"You don't look right," I shot back, as he laughed at my fumbling
attempt to fix it.

"Need a hand, bro? This one looks like it needs to be flipped,"
another friend said, bringing my attention back to the pan, where the
first kofta was beginning to smoke, the bottom of it charring though
the top of it was still raw.

"I got it!" It seemed so simple in my mind. But the kofta split open
when I grabbed too forcefully with the tongs, the bottom half sticking to the pan.

My friends laughed, but by the fourth piece, I'd gotten the hang
of it. I felt proud serving them something actually Egyptian, however
messy. That night, they tasted a piece of my culture, and it felt like a
small victory.

When I told Mama about it, she was thrilled. She listed ingredients
and cooking tips, all of which I tried to remember. I wasn't just learning to cook: I was connecting with a deeper part of myself, a part that
belonged to a long line of Egyptian women who passed down their
recipes by heart. I was tapping into a piece of my family's history,
something sacred that I could carry forward.

CAMPUS LIFE PRESENTED A STRANGE MIX OF LIBERATION AND DISIL-
lusionment. I attended a Muslim Student Association meeting, hoping
to capitalize on my newfound excitement for Egyptian and Muslim
heritage and connect with others who shared my background. But the
group was self-segregated between genders and held rigid attitudes.
It made no sense, I thought, to ask women to sit in the back of the

room a half-hour after we men had sat next to non-Muslim women in the cafeteria, in the dorm, and in class. Why self-segregate here? This frustrated me.

Worse yet, when one woman made her case to the group, a college junior told her it was not in the interest of Muslims on campus to "behave" like the non-Muslims we went to school with. I left the meeting feeling disappointed, not just with the group but with my own sense of belonging. College was supposed to be where I found my people. I thought I'd get to campus and discover a Muslim community that just clicked. Instead, I felt more out of place with them than with anyone else.

The Muslims I met around campus seemed so certain about who they were and what they believed. Meanwhile, I was still untangling what faith meant to me, and didn't see the point in performing what felt like rote conventions instead of exploring actual belief, like arbitrary customs dressed up as doctrine. Instead of finding answers, I just felt more disillusioned.

During my second year, while waiting for a bus at the student center, I heard a voice behind me. "Are you Sister Nadia's kid?" a girl asked, her eyes narrowing with curiosity.

I turned to see someone I didn't recognize. "Sister Nadia" was how Mama was known at Al-Ghazaly, the Islamic school where she'd taught for years. Her name was Haniya. She was younger than me and had been one of Mama's students.

"Are you Egyptian?" I asked her.

"Ew. No. I'm not," she said, cackling in her signature laugh. I thought it was charming.

"No, I get it. I'm avoiding Egyptians right now, too," I said.

Despite our age difference, Haniya and I bonded immediately, recognizing the other was wrestling with the same questions of faith and identity, wanting the most out of the world around us while holding on to our Muslim roots. We'd meet between classes or late-night coffees, confiding in each other the ways we'd chafe against our own boundaries as we flailed for balance.

Haniya became a close confidante, someone who got the tug-of-war I felt between tradition and self-discovery.

In time, she revealed her own internal conflict. Like many young Muslim women, she felt the unspoken expectation to find herself a husband in between her classes. She resisted it at first, but came to find the prospect of marriage as a chance to build a new life on her own terms, within the boundaries of what was acceptable in Islam. I encouraged her to just enjoy the freedom of campus life and worry about the consequences later, as I did, but Haniya became convinced that doing things the "right" way could work.

Years later, after we graduated, Haniya wasted no time and got married. Later, when she got divorced, we found our friendship only grew stronger.

"Okay, so that didn't work," she said to me over the phone late one night, and we both burst into laughter, the kind that left us gasping for air.

Haniya continued to be my confidante and fellow rebel. She was open about her experiences within her marriage and the perspective she gained after it was over. Just by being candid, she pulled me out of my comfort zone and tested the limits of what I was ready to hear about the complex lives Muslim women led.

Our conversations ranged from the absurd and silly to the deeply personal, debating whether love could ever truly be unconditional, dissecting the double standards Muslim women faced in relationships, and questioning what it meant to be "good" in Islam, or more specifically, in our families.

She wrestled with her own questions: Should she lower her high standards so she wouldn't close herself off from someone genuinely decent? Meanwhile, I struggled with my contradictions, wanting love and deep connections with women but fearing that my choices made me unworthy of one day becoming a proper Muslim suitor, or identifying as a Muslim at all.

We ranted, half expecting the other to make sense of our dilemmas, but more often than not, we just left each other with more questions than answers. And yet, with every late-night phone call, every challenge she threw my way, she forced me to reexamine the quiet beliefs I had absorbed—about Muslim women, about relationships, and about myself.

Haniya's insights hit hard because, throughout college and beyond, I had always considered Muslim women off-limits—untouchable in a way that had less to do with them and more to do with my own insecurities. I assumed I fell too short of the standards of a good Muslim man to ever be considered a suitable partner. But hearing about her struggles—both in marriage and in reclaiming her agency afterward—challenged me to look beyond those assumptions. She forced me to see Muslim women not as distant ideals, but as individuals navigating their own expectations, desires, and choices with power and self-determination.

But she wasn't just a mirror to my own growth. As I reciprocated and told her all about the messy details from my relationships, first with Divya then with the women who came after, she called me out, too. She warned me when my behavior was selfish or harmful, challenging me to be better than the emotionally immature Muslim men she encountered all around her.

"You can't just focus on your religious growth," she told me once. "If you don't also focus on your emotional growth, you'll never have a relationship that lasts."

Her words struck a nerve. I had been trying so hard to reconcile my faith with my desires, convincing myself that if I could just get my religious life in order, everything else would follow. The idea that I had to work on something as nebulous as "emotional growth" felt overwhelming, like one more thing I wasn't measuring up to.

"Why would I take dating advice from someone who's already divorced?" I shot back, more defensive than I intended.

Haniya just laughed, shaking her head. She knew me well enough to recognize my deflection for what it was. One of the reasons I thought we stayed friends was for her own amusement at how predictably I impulsively floundered instead of engaging with the harder truth she was trying to get me to see.

"Dude. That's exactly who you need to be taking advice from," she countered with a wide smile, her voice firm, daring me to argue.

COLLEGE ME LIKED THE PATH OF LEAST RESISTANCE. I DRIFTED between social groups but always made time to party with Mike. We moved off campus into a house with four other guys, each from a different corner of the world. Mike and I shared a room.

The house was a disaster almost immediately. Our lofty ideas of independence dissolved within weeks. The kitchen became a wreck, the bathroom something out of my mama's nightmares, and the whole place reeked of weed. Hazy sunlight filtered through broken blinds, thick with smoke.

My roommates smoked whenever and wherever they wanted. I never minded, but I never joined in. My faith had faltered, but I still believed alcohol and drugs were forbidden for good reason. It wasn't about piety. I just had no desire to regress into the mind of a twelve-year-old like my friends did after every session.

I had years of practice saying no. Being the only Muslim was something I had learned to own.

"You really not smoking, bro?" one of my roommates asked before class, passing me a joint with a lazy grin.

"Imagine me actually high. It'd be like double high. Overkill," I said. It always cracked them up.

The joint moved on. Saying no to pork all these years made saying no to weed second nature. I didn't need it. I already felt between worlds.

SHORTLY AFTER I GRADUATED COLLEGE, I WAS COMPLETELY TAKEN off guard when Mama suggested I meet a girl she had picked out for me. I didn't know how to react. I'd spent years avoiding this exact situation, terrified of how my two worlds—my family and my private life—might collide. But Mama was insistent about her new friend's daughter.

"I think you'd like her a lot!" she said. Mama had told the other family that I was a good Muslim, and I felt terrible that I had made her a liar, too.

"If you don't like her, just say so, and that will be that. But if you do like her . . ."

"That'll be the last date you set up for me?" I asked, seeking some incentive.

"Date? Astaghfruallah. Muslims don't date, Aymann," she interjected.

IT SURE DIDN'T *FEEL* LIKE A DATE, EITHER. THE GIRL AND I SAT ON THE floor of her living room while our mothers whispered in the kitchen. My "date" wore a traditional decorative flowy abaya and a pristine white hijab. I thought she was wearing way too much jewelry for a date in her own apartment.

She was devout in a way that felt foreign to me. I tried to make small talk, but every question was met with a short, religiously anchored response. It was boring, frankly. If this was the measured religiosity Mama hoped I'd aspire to, I was glad to have resisted it so fiercely.

I told Mama it wasn't a match. She accepted my response with surprising equanimity but suggested that we try again.

I was stumped. All my life, she'd instructed me to avoid even platonic friendships with girls my age, and now, suddenly, she wanted to find me a wife? Was it even possible for anyone to go from avoiding girls to becoming a competent partner?

The following week, Mama called again to invite me to a nearby restaurant. I suspected she might have wanted to talk to me about setting up another date, but when Mama didn't mention it, I wondered if she might simply have had fun seeing me and wanted to do it again, just the two of us.

The restaurant was empty when Mama and I arrived together,

except for one table where a Muslim mom sat with her daughter. It was a trap.

THIS GIRL, NOOR, WAS DIFFERENT. SHE WAS OUTGOING, EDUCATED, and seemingly less afraid of being part of a modern society. Her hijab perfectly framed her freckled face, with its radiant smile and inviting eyes. She wore a cool outfit, a baggy shirt with a floral pattern and ripped jeans. Still, I was afraid of leading her on, letting her believe that I was some eligible, religious Muslim bachelor.

"Sorry, this is kind of weird for me. My mom didn't even tell me we were coming to meet people here . . ."

She laughed. "You had no idea this was a setup?" she asked. Our laughter immediately caught the attention of our mamas, who were getting giddy themselves as they watched from the opposite side of the restaurant.

"Can I level with you?" I asked her. "I'm not really looking to get, you know, *married* or anything right now."

She surprised me with a look of relief.

"Oh, thank God. I'm only here to keep my mom off my back. She's been begging me to meet all these guys. She thinks that because I'm twenty-one and not married, I'm gonna die alone . . ."

This time I was the one who let out a cackle.

It was kind of fun. After a while, we said our goodbyes, and afterward, in the car, Mama couldn't contain her excitement.

"She's studying to be a doctor, you know?" Mama began. I could tell she thought this was the one.

"That's cool," I responded, but I explained to Mama that I felt like I was being pushed into something I wasn't ready for. Again, she was understanding—at least at first.

That evening, I got a text message from Noor. "Hey, this is my number."

For a moment, I began to wonder if going the halal route could work for me. I caught a glimpse of a relationship with a girl that Mama was excited about, and it seemed doable. Maybe I was wrong to write off Mama's suggestion that finding a life partner was possible without dating the way non-Muslim Americans did.

Noor and I texted and talked on the phone from time to time. I was beginning to like this girl a little bit. No big feelings or anything, but I thought she was the coolest Muslim girl I'd met so far. Still, my conscience weighed me down; I was afraid of deceiving this innocent girl into believing I was something I was not. I had no idea how to tell her I was actually not a great Muslim, and the prospect of having to confess that to her terrified me.

ONE NIGHT, NOOR TEXTED TO ASK IF SHE COULD CALL ME. SHE CAME right out with it.

"I think we should stop talking," she said in a hesitant voice. "It's not you, it's that I'm still studying, and I think getting married right now would be really distracting." She explained her reasoning like it had been weighing on her.

"Yeah, I agree," I said. "It totally would be distracting. You're right."

She seemed surprised.

"Hearing you say that is going to make me wonder if this was the right call," she said in a muted tone.

"It's definitely the right call. Go be a doctor," I told her. We said our goodbyes, and I never heard from her again.

Mama's efforts never led to a relationship, but they helped me set my sights on the kind of dynamic I wanted. I wanted someone who fit into both parts of my life—who could navigate the nuances of my shaky faith and my future without making me feel I was compromising one for the other. It was about finding a partner who could walk with me in the two worlds, who acknowledged the importance of both of them. And if it was someone Mama could get butterflies about, too, that'd be even better.

Chapter 6

Halal/Haram Ratio

I FIRST ENCOUNTERED PHOTOGRAPHY IN COLLEGE, WHEN CANON introduced a video recording feature on one of their professional photography cameras: the Canon 5D Mark II. It was as revolutionary for amateur filmmaking as the discovery of fire. After reading about an exploit online that let customers trade a broken camera for a discount on a new one, I managed to get my hands on one.

Mama had always kept a drawer in her dresser filled with loose family photos, and on occasional nights, we'd go through them together. Those moments felt magical. Each photo came with a story that made my grandparents, whom I'd never met, feel real. The idea of shooting my own photos—archiving moments for others to observe and wonder about—sparked something in me.

Photography quickly became an obsession. The satisfying click of the shutter made my heart flutter, and, ever the hustler, I used the camera to take on photography gigs I found online. Little League games, wedding receptions, actor headshots—I took every paid gig I could get, reinvesting the money in better lenses and accessories.

Around that time, I became curious about *The Daily Targum,* the student-run campus newspaper. It had become a battleground for dueling op-eds from pro-Palestine and pro-Israel students. In the back of one issue, I noticed a listing for a paid video gig with the paper. Within days of reaching out, I was invited to meet the editor-in-chief, Dan Bracaglia.

Mama posing by a camel near the Pyramids, 1960s.

Dan was a character straight out of a comic book: thick glasses, messy hair, and a wardrobe that looked entirely handmade. The *Targum* office was a chaotic maze of desks crammed with computers, papers tacked to walls, and printouts of faces defaced with mustaches and scratched-out eyes. It felt electric. Dan asked me to create a sample video, and soon after, I became the paper's first multimedia editor and video producer.

Suddenly, it felt like I'd been handed the keys to the university. I had backstage access to concerts, big sporting events, and more. I produced a video every day, calling it the Daily Targum Daily Video, and quickly became known around campus as "that kid with the camera."

Photography gave me a sense of purpose. I wasn't the best skater; I couldn't draw or paint graffiti like some of my friends. But having a camera made me feel grounded. When I wanted, I could retreat behind the lens and snap photos.

AFTER COLLEGE, I KEPT TAKING ON PHOTO AND VIDEO GIGS TO EARN a living and pay down my student loan debt. During our days at the *Targum,* geeking out over a shared obsession with cameras turned Dan and me into great friends. We moved into a charming apartment in Weehawken, New Jersey, perched on the edge of the Hudson River, overlooking the New York City skyline. Dan had landed a prestigious photography job at a major magazine, and I looked up to him like a mentor. He thrived on creative praise, and I showered him with it. In return, he taught me every trick he knew.

One day, I asked him how he became such a great photographer. "Just take a hundred photos every day for like, ten years and—you know—stop being a little bitch," he replied with his signature cheesy grin.

DAN'S INFLUENCE EXTENDED BEYOND PHOTOGRAPHY. ONE EVENING, I tore open a package to reveal a pair of Rollerblades I'd ordered online, planning to use them while I shot video like a human dolly. Dan snickered and made me promise to return them. "Dude, I can't be seen with you riding Rollerblades. Here." He handed me one of his old skateboards. "Trust me," he said with a wink, "chicks dig a skateboard."

For weeks, Dan took me out on the steep hills of Weehawken to practice skating and shoot photos all night. On one crisp autumn Friday night, as we looked out over the glowing New York City skyline, I remembered I had skipped the mandatory communal Friday prayers so many times I'd become entirely detached from the ritual. Dan reached into his jacket pocket and pulled out what looked like an ordinary pen. He removed the cap, jabbed it against the ground until the back popped open, and out slipped the skinniest weed joint possible. It was his trademark.

Dan had been smoking weed for years, but I was new to it. I accepted that smoking was a sin, but at that stage in my life, I'd stopped trying to be anything other than the tortured video and photo degenerate I believed I was.

As we smoked, I admitted to Dan that I hadn't been to Friday prayer in ages. "Fridays used to mean something to me as a Muslim," I said. "Now it's just the start of the weekend."

Dan shrugged, taking a long drag from the joint. "I want that," I told him. "The way you just can't be bothered by whatever."

As the weed smoke slowly crept in and took its effect, lifting our inhibitions, Dan revealed some of his own vulnerabilities. He confessed that he felt his magazine job, while prestigious, stifled his creativity. "I can't be the same person at work as I am outside of work. If they knew who they hired, they'd fire me!" he said.

His words reminded me of how I balanced being a "proper" Muslim at home, and doing what I wanted when Mama wasn't looking.

He deflected his seriousness with a joke: "One day, I'm gonna take over that magazine and call it *Dan Zine*." We laughed, but the moment would stay with me.

As we sat on that cliff, it seemed as if the city lights formed a crown over Dan's head.

Before the night ended, Dan threw his skateboard down and asked,

"Want to see me do a boneless?" I took photos of him trying to land the trick, feeling like a mini-Dan myself. In that moment, I thought we were the coolest kids in Weehawken.

AFTER ONLY TWO YEARS OF SHARING A PLACE WITH DAN IN WEE-hawken, I landed my first grown-up job with a salary in New York City. I moved into a dingy apartment in Brooklyn, sharing it with four other people. The place was a bit cramped, run-down, and in desperate need of repairs, but it was in New York, which meant we were rarely home to be bothered by any of that.

We had frequent visitors. Anyone who knew me was invited to swing by. So when a college friend of mine, a Muslim woman named Amani al-Khatahtbeh, asked if she could visit with a friend of hers, I didn't think twice about it.

In the fall of 2015, Amani introduced me to her friend Mira. "I feel like you two could open each other's worlds a lot," she said.

I was trying my hardest to disguise my nervousness. "I'm actually going to this opening at an art gallery tonight. I know the artists. They do graffiti and stuff. Should be cool. Want to come?" I asked them.

Mira seemed unimpressed. "No, thanks," she said. She walked past me, dropped her backpack on the floor by the couch, and made herself at home.

I was already packed, with my skateboard tucked beneath my arm, ready to leave, but I dropped my stuff and sat down next to her.

She was different—Egyptian American like me, but with a confidence and presence that were both intimidating and magnetic. Her style was a blend of street and sophistication, a combination that made her seem untouchable. She had these large Disney-princess eyes with long lashes, and the swagger of someone who hangs at the skatepark and moonlights as an editor at *Vogue*. When she looked me in the eyes, I wanted to run.

"You're Muslim?" she asked me.

"Yup. Went to Islamic school and everything. Retained only the questions. None of the answers," I said.

She seemed amused. "Everyone I know who went to an Islamic school is messed up," she said.

"Oh yeah. I'm totally messed up. It's to the point that when I see someone I went to school with, I tell them I'm actually Dominican."

Amani overheard this, and laughed. "Yo, I've seen him do it! He's all, Qué lo qué?" she chimed in. Mira cracked up, but she kept her arms crossed, like she wasn't ready to let her guard down.

One of my roommates came out of his room with a joint. I felt conflicted about this, still holding out for wanting to *feel* fully Muslim one day, but embarrassed to do so in front of another Arab and Muslim person. I didn't yet have a sense for Mira's halal/haram ratio.

Mira didn't seem fazed by the weed at all. She held the joint between her fingers and casually brought it to her lips. Then, in the next moment, she glanced away into space, like she'd rather be anyplace else.

FROM THE MOMENT WE MET, MIRA SHATTERED EVERY NOTION I HAD about what it meant to be a Muslim. I had expected that all my bad habits had made me radioactive. She was brash and funny, had a tattoo, yet was still somehow very, very religious.

"It drives me crazy," she said, "that Muslims have adopted the Christian deification of man in the way they personify Allah. I'm so tired of people saying things like 'Allah *wants* or *doesn't want* certain things.' Like, has it occurred to anyone that the way the Quran is written is meant to help us achieve a high level of understanding of something deeper? People imagine this invisible all-seeing *man* with feelings. And by doing that, they abandon the *actual* journey, you know?"

I'd never heard a Muslim talk that way. In that minute, Mira revolutionized my entire relationship to Islam. She seemed like an angel sent down to challenge mankind to be better, and I couldn't believe she was in my apartment, sitting on my couch, dispensing this priceless wisdom.

She continued her analysis, reciting verses from the Quran with perfect diction, entirely from memory. She made them come alive, applying them to the complexities of our modern world in a way that made me feel I was encountering Islam for the first time in my life.

When the last of the weed had turned to ash, Mira offered a du'a, an impromptu prayer. She hung her head down and held her hands up to her face.

"May Allah guide those who seek guidance, and protect those who haven't yet discovered the right path," she said. Amani and I responded in kind: "Ameen."

I invited them out to the art-gallery party once more, but the girls declined.

"Am I going to see you again?" I asked Mira. I didn't want her to see how terrified I was of even making eye contact with her enormous brown eyes.

She gave me a confused look, like I was speaking a foreign language.

"I mean, you can give me your number and I'll hit you up about parties in Brooklyn, or whatever. We can get to know each other better," I tried once more.

She smiled. "No, thanks," she answered politely. "That's not really what I'm looking for right now."

This was a bummer, but I'd made the kind of effort I thought my friends would have been proud to witness. Mike Molina would have been happy to see me shoot my shot, and JV and Haniya would have appreciated the way I didn't persist or make the situation uncomfortable for Mira. Something about her encouraged me to feel safe in being honest with her, and I was still grateful that she had taught me something new. As I skated between cars on my way to that gallery party, I imagined that, one day, I might meet someone who was open-minded enough to light a blunt, but also sufficiently in touch with Islam so I could bring her home to my family.

While at the art gallery, I contemplated that, just because I liked a girl and she wasn't interested in me in *that* way, this didn't mean there was no future for us. Mira was still a remarkable human being, and I didn't want my desire for something more to keep us from becoming friends.

A MONTH LATER, MIRA STILL LINGERED IN MY MIND. ON A WHIM, I reached out to her. If she didn't want a relationship, maybe she could just be a spiritual friend with whom I could contemplate questions about God. So, I texted Amani: "Can you ask her for me if she's down to just be friends?"

Two weeks later, I got a text from Mira: "Hey." I was thrilled.

WE'D SPEND THE NEXT FEW MONTHS IN DEEP CONVERSATIONS ABOUT Islam and our relationships to it. She was interested in my questions as a Muslim kid from Jersey, and I was interested in how she never seemed boxed in by Islam.

Although I had always been secretive with my family, I was open with Mira. I could so easily divulge my personal shortcomings—in fact, she encouraged it. Mira is someone who gets curious about hang-ups and wants to get into the heads of people working their way through major questions and doubts. She's fascinated with how the mind and spirit rationalize things that seem entirely at odds with rationality, like God and religion. She likes to see how people justify things to themselves.

When I was around Mira, Islam wasn't a distant concept; it felt real, tangible. Nightly phone calls became our routine. I'd get home, throw my bag on the floor, download my camera's SD card, and chat with Mira for hours while I clicked on my laptop, editing the photos I'd shot that day. Mira had this way of making complex ideas seem simple.

"It's not supposed to be difficult," she'd say, helping me to unlearn what I thought I knew about being Muslim from my experience in Islamic school.

"So what do you say to people who insist that this life is just a test to prepare you for the afterlife?"

"I'd ask them why God asks us to take care of the Earth if it doesn't matter," she replied.

"As a test?"

"God swears by his creations all the time in the Quran. 'By the dawn . . .' 'By the dusk . . .' And do you know what this means? بَنَأَيُّهَا ٱلَّذِينَ ءَامَنُواْ لَا تُحَرِّمُواْ طَيِّبَٰتِ مَآ أَحَلَّ ٱللَّهُ لَكُمْ وَلَا تَعْتَدُوٓاْ إِنَّ ٱللَّهَ لَا يُحِبُّ ٱلْمُعْتَدِينَ 'O believers! Do not forbid the good things which Allah has made lawful for you, and do not transgress. Indeed, Allah does not like transgressors.' Come on, Aymann," she'd say in an exasperated voice, effortlessly switching between lively Quranic reciter and critical thinker.

Every other child of Muslim migrants I knew was like me, associating our teenage angst with rebelling against Islam. Mira seemed to have solved the puzzle that all the rest of us had failed to. She'd found a way to feel religiously fulfilled without punishing herself for loving all of what life in America had to offer. She had three separate phone apps that tracked the daily prayer times, and when the Athan call to prayer went off, she pulled herself away from whatever she was doing and made time for it. I hated when Mama made me turn off the TV to pray, but Mira loved Islam the way Mama and Baba always wished their kids would.

When she wasn't taking classes to complete her master's degree in religion, Mira stayed with her younger sister and two younger brothers in their family home in Somerset, Kentucky. She talked about Kentucky lovingly, the same way I talked about Newark. One night, she asked me if I would like to see it for myself. I bought my plane tickets before we had hung up the phone.

MY EYES FELT STRANGE IN KENTUCKY, LIKE THEY STRUGGLED TO PRO-cess the landscape; was this the first time they had ever looked beyond just one city block? Living all my life in a city, I was so accustomed to streets framed by towering buildings and sidewalks teeming with busy people that the vast stillness of the countryside felt almost surreal. The uninterrupted sky made me feel both small and exposed.

But Mira's enthusiasm in showing me around grounded me in the unfamiliar setting.

"Where do you keep the cows?" I jokingly asked her.

"Down the road. They're my friends," she replied, with a twinkle of sweet sincerity in her eyes.

After a short weekend, I was glad to be back in New York, enveloped by its familiar chaos. I didn't think much of my trip at the time, aside from having new stories about the Bible Belt to share with my friends.

THAT WINTER IN 2015, WHEN MIRA RETURNED TO NEW JERSEY ONE last time to complete her master's, she met me at Union Square in Manhattan to get up to our usual antics—browsing the city and talking about Islam. But the mood took a terrifying turn when she revealed that her father had found out about my visit and was furious.

A pit grew in my stomach. One of her younger brothers had told her parents that Mira had invited a guy friend to their family house. Though it had felt entirely innocent—we mostly drove around town and played video games with her brothers—it was a total violation in Islamic terms.

This felt like a crossroads. We were clearly growing closer, becoming just a bit more than friends. If things were going to progress any further, it needed to happen the halal way, I thought.

"What's your dad's number?" I asked her.

Mira looked nervous, but she retrieved her phone from her pocket. "What will you say?" she asked.

"Just that I'm sorry. He's right to be mad. And he has the right to know who to be mad at."

I pulled out my phone to take the number down.

"But I've got another problem," I told her.

She raised an eyebrow in anticipation.

"My phone is at one percent," I said.

"Aymann!" she shouted, laughing. She looked like she was holding herself back from punching me.

"Chill! There's a Best Buy right here." Whenever I needed a little battery boost before jumping on the train, I'd charge my phone at the Best Buy phone displays. I'd unplug one of the display models and plug mine in.

I felt that knot in my stomach tighten. I didn't really have a plan besides saying that I knew I was wrong and I was sorry. But if I could look brave in Mira's eyes, it was worth the risk.

The phone rang for a bit, and no one answered. I got his voicemail, so I put on my LinkedIn voice. "Assalamualaykum Amo"—Hello, Uncle. I said this with all the formality and confidence I could muster. I decided I'd try to leave the message in Arabic: "My name is Aymann Ismail. I got your phone number from Mira. If you'd like to call me back, I'd appreciate the opportunity to discuss something important with you. Talk to you soon, Inshallah." I hung up, and Mira offered her approval. She quickly peeked at her phone to check the time.

"Maybe he's at work?" she asked.

"Was calling him 'Amo' a little too much?"

"He's going to love that," she said encouragingly.

We headed for the exit. But we had just gotten to the door when Mira's father called me back.

"What a power move," I said to her.

"Answer it!" she said, panicky.

"Assalamualaykum!" I said loudly, leaving out the uncle this time.

"Wa 'Alaykum Assalam," Mira's dad answered. His voice was silky but powerful, like that of an Arab Pierce Brosnan.

With Mira listening in, I apologized gently but profusely. "I'm disappointed in myself for not realizing sooner how wrong it was to do that. I know better. I'm very sorry that I crossed that line with you, and that you found out the way that you did. I feel awful about it," I explained in English.

"I can tell you are genuine about this," he said. "This of course was not the right thing to do, but I'm happy that you know that it was wrong and that you want to correct your mistake. It's okay," he said.

I looked at Mira with stars in my eyes. I saw them in her eyes, too.

The rest of the conversation with her father was tense, but by the end, he granted me his blessing to pursue a relationship with his daughter and an invitation to come back to Kentucky to meet him in person, provided that Mira's mother also approved.

"Inshallah! Can't wait!" I answered. "Shukran Amo!" Thanks, Uncle! "I can't wait to meet you in person and shake your hand!" I said.

"Inshallah, Inshallah," he answered.

I snaked my phone back into my pocket and jumped over to Mira. She had already pieced it all together. "I guess I'm coming back to Kentucky!" I told her.

Mira looked smitten, giving me loving eyes. "I guess you have to tell your parents now, too," she suggested.

"Good idea," I said sweetly. I pulled my phone back out of my pocket. "Crap . . . one-percent battery again."

"Back upstairs?" she asked.

"Back upstairs!" I cheered.

I TOLD MAMA FIRST. SHE WAS EXUBERANT TO LEARN ABOUT MIRA, AND about my impending visit to meet her father in Kentucky. But Mama was sure that the invitation extended to her as well.

"Aymann, they're expecting your family. This is the way this is done as Muslims," she asserted.

"Okay, but it's in Kentucky! You'll need to book flights and a hotel," I said.

"Of course!" she exclaimed excitedly. "Mashallah! Alhamdulillah! May Allah protect you and bless your future," she said in Arabic. Mira could hear it through the phone. "Ameen," she mouthed.

For the first time, I could imagine living unapologetically, knowing that Mama's love for me wasn't in jeopardy. At long last, I didn't feel I was doing something bad behind her back.

"So . . ." I started, turning my attention back to Mira. "Want to try out these new headphones while we wait for this phone to charge?"

"Yes!" she said. Off to a perfect start, I thought.

JUST A FEW WEEKS LATER, MY PARENTS AND I BOARDED THE PLANE to Kentucky. I tried to swallow my fear, but it didn't go down easily.

On the way to Mira's family home from the hotel, Baba insisted on driving, because he wanted me focused on meeting Mira—as if it was my first time meeting her. He wasn't showing excitement outwardly, and didn't pull me aside to give me a pep talk or anything, like you might see in the movies. Instead, he showed support in his own stoic way, with his eyes trained on the road.

Fighting off nerves, I gently pulled out a small box and carefully removed it from the miniature gift bag. I thumbed it around in my palm for a minute, mulling over whether I could trust my parents enough to let them in on my little secret. I turned around and revealed it to my mom, who was smiling as she looked out the window in the back seat.

"What do you think of these?" I asked, as I opened the case and showed Mama a set of modest-sized rose-gold double-hooped earrings with tiny diamond studs.

"Allah!" Mama exclaimed joyfully. She pulled them out carefully to take a closer look. "She wears earrings?" she asked me.

"Don't all girls?" I asked. Was I an idiot for buying a girl earrings?

"How much did you pay for them?" Mama asked in a changed tone.

"Mama!" I exclaimed. I withdrew the earrings and turned back to face front, feeling shamed and judged.

Baba scoffed loudly. "Who did you hand your money to? Did you pay cash?" he questioned, his eyes on the road still.

"I bought them at the diamond district in Manhattan," I said. Baba shook his head in disapproval but remained silent.

"Aymann! You should have asked me first! I saw earrings just like this at Costco! And for less than five hundred dollars!" Mama exclaimed. She was right that I had overpaid, which didn't make me feel any less under attack.

"They're really nice, though," Mama said. "Mashallah. Bravo, habibi," Mama comforted me, obviously having noticed that I felt vulnerable. She placed the earrings gently back into their case and tapped my shoulder to hand them back to me.

Nobody said another word. We don't hash things out in our family. We let them go.

WE ARRIVED AT MIRA'S HOME EARLY. IT WAS A BEAUTIFUL SUMMER morning, with just a few clouds in the sky, like floating ornaments. Mira's two preteen brothers rushed over to answer the door.

I took off my shoes, and when I looked up, I saw Mira. I was used to seeing her dressed in a hoodie and jeans, but today she wore an emerald-green dress with hand-embroidered designs that gave it away as an import from Egypt. Her eye makeup made her look even more like a Disney princess. Her hair was up in a bow, with long curls streaming out in back.

My mouth went dry. Mira smiled at me like she thought I was being silly. And then I noticed something else. *Shit, she's not wearing earrings,* I thought to myself.

"Hi," she said faintly.

I froze. "Hi . . ." I said staring forward. Though Mira and I were already an item at this point, I felt like I was meeting her for the first time. After all, I'd met her less than a year ago.

"Come in! Come in!" called Mira's mom, Tant Maha (*tant* is Arabic for "aunt," but also a term of status for a woman you want to address affectionately, as a relative), welcoming us into the foyer. She waved her arms in excitement, gesturing for us to follow her into the living room, where Mira's dad, Ashraf, was standing, wearing a very sharp black suit. I hadn't forgotten our phone conversation. Tension weighed heavily on my mind, but he offered me a warm and inviting smile.

Behind them was an elaborately set-up seating arrangement. I walked over to shake her dad's hand. "Hamdila Alsalamah!" he said firmly, thank God for your safety. "How was your trip?" he said to my baba as both my parents shuffled in.

"Alhamdulillah," they both answered in unison.

Mira guided us to where she had set up two very stylish European dining chairs in their massive living room, with an ornate side table between them holding a Quran. The parents and Mira's brothers sat on couches across from us. Mira and I were on a stage, with our families positioned as audience.

Her dad—Uncle Ashraf, as I called him—began formally.

"Mira agreed to this meeting, to get to know you and your family better. And for you to get to know us better. With Allah's blessing, I will read the Fatiha."

The Fatiha, "the Opening" in Arabic, is just the opening chapter of the Quran. But in this context, reading it would initiate something of an engagement between Mira and me. Was I ready for this? I wondered. But I suppressed my doubts. "Inshallah," I said, trying to match Uncle Ashraf's directness and candor.

Mira and I watched as our parents engaged in conversation, sharing where they were from in Egypt and telling embarrassing stories about their kids. I winced as Mama described me as a fumbling baby who climbed the furniture and always landed on my diaper.

BUT I HAD ANOTHER THING ON MY MIND. I PRESSED MY HAND AGAINST the small box in my suit jacket pocket. It felt electric.

"Diamonds, baby," I whispered to myself, trying to summon some courage to present it to the beautiful girl on the other side of the little table. I withdrew the box from my jacket pocket.

"You wear earrings, right?" I nervously asked.

"Yeah, sometimes," she replied. I handed her the box.

"For whenever you *do* wear them," I said.

She opened the box slowly and gazed at her new earrings with adoring eyes. "Oooh," she ogled. Both our moms looked over with great interest, while the dads just sat and smiled at each other.

"I *love* rose gold!" Mira exclaimed.

Maha jumped out of her seat and came over to inspect the earrings herself. "Wow! This is really nice, Mira!" she affirmed, as she offered me a glance of approval. I looked over at my mama and shrugged. She wore a thick grin—the happiest I'd ever seen her.

After the gifts, Uncle Ashraf sat up a bit—a slight movement that shifted the mood of the room, commanding everyone's attention. "It's almost time for Duhr. Yalla. Would you all like to read the Fatiha?" I glanced over at Mira. Her eyes confirmed what I was feeling: overwhelming excitement. We were ready.

Uncle Ashraf cupped his hands and tilted his head forward. The rest of us did the same. He recited the ceremonial verses:

بِسْمِ ٱللَّهِ ٱلرَّحْمَٰنِ ٱلرَّحِيمِ (١)
ٱلْحَمْدُ لِلَّهِ رَبِّ ٱلْعَٰلَمِينَ (٢)
ٱلرَّحْمَٰنِ ٱلرَّحِيمِ (٣)
مَٰلِكِ يَوْمِ ٱلدِّينِ (٤)
إِيَّاكَ نَعْبُدُ وَإِيَّاكَ نَسْتَعِينُ (٥)
ٱهْدِنَا ٱلصِّرَٰطَ ٱلْمُسْتَقِيمَ (٦)
صِرَٰطَ ٱلَّذِينَ أَنْعَمْتَ عَلَيْهِمْ غَيْرِ ٱلْمَغْضُوبِ عَلَيْهِمْ وَلَا ٱلضَّآلِّينَ (٧)

In the name of Allah, the Entirely Merciful, the Especially Merciful.
All praise is due to Allah, Lord of the worlds—
The Entirely Merciful, the Especially Merciful,
Sovereign of the Day of Recompense.
It is You we worship and You we ask for help.
Guide us to the straight path—
The path of those upon whom You have bestowed favor, not of
    those who have evoked Your anger or of those who are astray.

The knot in my gut loosened. For a moment, inviting God into the room helped me feel I could relinquish control. It was the perfect opportunity for me to acknowledge that I had never really had control in the first place.

"Yalla. You lead the prayer." Uncle Ashraf gestured his arm forward, inviting my baba to be imam, but Baba didn't bite.

"Go ahead," he responded in Arabic, as he wrapped his arm around Uncle Ashraf's back and physically shoved him forward. Eventually, he won the bout and lined up with his two boys and me behind my baba. The two mamas and Mira lined up behind us in the back, all draped in long isdals, oversized hijabs.

Afterward, Tant Maha invited us into the kitchen. On the table was something that looked like a chocolate birthday cake with Mira's and my names written on it in thin red icing, a heart conjoining us. "It's on a cake, so now it's official," Mira playfully snickered at me. I took a long look at the cake and started to laugh.

My name on the cake was misspelled, missing the second "n."

"Who the hell is that guy?!" I joked. Mira shook her head at me, trying to conceal her smile.

"LULULULULULULULULULULEEEEEEE!!!!" Tant Maha let loose a zaghroota while she pulled the foil from four massive trays of food. There was about a tray-full for each of us there, including rice, chicken, mashed potatoes, salad—the works. Without a second thought, Mira and I dived in.

My parents left pretty soon after they finished their meals; Baba couldn't turn down too many jobs without it costing him return clients. I opted to stay another day, now that I had permission from Mira's family to pursue something romantic with her. But I'm not sure I did myself too many favors.

That night, Mira's dad again gathered everyone to pray. He insisted that I lead the prayer.

"No, no, I couldn't. It's your house!" I shot back, playing the same game my baba had played.

"No, no, no, you're our guest," he lobbed back. We volleyed back and forth way too many times for it to feel polite before I crabbily relented.

I'm the youngest boy in my family. Growing up, I was asked a grand total of zero times to lead the prayer. And after five years in New York, I was badly out of the practice of the daily ritual prayer and in no shape to lead one.

Uncle Ashraf lined up with both of his sons on either side of him, as Mira and Tant Maha donned isdals and stood behind them. They tilted their heads in anticipation of my command to initiate the prayer.

I silently gave myself a little pep talk. It's just "Allahu Akbar," like twenty times. Easy.

I took a breath. "Allahu Akbar!" I said loudly.

I recited Surah Fatiha, the same chapter we had recited earlier in the day. So far so good. Then Surah Al-Asr—literally the shortest chapter of the entire Quran, only three verses long. My inner voice creeped in. *Oh God. Al-Asr? Seriously?* In the second rak'a, I went with Surah Al-Nas, which might have been the first surah I had memorized, as a baby. There are only six verses, and they all end with the same word, like a nursery rhyme.

Verse one. *Easy. Slow and steady, Aymann.*

Verse two. *Muscle memory. I got this.*

Verse three. *Keep going!*

Verse four. *I remember being taught this one was about witchcraft . . .*

Verse five. *You're pulling it off—*

From behind me came a commanding voice: "Al-la-*thi*!" It was the elder of Mira's two younger brothers. Oof. What had I said? "Al-la-*zi*"? I started the verse over, trying to recuperate. "Al-lathi . . ."

At the end, in the final position of the prayer, my mind was still on how I'd chosen to go it the easy way and still gotten the verse wrong. But things got worse. At the end of the prayer, I blanked. I somehow forgot how to close out of the prayer.

No. No, no, no, no, no. No, Aymann. No. Think. What was it? Aymann! No. No, no, no, no, NO. Muscle memory? Help! NO!

The whole family were sitting in that final position behind me for what felt like ages. It was quiet. The sounds of people murmuring their prayers had died out, and I still hadn't ended the prayer. The agony!

I panicked. I had to do something. I turned my head to the right and muttered "Allahu Akbar," turned my head to the left and muttered it again.

Mira's dad took over. "Assalamualaykum, Assalamualaykum," he said loudly in his commanding voice. Assalamualaykum! That's what I'd forgotten. The words for greeting and saying goodbye. It's literally the simplest Muslim phrase in all of Islam. *Assalamualaykum!* Are you kidding me?

I turned around to face Mira and her family. Mira remained focused on the prayer, making du'a, personal appeals to God. Nobody said anything to acknowledge what had just happened, or even looked up. They all continued their prayers. Mira's dad might have refrained from commenting out of kindness, but it didn't matter. I was beyond embarrassed. Then it got worse.

"Okay, time for Isha," Mira's dad declared, rising to his feet. It was the last prayer of the day.

"You lead this time," I said nudging him into my place at the front. And, this time, he didn't resist. He led us through the prayer immaculately, reciting longer surahs with ease, with his eyes closed in concentration; he meant every word.

Despite the familiar cadence of the prayer, my mind raced with thoughts of inadequacy and shame. I'd mastered living a double life inside my own family, but it seemed to have taken no time at all for me to be discovered as a fraud by Mira's family.

"Allahu Akbar," Mira's baba intoned, his voice commanding as he and his children bowed forward in synchronized prayer. Would Mira's baba now doubt my worthiness to be with his daughter? Had my failure to lead a single prayer irreparably damaged my standing in his eyes, revealing me to be a hypocrite, unfit to guide his future grandchildren?

In the midst of my inner turmoil, I couldn't help gazing at Mira's baba with admiration. It was like I caught my first glimpse into the kind of father I hoped to become for my own children: a commanding leader who could inspire within them a genuine yearning for a deep, meaningful relationship with Allah. It wasn't just a routine for them; it was a sacred ritual—a moment of communion with the divine, something they *needed* to break free from the confines of the world we lived in. I was stunned.

After the family was finished, Mira's two younger brothers folded everyone's prayer mats and stashed them aside. I sought to clear the air with Mira's baba.

"Uncle, I'm embarrassed," I said to him.

"It's okay," he acknowledged. "Do you know why prayer is so important?" he asked.

"Because it's what separates us from the non-Muslims," I said, echoing my parents.

"Because, if you make it a habit, it makes it so everything else in Islam comes naturally," he said. "If you pray five times a day, all the other struggles—for focus, for honesty, for patience—all of it requires your morality to be strong, and prayer is how you practice and ready yourself for those moments. We pray to God. But God doesn't need our prayer. We pray for our own good," he explained.

I was touched. Mira became a little bit less of an enigma, and Islam as a religion along with her.

THE NEXT MORNING, MY WEEKEND IN KENTUCKY WAS OVER. I NEEDED to return to the hustle in Brooklyn. I felt I had been cut by the very tip of a sword, had felt the edge of something powerful that could literally have killed me. I brought a prayer mat to work the next Monday, with new conviction.

I got to my desk and ran through my morning routine. Around lunchtime that day, I found a quiet corner of the office and prayed. If I hadn't been so focused on how proud of myself I was for praying, maybe I would have benefited from it.

THE DAYS THAT FOLLOWED SEEMED TO BLUR TOGETHER. THINGS WERE moving quickly with Mira, and my mind raced with the possibilities of how this new connection could coexist with my only passion at the time: exploring the off-limits corners of New York City, and documenting graffiti writers unleashing their artistry then vanishing into the night. This time, unlike the night we met, when I invited Mira to join me on a night out, she said yes.

Near the Manhattan Bridge, we joined one of my best friends, a graffiti artist who went by the moniker VEW. The plan was simple: climb the fence, cross the tracks, and explore the hidden corners of the city.

"This is Mira. We're basically married now," I said, joking about how she'd met my family.

"You guys got here at the perfect time. I've been watching the foot traffic, and it's dead right now."

I positioned Mira in front of me and pointed to the train track on the Manhattan Bridge that tunneled underground, beneath the streets of Manhattan.

VEW nodded his head and sank his bare fingers into the splits in the chain fence. The fence rattled loudly back and forth, swaying rapidly against the hand railing on the walking path with the weight it wasn't built to hold. I snapped a photo of VEW as half his body swung around to the top and he plopped down to the bottom on the other side, nailing the superhero landing.

I put my camera away to free up both hands and gestured toward Mira to help her get her footing, but, before I'd even turned, she was already at the very top of the fence. She turned around and looked at me—my jaw agape, at the base of the fence—shrugged, swiveled her body around, and climbed down, barely rattling the fence at all.

"It's like that?" I murmured as I made the climb up and down myself.

We ran out of view and into a pitch-black corner of the cavernous space beneath Manhattan. I leaned into Mira's ear and whispered, "Okay. There are some rules down here. Avoid the third rail. Step only where I step. And stop only in the darkest spots. Got it?" I could feel Mira's adrenaline pumping.

VEW went first, moving back deeper into the darkness of the tunnel. He skipped swiftly over the track. I moved slowly so Mira could see where I was stepping and follow.

We heard rumbles coming from behind us and crept into the darkest corner. As the train passed, I let corniness take over. "This would be a cool spot for a kiss, right?" I said.

She smiled, leaned in, and planted one right on me. This was my first halal date, but it was also illegal, I thought.

We explored a bit deeper into the tunnel. VEW took out two spray-paint cans, wielding one in each hand. Mira looked over his shoulder, studying his hand waving as he painted perfectly consistent streaks of white and yellow high above the other tags. He was finished in an instant.

"Dope," Mira whispered. I took photos of VEW as he leaned toward the edge, closing his eyes just as another train brought a gust of wind mixed with steel dust. Mira crouched behind us. When the train had passed, we made our way back down the tunnel toward the bridge, and over the gate again.

On our way back to my apartment in Brooklyn, aboard the J subway train, I whispered into Mira's ear, "Nobody knows what we just did." I could see in her eyes a sense of contentment. I had wondered if that experience would scare her off. It did the opposite.

AS WE REACHED THE MIDWAY POINT OF THE WILLIAMSBURG BRIDGE, Mira turned to me with a grin.

"That was insane," she said.

"Want to see something else?" I asked her. I grabbed her by the hand. Sensing that we still had the rush of the night coursing through our veins, I led her to the end of the subway car, opened the door, and stepped out with her to the space between the cars. The city lights shone like fireflies on the river beneath our feet. The wind swirled her hair, and our clothes fluttered as if they were dancing. The metal beams rushing past above synchronized with the sound of the train hurtling down the steel tracks.

We kissed for only a second, but that memory is seared into my brain. I watched Mira staring off, her eyes wider than I'd ever seen them. When the train crossed the bridge, we went back into the car. Nobody even looked up.

"That right there is why I love this city," I murmured to myself as Mira and I went to look out the window at the river. New York is magical.

IN THE MONTHS THAT FOLLOWED, MIRA AND I CONTINUED TO EXPLORE the city together. We climbed rooftops, wandered through abandoned buildings, and even sneaked into a few concerts. We read KEEP OUT signs like invitations.

LATE ONE NIGHT, ON A ROOFTOP IN BROOKLYN, MIRA AND I GOT TALK-ing about the kind of future we wanted with each other. She turned to me but remained quiet.

"My mom asked me how I felt about you," she said.

I swallowed so loudly I could have sworn she heard it. "What did you tell her?" I asked.

Mira explained that her mom had encouraged her to keep it halal, and for us to get religiously married, especially as we continued to see each other more. But even though we'd grown close, it still felt to me like this came out of nowhere.

I hesitated. "Are you asking me to marry you right now? Like, for real?" I said, nervously laughing.

Mira laughed, too, which helped alleviate some of the awkward-ness. "Do you *want* to marry me?" she asked.

Maybe I should have thought about it for a second, but the answer just came tumbling out. "Honestly, if I'm going to take that leap of faith with anyone, it'll be you."

We both sat quietly for a moment, letting what I'd just said ring out.

"Yeah. Me, too," she said quietly.

"Ugh . . . my family is going to be so excited," I said. We both laughed.

But after the initial excitement subsided, I unleashed my emotions about marriage, hoping they wouldn't scare her away. "I guess I'm worried about ending up like my parents, putting religion at the center of everything, to the point where we end up like robots carrying out this programming—having kids when we're supposed to, raising them the way we're supposed to, all that."

What Mira said next I carry with me so deeply that it has become a part of who I am.

"The reason I'm ready to try something like this is not because I love who you are today. It's because I love how you think. Everything else just matters less to me," she explained.

Mira seemed to understand, in a way I hadn't yet, that real growth often means letting go of one part of ourselves to make space for another, and allowing the other person the freedom to evolve. She wasn't just caught up in the excitement of our days in New York; she was looking ahead, imagining the kind of life partner she wanted. It took me a few weeks to fully process what I had agreed to, but as her words settled in, I found myself ready to embrace it.

THE NEXT SUMMER, IN 2016, I WAS BACK IN SOMERSET, KENTUCKY, BUT this time I was wearing a tux, surrounded by family and friends, and waiting at the bottom of the staircase for my bride. Mira floated down in a gorgeous white dress, making each step glow as she blessed the room with her arrival. For the entire party, I was completely outside of my body.

Some of my friends had come from New York, too. As my best friend Mike Molina fixed my bow tie, he whispered into my ear: "You're the only person I would ever come all the way out to Kentucky for, bro."

Not even one year after meeting Mira, she and I were religiously married. We got our paperwork filled out with the nearby registry in Kentucky, and in the eyes of the state, and also Allah, Mira was my wife, and I was her husband. But in the eyes of our family, it was a whole other story. As Egyptians, we wouldn't be considered a truly married couple until I, as the man, got a place ready for us to move into together. Without that, the second ceremony—a big party formalizing the marriage with our families—would have to wait.

Thanks for everything
Aymann! Please take
good care of beautiful
Petunia until I
come back :")

♡ Mira

P.S. Didn't have enough space for
the contact solution : lol

Handwritten note from Mira asking me to care for the
impulse-bought plant she'd left at my Brooklyn apartment, 2016.

Chapter 7

No Lens Cap

THERE WAS ONE PERSON WITH WHOM I COULDN'T WAIT TO SHARE the news of my marriage: Haniya. In college, we'd both gone through parallel crises of faith. She'd married a Muslim man, only to divorce. Now, single again, Haniya seemed freer than ever. After graduating, she got a job in Manhattan. Whenever she could, she'd drop by my Brooklyn apartment, where she'd start her night before enjoying the trendy neighborhoods nearby.

I giddily delivered the news of my marriage. Haniya, as always, didn't miss the chance to take credit.

"You're welcome for preparing you for a girl like Mira. You were so sheltered when we met. Honestly, you should be kissing my feet right now."

My roommates laughed, egging her on.

"Oh, please," I replied, shaking my head. "Do you even remember what you said when I first told you about Mira?" Haniya raised an eyebrow; clearly, she'd forgotten. "You said she was too much woman for me." I laughed.

"She *is!*" Haniya bellowed, letting out one of her deep, contagious laughs.

I grinned, but I couldn't let it go. "And what about you? You got married to be free, and now look at you."

It came out sharper than I intended—blunt, almost cruel. But that was our dynamic, trading jabs like old friends who had long stopped sugarcoating things. At least, that's what I told myself. Maybe it was just another defense mechanism, my way of resisting how often she challenged me. Or maybe I'd grown so comfortable that I forgot she wasn't immune to my carelessness. Either way, I knew the words had landed wrong.

Haniya shrugged. Though she was clearly insulted, she had gotten accustomed to giving me grace. "I gave up on it, honestly," she said. "But seeing you and Mira gives me hope. Like, maybe it's possible to find a decent Muslim who isn't expecting his wife to pick up where his mom left off." She giggled, but I could sense the truth beneath her words.

"I guess I got lucky," I said, cautiously.

Haniya snapped her fingers. "Say Mashallah and Alhamdulillah," she scolded. "And recite Mu'awwizatayn!" referring to the two protective surahs from the Quran. "Be grateful to Allah, and watch out for jealousy. Now that you've got a wife, you need to protect yourself from envy."

Haniya's faith had evolved, too, though in another direction. She became captivated by North African spiritual traditions, drawn to the ways they diverged from the more rigid Arab practices of Islam we had both grown up with. She explored the idea that her misfortunes were the result of unseen curses, and sought out mystic healers who performed ruqyah for her, warding off evil spirits from her body and orbit.

Her curiosity led her deep into histories and rituals I never heard of. She became intrigued by the tradition of ornamental face tattoos once worn by Indigenous women before stricter Islamic practices spread, as a way of protecting themselves from evil jinns. I was taken aback. I had always been taught that tattoos were flatly haram, considered an unholy mutilation of the body.

Given my own North African heritage, I asked my parents the next chance I got if any women in our lineage had worn them. I was stunned to learn that they had—as recently as my great-grandmother. It was a revelation I would have never encountered if not for Haniya's relentless curiosity, and her willingness to explore faith in ways I had never considered.

"Thanks," I whispered, and quietly recited the verses to myself. "Got any advice for me?"

"The fact that you're stopping to ask means you're ready," she said, her tone softening. "The problem with most Muslim guys is, they don't think. They just want. If I can give you any advice, it's this: want *less*."

I paused, letting her words sink in. She was right—wanting less would ease both Mira's burden of having to perform, and mine of constantly yearning for something more. I nodded, impressed, but I avoided feeding her ego. She already acted like she ran the place when she was at my apartment.

BY THE TIME I WAS FINISHED WITH COLLEGE IN 2011, I HAD GOTTEN something perhaps more valuable than a college degree: a massive portfolio of video and photo work. The following year, in late 2012, I caught a big break when a friend from Rutgers reached out. He worked at an art-focused magazine in New York called *ANIMAL New York,* and he told me that they were looking to expand their video team and that I came to mind. After just one interview, I was making all kinds of crazy photos and videos, and getting a salary to do it felt like a miracle.

The magazine team included only about five people, but the energy in the room felt like a bustling newsroom of fifty, thanks largely to Bucky Turco, the editor-in-chief and founder. Bucky was a classic New Yorker, loud, relentless, and hilarious. He grew up on Long Island but had called the city home since the early 1990s. His voice boomed through the office, whether he was barking out assignments, cracking jokes, or passionately debating the finer points of the newest meme to go viral. His desk was a shrine to controlled chaos, blasting reggae or hip-hop at an obnoxious volume throughout the day. He had a kind of magnetism that made you want to match his energy, even if it exhausted you.

Bucky was always in motion, throwing pens across the room to get your attention, demanding the best from everyone with a bluntness that could border on brutal. I believed it was linked to his mysterious and rough upbringing. He sometimes shared stories involving drug heists and armored trucks that were so out there that some of them were hard to believe. Growing up in Newark, I'd learned to love people who had an edge, and Bucky was like a human box cutter. To me, he was the last of a dying breed—a relic of New York's rawer days, a living legend.

A FEW MONTHS INTO THIS GIG, I COULDN'T IMAGINE DOING ANYTHING else. It wasn't a job—it was an adrenaline-fueled daily dive into the beating heart of New York's underground. Bucky introduced me to graffiti kings and street art legends who made the city their playground. Every photo and video I captured was a one-of-a-kind piece of art, preserving fleeting masterpieces before they were painted over and lost forever. Each day, I was dodging security guards to sneak into abandoned warehouses, scaling rooftops to document murals in progress, and following artists as they graffiti-bombed subway cars.

After that first year, I stopped waiting for Bucky to dispatch me. I spent every night wandering around every borough of New York, camera in hand, which began to look like it'd gone through war. The lens was scratched up, the body was chipped and battered, and it hadn't seen a lens cap or strap in months. Trailing nocturnal graffiti-writers deep into the forbidden worlds of subway tunnels became all of who I was. The hiss of distant trains, the echoes of footsteps on steel tracks—I could hardly sleep without the nagging feeling that I belonged out there.

I was at home underground, but the city's bridges—those towering giants piercing the skyline—looked like jewels to me. When a younger photographer reached out to the magazine, boasting about his escapades climbing to the peak of the Williamsburg Bridge, I didn't hesitate. I knew instantly I had found my ticket up.

———

THIS YOUNG PHOTOGRAPHER, LUCAS, TOLD ME TO MEET HIM ON THE Williamsburg Bridge. With baseball gloves in my backpack (for a better grip), my *ANIMAL*-branded baseball cap (to hide my face), and my backpack stocked with camera gear, I set out to meet him. It was already 11:00 p.m. when I arrived. He appeared from above, dropping down like Spider-Man.

I followed him up as we scaled the diagonal beams high above the East River—nothing beneath us but hundreds of feet and water. As I looked down, I noticed that my shoe had come untied. I pressed my foot down against the bridge, using all of the strength in my toes to widen my foot and keep the shoe in place. I tried to keep my eyes on Lucas and climb exactly how he climbed, and I stayed focused on the prize: a perfect shot from the top of the bridge.

The climb was much more difficult than he'd let on. We needed to pull our body weight up through gaps between the beams. As we climbed higher, the wind grew stronger, buffeting us and threatening to knock us off balance. At one point, we had to walk across a narrow beam, an iron tightrope, my arms stretched out for balance. My eyes were locked on Lucas, who looked like he was playing on a jungle gym.

Finally, we made it to the top. My legs were wobbling, and I was gasping for breath, but I felt exhilarated. The view was breathtaking. The lights of the city stretched and winked before us. I could see for miles in every direction.

"Even if they arrested us now, they could never take the view," Lucas quipped. I smiled. He was right.

Instead of going to bed when I got home, I booted up my laptop and started editing my photos right away. They turned out to be amazing. It wasn't until a week later that reality hit me. As I was flipping through the photos, reliving the climb, a pang of fear struck me. What if I had slipped? And for what? A few photos, some likes on Instagram, and a moment of fleeting recognition? It wasn't worth the risk. But as I looked back at those photos, the rush of adrenaline and sense of accomplishment returned. Maybe it *was* worth it? Maybe it was both.

That thrill became the bud of a new piece of my personality blossoming. It meshed perfectly with my newfound love of journalism and storytelling from the front lines.

I'd continue to push the limits, summoning courage by telling myself the photos would be worth it. This work even led me to Egypt: Bucky texted me saying he had bought a ticket to Cairo to witness the tenuous period after the 2011 revolution firsthand.

"I'm coming with you," I texted back immediately. He refused, saying it was too dangerous for him to greenlight. I booked my flight that very day anyway.

Soon enough, we were both in Cairo.

We ended up staying in a hotel right inside Tahrir Square, which had become a sprawling encampment after the area functioned as the beating heart of the protests fueling the ousting of the decades-long regime headed by Egyptian president Hosni Mubarak. Bucky couldn't believe the atmosphere—chaotic but festive.

"Look at that! One guy's eating ice cream while another's doing doughnuts on his Vespa. And all around them, people are chanting! What the hell is going on? I love it!" he shouted, fully embracing the madness. My cousin Osama agreed to help us avoid getting into too much trouble. Osama was stoic, like all of my Upper Egyptian family. Even though we'd met in person only once before, he took it upon himself to help me however he could.

At one point, when we were deep in Tahrir Square, interviewing a protester about Egypt's first-ever democratic election, we were interrupted by loud bangs reverberating from a nearby alley. Instinctively, Osama, Bucky, and I hurried toward the noise—until we emerged into a battle. On one side, security forces were advancing, with guns slung over their backs, and taking cover behind an armored vehicle. On the other side, the protesters were hurling stones and Molotov cocktails. The air was thick with the acrid scent of tear gas, the sharp crack of rubber bullets ricocheting off buildings, and the desperate cries of injured protesters who were being dragged away.

I positioned myself as close to the front lines as I could and frantically snapped photos while Osama kept watch over my shoulder. At one point, protesters with large sticks were banging on a burned-out car in rhythm, creating an eerie, thunderous beat. Above them, two flags waved: the Egyptian flag, marked with both a crescent and a cross, symbolizing unity between Christians and Muslims; and a red flag spray-painted with the face of Khaled Saeed, whose death had sparked the revolution.

I switched between video and photo modes on my Canon 5D, capturing the charging security forces, the protesters retaliating, and the mayhem unfolding in real time. Osama's voice cut through the noise whenever danger approached, yelling, "Yalla ya Aymann!" I let my body move on autopilot, trusting his lead. The protesters chanted, "Horeya! Horeya!"—Freedom! Freedom!—with an intensity that made my heart pound.

AFTER WE RETURNED TO NEW YORK, BUCKY AND I PUBLISHED A DIS-patch series for the magazine. But nothing would compare to what happened when I returned to Egypt the following year for Osama's brother's wedding, this time without Bucky.

I arrived to find Cairo in turmoil again. A massive protest erupted near El-Hegaz Square, where my mama, sister, and I were staying with my aunt. The protesters barreling past our balcony were so loud they sounded like a freight train. The previously outlawed Muslim Brother-hood emerged from the shadows after the revolution in 2011 and won the presidency in the country's first-ever fair democratic election. The streets were filled with their supporters after the Egyptian military arrested the president and seized back control of the country. It was a pivotal moment in Egypt's history. I couldn't resist my intense crav-ing to document it in any way I could. I told my family I'd be back in a minute, grabbed my camera, and headed toward the commotion.

AS I MADE MY WAY THROUGH THE THRONGS OF PEOPLE, I FELT ELEC-tricity in the air. My Arabic isn't perfect, but I loved being out navi-gating on my own. I spotted a dozen men on the sidewalk walking parallel to us, writing graffiti on the walls, awnings, buses—everything. They wrote slogans like "Morsi is my president," "No CC," and "CC is a murderer," phonetically referring to the current leader President Abdel Fattah El-Sisi. It was the perfect convergence of all my interests up until that point. I was there, capturing the moment as people painted graffiti in Cairo in the heat of a protest. I jumped down from the truck and ran over to ask permission to document one of the protesters. "Yeah, we're not afraid," he replied. "We're ready to die for this!" I took that as license to follow and document what he was doing. As I followed the man, I was amazed at how easily he moved through the crowd, tagging walls and shouting his message. He was fearless and confident. I took picture after picture, capturing the defiance and power in their message.

Then another man stood out for me—he was older than the others, wearing a traditional galabiya instead of jeans and a T-shirt. I watched as he prepared to tag the door of a gorgeous, old cathedral, the Cathedral of Our Lady of Fatima. I took picture after picture as the man spray-painted the door with "Islameya," short for "Masr Islameya," or "Egypt Is Islamic."

I crept closer to get better photos, when suddenly the vandal noticed me. His face twisted with anger, and in an instant, he lunged at me and sprayed black paint all over my face and neck. Within seconds, I was surrounded by a mob. I felt as though they were trying to tear me apart. I braced, tucked my chin downward into my chest, and wrapped both my arms around the body of the camera in a cradle, a technique I learned from my short stint playing football in high school. All I smelled was sweat and spray paint.

"Erase the photos!" the vandal demanded, his sweaty grip tightening around my neck. I struggled to comply, my fingers fumbling over the camera buttons. But even after I showed them that I'd deleted the images, they weren't satisfied. They wanted my camera.

"Smash the camera!" yelled one person in Arabic. "Gasoos!" Spy! Just one person accused me of being a spy, and the mob intensified their assault. Blows rained down on me as I struggled to protect my camera. A man I couldn't see reached from behind to pry my hands off it. Another man headbutted me, and finally, my grip loosened. When they were through, and I was empty-handed, they shoved me to the side. But now, I was the one unsatisfied.

"Haramee!" I screamed. "Thief!"—hoping to draw the attention of protesters who weren't part of the mob. "No, we're Muslim. Muslims don't steal," a man who had just been a part of the mob that robbed me told me in an unsettlingly calm voice. Another man took pity on me and pulled on my arm to drag me away from the scene. "Khalas. Imshi." Enough. Just go.

But I couldn't leave. I spotted the vandal with my camera stuffed into his galabiya pocket.

I chased after him, demanding my camera back. He wasn't having it, telling me it belonged to him until he could verify he wasn't in any of the photos. As I pleaded with him, his attention suddenly turned acute.

"What country are you from? Your Arabic is off," he interrogated me.

I knew I had to hide that I was American, and fast. "I'm from Alexandria," I lied, hoping the regional differences in accent could provide enough cover. But the deception only added to his suspicion.

"Do you work for CNN?" he asked in Arabic, his tone menacing.

I could feel the weight of his gaze bearing down on me. "I'm just visiting family," I said, trying to keep my voice steady.

"I don't believe you," he shot back, his tone almost gleeful. A chill ran down my spine. "You'll get it back in Rabaa," he threatened, referring to Rabaa al-Adawiya Square, where supporters of the Muslim Brotherhood were defying a military curfew, which the military announced earlier would treat anyone caught near the square after hours as a terrorist. It was the last place I wanted to be suspected of being a spy. Desperate, I dug through my pockets hoping to find something that would help me escape the situation. Miraculously, my hand found my mama's Egyptian phone. It was my only hope. I called the last number dialed, my aunt's, and my mama answered.

"This guy took my camera and won't give it back. He thinks I'm not Egyptian," I said, explaining the situation.

My mama's reaction was immediate. "Who is he?" she demanded. "Give him the phone!" I passed the phone to the vandal, feeling a sense of triumph as he looked at me with confusion. "Who is this?" he asked skeptically. "Mama," I replied, smirking. The man's face fell as he nervously took the phone from me.

Mama's voice roared, somehow cutting through the noise of the protest. I could only catch bits and pieces of what she was saying, but the man's face grew redder by the second. I think I heard her say something about tearing at his face with her bare hands and chewing on the skin caught in her fingernails. I could see the fear in his eyes. He squinted as he struggled to keep the phone up to his ear. "I'm sorry, Mama!" he said over and over again. "I will bring him home myself! I promise!" he said trying to get a word in underneath my mama's yelling. "I promise you! You are like my mama! I promise I will bring him home!" he begged.

The man handed me back the phone, his face still flushed with embarrassment. "Why did you have to call your mama?"

"Give me back my camera," I demanded, my anger rising again. After a few tense moments, he still refused to hand me back the camera, or to release me.

Just when I thought all hope was lost, Hebah appeared, running toward us in a flurry, with her pristine white hijab billowing behind her like a superhero cape. She wasted no time and immediately confronted the vandal.

He turned to her, his face twisted in anger. "Who are you?!" he screamed.

I moved to stand in front of Hebah, ready to defend her. But I didn't have to. A group of women protesters in black niqabs, with only their eyes showing through, surrounded us, and started ferociously shouting the man down. "How dare you raise your voice at this woman!" they scolded.

The man, taken aback by the sudden appearance of the women,

stepped back, his eyes darting around, looking for a way out. Hebah told the man that there were family photos on the camera, some of which showed women without hijabs, making it haram for him to see. I couldn't help but grin at her clever tactic. And it seemed to be working.

Finally, as the vandal was feeling the walls close in around him, Hebah played her last card and revealed we had familial connections to the Muslim Brotherhood. She called a cousin and after a brief cordial discussion with the vandal, he got the confirmation he needed.

We did get my camera back, and I couldn't help but feel a twinge of guilt. I was sorry for getting Hebah into this mess. But there was no time for self-pity. We needed to get out of there, and fast. The streets were still crowded with protesters.

Another protester walked us back toward a busy street where vehicular traffic wasn't interrupted and hailed us a taxi, but not before menacing us with one last threat. "Don't ever come back to Egypt," he said.

As we drove away, Hebah turned to me and said, "I can't believe that actually worked."

I grinned at her. "You're a genius. Let's do that again!" I said.

She laughed. "Go ahead, but I'm not saving you next time."

When we returned to my aunt's apartment, I immediately ran my recovery software and retrieved the deleted photos. The last image felt surreal to look at. It was a haunting shot of the vandal mid-lunge, spray can in hand pointed at the lens. His expression was contorted, his jaw open. You could see the anger in his eyes. Right over his shoulder is the evidence of his crime: the church door marked "Islameya," the paint still wet.

What happened next was nightmarish. That night, the Egyptian military made good on their threats and raided Rabaa al-Adawiya Square, carrying out one of the world's largest killings of demonstrators in a single day, according to Human Rights Watch. The crackdown left at least nine hundred protesters dead, though no official toll was ever calculated. I narrowly escaped being caught in the massacre—a chilling realization that still haunts me. I often joke with Hebah about how she saved my life that day, but the truth is, she really did.

I wasn't an experienced writer, so an editor at *ANIMAL* helped me put the story together along with my photography. And my final photo of the vandal spread like wildfire online. Later on, I heard from one of my cousins in Egypt that the man had become famous in Egypt, and the photo was used to incite fear of the Muslim Brotherhood. I couldn't help feeling a little sorry for the vandal after learning he was caught and jailed, but not bad enough to stop me from framing the photo and offering it as gifts to some of my favorite people to hang on their walls.

After that near-death ordeal, if I was supposed to have learned some grand lesson about staying alert to the dangers photography and journalism could pose, I hadn't even come close.

A FEW YEARS LATER, IN 2015, WHILE BUCKY AND I WERE IN BALTIMORE covering massive protests after police killed a Black man in custody, one of my Brooklyn roommates called me in a panic.

"There are four detectives at our door right now. They're asking for you," he said.

He texted me a picture of the business card they'd left behind. I showed it to Bucky, who pulled his phone out right away to dial a lawyer on my behalf. The worst part was that I had no idea what the cops wanted with me.

My life in New York had always been defined by a sense of freedom—skateboarding through the streets, camera in hand, capturing the city as I saw it. But that sense of freedom shattered the day I found myself in the crosshairs of the NYPD.

I was being charged with trespassing, and I was being ordered to surrender myself. I felt my stomach knot. Bucky and I returned to New York, and he escorted me to the precinct. We didn't get there until the dead of night, when the streets were mostly empty. Everyone was either home or on their way home, except me.

As two detectives led me into a small, cramped room for questioning, the weight of their gaze felt suffocating. They had me on camera trespassing, and my social-media posts from the top of the Williamsburg Bridge were the smoking gun.

"I'm a journalist," I retorted, trying to sound confident. But the lawyer's hand on my shoulder urged me to stay quiet. I slumped back in my chair, feeling small and powerless.

THE LEGAL PROCESS WAS A BLUR—A WHIRLWIND OF FORMS, MUG shots, and handcuffs, as I was herded from location to location against my will. While they were leading me to a holding cell, I caught a glimpse of the news playing on a TV. Baltimore was burning.

The detectives led me beneath the New York City courthouse to a holding facility known as "The Tombs." It seemed packed to twice its capacity. I took a deep breath, stepped inside with my right foot, and timidly said to myself, "Assalamualaykum." To my surprise, like a choir, half the men in the cell returned the greeting: "Wa 'Alaykum Assalam." The Newark kid in me felt the safety in numbers. If this was going to be anything like what I had heard about jail, I was sure that being a Muslim among Muslims would keep me at least a little safer.

I scanned the room for Lucas, the photographer who had been with me on the bridge, and there he was, in the corner, chatting with another inmate. He caught my eye and called out, "This is who I was talking about!" He pointed directly at me. When I made my way over to him, he introduced me to his new friend. "This is Aymann; he climbed the Williamsburg Bridge with me. So, anyways, Police Commissioner Bratton had to release a statement basically calling us bozos," he bragged.

EVERY FEW HOURS, A COP WOULD SAUNTER IN AND LAZILY READ OFF some names from a clipboard: prisoners the judge was ready to arraign. After Lucas's name was called, I was sure mine would be next. But I had to wait another twenty-four hours before my name was called. And then, rather than being taken to see a judge, I was led to an empty cell where a plainclothes detective waited for me.

"You seem like a good kid. If you answer my questions, I can put in a good word with the judge and get you out of here."

I nodded, though I felt uneasy about what was to follow.

The detective shuffled through her notes as she asked me what mosque I prayed in, where my family had emigrated from, and whether I would cooperate with the police if I heard about any terrorist plots.

My eyebrows shot up. I couldn't hide my shock. "What, you think we're sitting in the mosque, scooping hummus, discussing acts of terror? This is our city, too. You realize that, right? Of course I'd say something. Anybody would say something."

She nodded, and handed me her card. "I'm going to write in your file that you're cooperating, and that should look really good with the judge," she said gracefully. I took her card and thanked her to be polite. But I left the card in that empty cell when I was escorted back to the bigger one. None of what had just happened felt right to me.

Finally, after I'd waited the entire weekend underground, it was my turn to face the judge. The room was mostly empty except for Bucky and a few others, who had come to witness the proceedings from the stands.

I approached my lawyer, who directed me to turn toward the judge and whispered, "This will be over soon." I took a deep breath and tried to remain calm.

The judge took a cursory glance at my case before lifting his gaze to meet mine. "How will Mr. Ismail plead today?" he asked my lawyer.

"Not guilty," he firmly replied. I was utterly spent.

After briefly scanning through the papers in front of him, the judge looked up at me and read aloud the charges against me. "Criminal trespassing, base jumping": to me it was just a jumble of meaningless words.

My lawyer made a statement. "Your Honor, my client has no prior convictions. He lives and works in New York City. We're requesting an ROR."

"It says here that he evaded arrest, used an alias, and encouraged others to break the law," the judge replied. The accusations were so absurd that I couldn't help smirking. I leaned over to my lawyer and whispered, "Can they just make stuff up like that?"

Abruptly, without further consideration, the judge made his decision:

"Bail is set for three thousand dollars," he announced as he banged his gavel.

I looked at my lawyer, confused. He looked back at me in shock.

Before I could turn to see Bucky's reaction, a police officer grabbed me and pulled me back toward the door behind the judge. I knew what that meant. If my bail wasn't paid, I was going to have to wait for my trial, for what could be months or even years, at Rikers Island, a notorious New York City prison known as one of the worst in the country.

My eyes stung from lack of sleep. The officer guided me into another cramped cell. I scanned for Lucas's familiar face, but my heart sank when I noticed the reek from another inmate smoking something that smelled like burning tar. Lucas wasn't with me anymore, and I assumed he was granted his ROR. I was terrified of what might happen next.

I looked around the cell, trying not to make eye contact with anyone; I knew I needed to rely on what I'd learned growing up in Newark and keep my head down. I thought of how my parents would feel if they found out the trouble I was in.

Eventually, we were all lined up, and I was tightly shackled to the prisoner in front of me by my wrists and ankles.

The officer at a desk nearby let out a sigh. "Aymann Ismail?" she shouted into the echoey cell.

"Yeah?" I yelled back. She addressed another officer, using a commanding voice: "Take him upstairs."

My bail had been paid, by Bucky. But the relief I felt was mixed with guilt at leaving all the other people behind. Though my autonomy had been returned to me, I found I wished I could do the same for the others, especially one guy I overheard complaining that his bail was set for just one dollar. None of it seemed fair. Without Bucky, I'd have gone to Rikers Island, too.

The police returned my belongings, and I checked my phone first. Bucky had texted me to meet him at his place when they released me. I laced my shoes back up, slapped on my belt, and took what felt like my first-ever breath of fresh air.

When my phone was returned to me, I saw that I had missed a call from Mama. I called her right back, and she told me she sensed something was wrong.

"Everything's fine, just a crazy workweek," I lied, not ready to worry her with the truth. Next, I called Mira, who was only a friend at the time, and tried to play this whole thing off as an adventure. But deep down, I was rattled, and I knew I'd need more than a few jokes to shake the feeling. If I'd ever seen myself as a tough guy who thrived in dangerous situations, this judge forced me to see who I really was—someone vulnerable, so accustomed to putting on a show for everyone else that I felt like a stranger to myself when I was alone.

I felt even worse when I got home and found that my entire room had been taken apart by NYPD detectives. My bedsheets had been tossed onto the floor. The art on my walls had been ripped down. The contents of my desk and clothing drawers littered the room. I was shaken, imagining the police going through my personal belongings and finding a Quran and my prayer rug, and thinking they'd put two and two together. The implication was obvious, and I'd never known the police to be any kind of clever.

They had taken with them several things: a new laptop I'd bought, still in its box and sealed with plastic; my Nintendo DS; and a bunch of camera equipment. They even took an art piece as evidence: a framed poster I'd gotten from an Arab American artist, Essam Attia, that depicted a silhouetted cartoon drone branded with the NYPD logo that was shooting a missile.

"I guess they're art critics now," Bucky joked when I told him.

For some reason, they didn't take the New York Bridge and Tunnel–branded helmet that I had found on a subway track. And they also never found what I was sure they were truly after, since the hard drives that stored my archive of footage of people doing illegal graffiti and trespassing was safe someplace else.

I picked up everything and put my room back together, but I never slept comfortably there again.

A FEW WEEKS LATER, I WAS HANGING OUT ON MY STOOP IN BROOKLYN when a neighbor called the cops on me for speaking too loudly on my phone. I figured all I'd have to do was show my ID and prove that I lived there, but as soon as the officer scanned my card, he said I was needed for questioning at the station. Before I knew it, I was in cuffs, and imprisoned for hours, only to be released without being asked a single question.

This became a regular thing. It seemed like every time I turned around a cop was there, ready and waiting to slap cuffs on me for some minor infraction. Standing on my skateboard at a subway station? Jail. Jumping a turnstile? Jail. Each encounter felt like a test, a reminder that the freedom I cherished was always one misstep from being snatched away. It was enough to make me want to pack my bags and leave, not just New York but America. I was born here, and I resented that fact.

The paranoia lingered, but I craved self-determination. One day, from the elevated J train, I spotted my favorite rooftop in Brooklyn, a red brick building covered in huge roller-painted letters. If the graffiti artists could make it up there, I told myself, so could I. Using a trash can to reach the fire escape, I climbed up and snapped photos from every angle. I sent Bucky a selfie with the rooftop art behind me. "Look familiar?" I texted.

He replied, "You're crazy!" I basked in his approval, happy to feel that I had seized back control.

———

THE FOLLOWING YEAR, JUST AFTER MIRA AND I MARRIED, I AGREED to plead guilty to trespassing on the bridge to settle the case, which seemed fair compared with all I'd actually done as *ANIMAL*'s graffiti documentarian. At the sentencing, I invited my sister, Hebah, to come witness it. She was in New York attending medical school at the time, after earning a law degree from Harvard Law School, and I thought she'd be interested.

Hebah, wearing her hijab, stood out in the courtroom. I expected her to be nervous for me, but instead, she looked defiant, as if daring anyone to mistreat me and deal with her wrath. Seeing her there reminded me of how she once handled her own legal troubles.

She was detained at an airport in Israel while on a research trip with Harvard Law School. During her nine-hour interrogation, Israeli soldiers demanded access to her email accounts. Aware the Israeli Supreme Court had recently ruled such demands illegal, she refused. Eventually, they cleared her and gave her a visa.

But upon finalizing her entry, the immigration officer once again asked for her email passwords. When she again refused, he crossed out her visa with a pen and slated her for deportation. But instead, they confiscated her belongings, including her phone, cutting off her communication, and held her in a detention center. It took the professor—a Palestinian citizen of Israel and lawyer—three days to locate Hebah and push for Israel to follow through with deporting her rather than continuing to hold her.

During her detention, Hebah was denied basic rights: no embassy access, no phone calls, and no updates on her fate. Later, Hebah shrugged off the ordeal, saying it was routine for Arab Americans traveling to Israel and that she had never been afraid. Though I already admired her resolve, this experience cemented it.

BACK IN THE MANHATTAN COURTROOM, THE JUDGE SEEMED CERTAIN and focused, but the next thing he said made me want to burst out laughing. "You better get your act together or the next time you're in front of me, I'll look into deporting you."

Deport me to where? I had been born within walking distance of this courthouse, just on the other side of the Holland Tunnel. I could get a courier to walk my birth certificate over.

I shot Hebah a look to silently confirm that she had also heard the judge say it. With a single eyebrow raise and a half-smile, she said all she needed. It was the kind of expression only a sibling could perfect—equal parts "Can you believe this?" and "Don't make a scene." She knew that this city judge had no power to follow through with his ignorant threat. In her gaze, I saw both her defiance and her unshakable belief that, no matter what, we belonged here. It made me want to laugh even more, but this time, with a sense of solidarity. Hebah didn't need to say anything; she let her composure do the talking, as always.

I WAS SENTENCED TO A HUNDRED HOURS OF COMMUNITY SERVICE, most of which I spent picking up trash in Battery Park in Lower Manhattan. It wasn't all bad. I figured I could hide out of sight and read a book and listen to music. When Ramadan came, I brought my Quran, thinking this was a good chance to study up so I could avoid embarrassing myself in front of Mira's dad, Uncle Ashraf, again.

Being mandated to sit in the park finally gave me the opportunity to take the Quran seriously. It was exhilarating to think of myself as a real Muslim for a change, approaching the Quran for the very first time without being told to.

Pondering my new role as a husband, I skipped to Surat An-Nisa, the chapter named "The Women." Perfect, I thought.

My version of the Quran had been recommended to me by Mira and included translations. I scanned through the chapter and landed on verse 34. Before reading the English, I took a deep breath and attempted to recite it in Arabic.

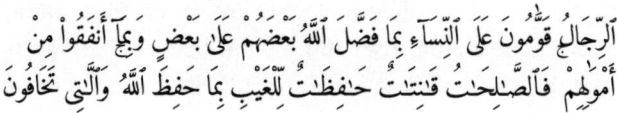

نُّشُوزَهُنَّ فَعِظُوهُنَّ وَاهْجُرُوهُنَّ فِي الْمَضَاجِعِ وَاضْرِبُوهُنَّ ۖ فَإِنْ أَطَعْنَكُمْ فَلَا تَبْغُوا
عَلَيْهِنَّ سَبِيلًا ۗ إِنَّ اللَّهَ كَانَ عَلِيًّا كَبِيرًا (٣٤)

My Arabic skills weren't even close to good enough for me to understand what I was reading. "Well, that's embarrassing," I muttered to myself, feeling foolish for even trying. Unsatisfied, I turned to the English translation of the verse.

> Men are in charge of women by [right of] what Allah has given one over the other and what they spend [for maintenance] from their wealth. So righteous women are devoutly obedient, guarding in [the husband's] absence what Allah would have them guard. But those [wives] from whom you fear arrogance—[first] advise them; [then if they persist], forsake them in bed; and [finally], strike them [lightly]. But if they obey you [once more], seek no means against them. Indeed, Allah is ever Exalted and Grand.

I felt my skin crawl. The idea of being *in charge* of Mira or *striking* her contradicted everything that I felt about her. I was left feeling confused, disgusted, and overwhelmed.

I instinctively looked away and skimmed around the Quran, then returned to the smaller chapters I was familiar with near the end of the book. The crisis of faith that I had been grappling with for most of my life—the one I was certain I'd made up ground with—was creeping back in. My mind raced with doubt and horror as I wondered how any of the many abusive men around the world might feel if they read the same verse—they could feel vindicated in their treatment of those they should protect and love unconditionally.

Later that night, I asked Mira how she made sense of such verses.

"You think there's only one way to interpret the Quran? We're talking about the *Quran*, Aymann. If you believe that this is really divine and the voice of God, wouldn't it be limiting and insulting to suggest there's only ever one way to understand any one word, let alone a whole verse or chapter? How could it be for all humanity, for all time, if you limit it that way? Don't take away an essential piece of what makes our religion so beautiful," she explained.

Mira insisted those verses didn't give men permission to hit their wives. She reverted to the original Arabic, reciting fluidly, switching seamlessly to English as she translated word by word. The verse, she explained, enshrined men as protectors of women—not out of dominance, but as a responsibility bestowed by Allah. It was about justice and a woman's right to safety and security, making harshness a last resort.

She also challenged the translation of daraba as "hit." In the Quran, she pointed out, the word appears in multiple contexts, many of them nonviolent. In some verses, it means to make something clear, like when God "shows you a sign." If daraba could mean different things elsewhere, she argued, why not here? "Using violence against the very person God commanded you to protect doesn't make sense," she said. "Wouldn't that contradict the entire spirit of the passage?"

Her perspective helped, but my discomfort lingered. Those verses still weighed on me like anvils. I was drawn to the Quran because of Mira's curiosity and openness, but after that conversation, I couldn't shake the thought of how little most Muslims globally might connect with our approach. Accepting that the meaning of verses was open-ended meant abandoning what I was taught, that the Quran was dense, impenetrable, and could only be understood by scholars who had spent their lives decoding it.

I could almost hear Mama's voice in my head, questioning how I could be so arrogant as to believe my understanding of the Quran could surpass that of scholars. Mira's way of seeing the Quran was beautiful, but that voice made me wonder if she was sidestepping the discomfort I was drowning in. Was she embracing interpretation because it was right, or because it was easier than confronting an inconvenient truth?

And yet, as much as that gnawed at me, I felt something else too.

That rigid way of understanding Islam had always felt artificial to me, like an obligation not a religion, and it eventually pushed me away. With Mira, learning, questioning, and discovering felt more like faith than anything I had ever known. And I wouldn't have found that without her. For now, I would set aside my discomfort and see how much faith I could find in starting over and learning to be Muslim again from scratch.

But maybe because I was so consumed by my own faith journey, I missed the signs that Mira was having second thoughts of her own. We were religiously married, but as Egyptians, we still needed a formal wedding. And when we talked on the phone, a call I expected to be about planning took a sharp turn when Mira revealed a struggle of her own.

"What if this doesn't work out?" she asked me. Her voice had an edge to it, like she was holding something back.

I already knew what was wrong before she said it. Things were moving too fast. We were both nervous about the future. She sighed, and I could imagine her sitting there, weighing her words carefully.

"We've already invested so much, but now I'm wondering if this is really what I want. Don't you worry that you'll blink and we'll both be ten years older, and we'll both be wondering what the hell just happened?" she asked.

I felt my chest tighten. She was making a good point, and I didn't know how to respond. The next thing she said felt like a kill shot: "I just don't see myself as the type of woman to get married."

I could feel the tears welling up in my eyes, and I tried to blink them away. This wasn't the Mira I thought I knew—the confident, self-assured woman who had jumped into marriage with me. But I was also glad to see another side of her, her feeling safe enough to show vulnerability.

I took a deep breath and said softly, "Mira, I have no idea how we got here, but I'm glad we did. This is our first real obstacle, and it's terrifying. But I'm here. I'm not going anywhere. We can't predict the future. All we can do is promise to be kind to each other, no matter what."

There was a long pause before she finally spoke. "I don't want it to end, either," she murmured, her voice cracking.

This wasn't just a leap of faith anymore—it was a commitment, a promise we were making to each other.

"There will be moments when we hate each other's guts," I said with a small laugh, trying to lighten the mood. "But as long as we have each other's backs, we'll be okay."

"I know," she said quietly, and I could tell she was smiling.

When I hung up the phone, I felt more secure in our relationship than ever.

MIRA PLANNED OUR WEDDING FOR THE FALL OF 2017, AND BOOKED us a yacht, on which we entertained twenty-five friends and family, cruising the Hudson and East rivers with an oud player covering old Umm Kulthum favorites. The celebration blended both Egyptian and East Coast flavors. There was a little bit of dancing, just enough to piss off my parents, but even they had a great time. And the best part about having a wedding on a boat? When we docked, it was time for everyone to go home. No long goodbyes allowed.

The moment my bride, Mira, laid her eyes on our new house, she gave it its forever nickname.

"Minty," she said profoundly, gazing at the pale green exterior.

As we explored our new home together, I teased her. "Are you having fun yet?"

She looked at me with gleaming eyes. "Yes."

"Now imagine how much fun we're going to keep having the rest of our lives," I said.

"I'm so fucking excited," she said, wearing the corniest grin ever.

Baba on a New York City subway platform, with
graffiti-covered trains in the background, 1970s.

Chapter 8

Through the Grapevine

IT WAS 2017, I WAS TWENTY-SIX YEARS OLD, AND I WAS FEELING QUITE proud of myself. I had a wife, and I'd somehow managed to buy a house and fulfill my promise to build a home for us, and returning to the city that had made me felt like the cherry on top. I exceeded all of my own expectations my younger self had for my future. But my happiness faded each time I thought about what had driven Mama to flee this city, and what it meant for me and my wife to begin our future here.

I had brought her to a city with a serious crime problem. I could still remember the smell of burning trash cans, and recalled staying up at night wondering if the loud pops in the distance were fireworks or gunshots. I thought about the day when my favorite high school teacher, Mr. T, came to class with a bruised eye, having been robbed and pistol-whipped on his way in. It started to hit me that I might have romanticized a place about which none of my siblings had a single nice thing to say.

Now, with Mira, my instinct to protect was in overdrive. The sound of police sirens outside our window felt sharper and more urgent. I tried to bury my fears, but I couldn't stop myself from flinching at every tire screech. I was afraid of the packs of boys who looked just like the ones I'd grown up with. I began to wonder if Mama had been right to move her family away when she had the chance.

Each morning, despite the sirens, Mira woke up with a smile. She would brew the strongest coffee I'd ever tasted, and she still dropped an extra shot of espresso into her own cup.

One morning, I stepped outside to finish my cup and watch the traffic go by. A neighbor two doors down caught my attention as he sat on his stoop enjoying an extra-long can of beer to start his day. He waved me over.

"Ayo! You live here now?" he called out to me.

He was a roughed-up middle-aged white guy who dressed like a teenager. The house he lived in looked worn down. When he set his can on the stoop, I noticed he was wearing an ankle monitor.

"That house you're in has some stories, man," he said, shaking his head. I explained to him that I wasn't new in town. I couldn't help code-switching, dialing my Newark/East Coast accent up to eleven.

He couldn't believe my story. "You moved *back* to Newark?" he said, laughing.

The house we had just bought had been shot at by his father when he was a kid, he told me, and he showed me the bullet hole to prove it. Just like he said, it was right in the side of the house, clean through. But when he asked me if he could "borrow some money," I told myself it was time to say thanks for the story and step back inside.

I was desperate for a fresh start and wanted to reconnect with my local mosque. That Friday, I decided to attend prayer. My childhood mosque was attached to my elementary school in Jersey City, but when we were running late, Baba and I would go to the one in downtown Newark.

I skated down Ferry Street and into the heart of Newark, a city that still bore the scars of its infamous rebellion in 1967. After decades of systemic racism, poverty, and police violence, the rebellion was sparked by a single act of police brutality but quickly escalated into five days of unrelenting confrontations between residents and law enforcement. Tanks rolled through Newark's streets as the National Guard was called in to restore order. By the time the violence subsided, twenty-six people were dead, hundreds more were seriously injured, and large swaths of the city had been devastated by arson.

The rebellion triggered the flight of Newark's white middle- and working-class residents, leaving behind a city crippled by disinvestment and soaring crime, deepening the poverty that fueled the uprising in the first place. But Newark's story didn't end there. Over time, the city became a hub for African American culture and resilience—a place where creativity and activism flourished.

As I skated through its streets, my eyes traced Newark's layered history. The gorgeous architecture from the city's wealthy past stood alongside burnt-brick textures that marked its decline. The mosque I was heading to was no exception. Housed in the city's former Chamber of Commerce building, it was a nine-story relic from Newark's golden age in the 1920s—once one of the tallest buildings in the city. In 1982, a Saudi philanthropist gifted the building to the congregation, transforming it into a spiritual sanctuary amid a city of change.

When I entered the mosque, I greeted everyone with "Assalamu-alaykum," but the response was muted. I felt like a stranger.

On the second floor, familiar scents filled the air as men slowly made their way to the carpet. The mosque was humble, offering only the essentials: a worn carpet, a few Qurans, and a barely functioning sound system. I found a space, sat down, and tried to silence my anxious thoughts.

A man dressed in the traditional white garb, sporting a dapper tarboosh, began the Athan. His voice echoed throughout the mosque, stirring something deep inside me that I hadn't felt in years. For a moment, I melted into the ummah, no longer just myself but part of something greater.

The sermon began in English, a welcome change from the Standard Arabic I'd grown up with. The imam spoke passionately about the plight young Muslims face, blaming the media and the internet for turning them into hypocrites. I couldn't help feeling that the sermon was directed at people like me.

Afterward, we lined up for prayer. My body vanished, becoming one of a hundred in the lines. As I went through the motions, I wrestled with my fears. Would I ever feel part of a Muslim community again? Would I ever be enough of a Muslim for someone like Mira or our future children? I had hoped that, by the prayer's end, I would feel I'd come home. Instead, I felt like an outsider in my own community.

Skating back home to the Ironbound, I clung to the back of a bus, and this gave me a brief surge of control. But as quickly as it came, that feeling faded.

AT HOME, I JOINED MIRA IN TACKLING THE OVERGROWN PATCH behind our house. A massive grapevine stretched across the fence, and when spring came without a single green leaf, I figured it was dead. I bought us two shovels, and we hacked at the thick roots buried deep in the dirt.

THAT NEXT WEEKEND, MIRA INVITED MY FAMILY FOR DINNER. WHEN Baba arrived, he headed straight to the backyard; it almost seemed that checking on the vine was the reason he came over. When he saw what I had done, he looked as if he could collapse and weep. This was the most intense emotion I'd ever seen from him.

"What did you do?" he demanded in an angry tone.

"The grapevine? It was dead," I answered, confused by his reaction. "I pulled it out. I was thinking of planting flowers or something. Maybe roses."

"Where is the stump?" he asked quickly, the words tumbling out.

I led him to the plastic bag where I'd stuffed the remains, hoping he'd see for himself how dry and brittle the vine was and accept that it was a lost cause. But when Baba saw it, his expression shifted into a deep scowl.

"I tried to water it," I protested, hoping to explain myself.

"Vines this old don't need your watering. They drink from deep underground. Do you have any idea how long it takes for roots to grow this thick? Look, feel it," he said in Arabic, his voice filled with a quiet pain as he reached into the bag. "Feel the roots."

I was left speechless, as was Baba. His droopy eyes looked dazed.

He kept to himself for the rest of the visit, and after he left, neither of us mentioned it again. He returned to his usual stoic self, speaking only in prepackaged religious phrases. But the memory of that moment would stay with me forever. I had no idea that, of all things, cutting a vine would trigger such a reaction from him. I couldn't help feeling like I had no idea who Baba was at all.

BY THIS TIME, *ANIMAL NEW YORK,* THE MAGAZINE THAT HAD BECOME a part of my identity, had run out of funding. Way back in the late summer of 2015, Bucky and I reveled in our accomplishments together one last time, and I set off to look for a new job. I cast a wide net, unsure if anyone would be interested in my chaotic graffiti-focused work at *ANIMAL.*

Slate magazine felt like a long shot. To me, it was a prestigious platform for sharp political writing and opinion pieces. But just a few weeks after *ANIMAL* shut down, I got a phone call from an unknown number while I was out at Coney Island with Mike Molina. We'd both taken an edible and were euphorically enjoying the ocean breeze. Needless to say, I was not anticipating a work call, and answered the phone aggressively. "What's up?" I barked into the receiver.

"Oh . . . Hi, is this Aymann?" the voice on the other end asked, clearly taken aback.

Realizing my mistake, I scrambled to sound friendly. "Yes, this is he. Who's calling?"

Meanwhile, Mike was losing control of his body as he tried to stifle his laughter.

IT TOOK ME A WHILE TO FEEL AT HOME AT A PLACE LIKE *SLATE.* AT the first interview, I showed up with a skateboard tucked beneath my arm, to find that most other people were wearing button-down shirts and slacks. I didn't really begin to find my rhythm until the Republican National Convention a year into the job, in 2016.

Donald Trump, the political outsider and presumptive nominee, bullied reporters with as much ferocity as he told lies about Muslims.

But I was surprised by a confrontation before the convention even began.

While I was waiting in line to get inside the secured perimeter, a man dressed in Colonial Era cosplay moved to get my attention. His hat and ruffles looked historically accurate, and I would have complimented him on the outfit if he hadn't turned out to be such a pest.

"Are you a Moslem?" he began bluntly. I know I look Arab, but this guy hit the nail on the head. I'd figured it would only be a matter of time before I was clocked as a Muslim, but I'd never expected it would happen before I had even entered the convention area.

I took a cautious step forward. "Yeah. I am Muslim."

I was taller than he was, which made me nervous. I was conscious of the awful stereotypes about Arab men—that we're seen as hot-headed and quick to justify violence. I was careful not to come across as too aggressive, because I really wanted to avoid reinforcing those views.

Unprompted, the man began dressing me down. "Don't you realize that *Izlam* is evil?" I was more bothered by his mispronunciation of "Islam" than by anything else in that moment. It's spelled and pronounced with an "s," not a "z." He could pronounce "kiss," right?

I asked the man why he thought Islam was evil.

"Well, in *Izlam,* you have the Shariah. Which is evil," he contended.

I crossed my arms as he explained to me how bloodthirsty and backward my religion was.

"How do you explain the fact that I've never killed anyone in my life?" I replied.

He shook his head, his colonial hat comically wobbling. I tried to explain to him how regional differences in how Islam is practiced proves the foolishness in judging individual Muslims based on cherry-picked verses.

"Muslims don't all agree on Shariah. Shariah is the *human* interpretation of Islam. Know what I mean? There are councils that come out with new rulings and change the law every so often. If they were really God's rules, then we couldn't be changing them," I explained.

I surprised myself. I'm a lot of things, but I wouldn't put "expert Islam interpreter" anywhere on a list.

Unsurprisingly, the man in the cartoonish outfit stuck to his own opinions about what I believed. "Well, you also worship a pedophile!" he shot back.

I could tell he was just trying to get a rise out of me, but I'd played this game before. "You're dressed as a founding father, right? Who are you supposed to be right now?" I asked, looking him up and down.

"I'm Thomas Jefferson," he answered proudly. I looked back at my colleagues, and we started laughing. We all knew where this was going.

"You're dressed head to toe like the most famous rapist in American history. And you're moralizing about the Prophet Muhammad, a man that lived in tribal Arabia in the seventh century? You must be joking."

"That's not true!" he protested.

Another reporter chimed in, chuckling. "It's well documented," she said.

"Google Sally Hemings," I said, and turned my back on him. The conversation was over. One of my colleagues from *Slate* captured the interaction on camera. In line, as we continued to wait to be cleared to enter the convention, they suggested I simply do a similar thing at the convention: film Trump supporters answering questions about Islam.

I spent the rest of the day talking to anyone willing to engage while my colleague filmed it. I argued with a man distributing anti-Muslim pamphlets who insisted that I had been commanded to kill non-Muslims. I countered his argument by asking how his theory accounted for Muslim American doctors and veterans. Similar conversations followed, including one with a rhinestone-clad woman who, after some gentle prodding, acknowledged that Republicans could be more specific when they said things like "Muslims are terrorists." That exchange ended with a high-five.

Later, I edited the footage into a video I tentatively titled *The Party of Jesus Meets a Muslim*. To my surprise, it ended up on *Slate*'s homepage. It was rewarding to expose the contradictions, but I also felt anxious about the potential backlash. My friend Amani had warned me about the risks of being visibly Muslim in media; she was frequently targeted by both Muslims and non-Muslims alike. Still, I figured that, if it advanced my journalism career, I could handle some hostility.

I JUST DIDN'T EXPECT THE HOSTILITY FROM MAMA. SHE CALLED ME in a panic.

"Aymann, you can't talk about Islam this way. People will think you're some kind of authority when you're not," she explained in Arabic. Mama knew I was plagued by religious shortcomings and scoffed at the thought of my teaching people what Islam is or isn't.

"Subjects like Shariah require an expert to explain!" she exclaimed.

"I don't say I'm an imam or anything," I replied, trying to soothe her. But Mama persisted. As ever, we were no good at understanding each other. I quickly told her I had to go. Sad to say, this was where most of our arguments ended.

"Mashi"—Fine—she said, her voice heavy with resignation.

I called Mira to vent about Mama's criticism, explaining that Mama thought I was doing the global Muslim community a disservice by trying to represent a Muslim perspective on video. I expected Mira to console me and massage my bruised ego, but that was never her style.

"She's right, you know. You don't even explain it right . . ." Mira's voice trailed off.

"I couldn't just not answer," I replied, after admitting that I'd gotten caught up in the moment.

"Aymann, have you read the entire Quran? Like, from front to back? Honestly?" Mira asked, her tone turning more serious.

"In English?" I joked, trying to lighten the mood. "I intend to! Someday!"

She groaned. "You should call her and apologize," Mira suggested.

I felt exposed, sure that Mira now saw me for the stubborn idiot I was. But I knew she was right. So I called Mama back. She picked up on the second ring.

"Asif, Mama"—Sorry. "You're right. I'm no authority on Islam. I know that."

"It's okay, habibi," she said. "Next time, talk to a sheikh."

The tension lifted immediately. I'd usually just give Mama space when she was upset, hoping time would sort it out. I hadn't known she was capable of being vulnerable with me. And without Mira's influence, I might have never known. For the first time, I wondered if I needed to keep hiding from Mama. Maybe I could be honest and open with her about my feelings and insecurities, especially when it came to religion. Maybe she would be more willing to be vulnerable with me if I asked about Islam. There was hope for us, I thought.

"Maybe I can call you and ask you questions about Islam?" I suggested, feeling brave.

"No, Aymann. Not even me. If you're going to talk about Islam, it needs to be truthful. The worst thing you can do is fill in the blanks yourself," she advised.

Her answer was satisfying. It was the kind of humility I saw in Mira. But, even as I hung up the phone, I couldn't shake the pride of having made a video that positioned me as a chronicler of Islamophobia and receiving the praise that came along with my journalism. I knew that I wasn't going to stop making videos like this. They gave me too much purpose.

At the same time, something Mama said rang in my head. Talking to a sheikh was a good idea. Maybe I could do more of what worked in this video—having Islamophobes rationalize their bigotry in the presence of a Muslim—while bringing in someone qualified to address their concerns. I accepted that I wasn't equipped to dive into religious doctrine, but it would feel more genuine, and grounded, to focus on how Islam manifested in the lives of those who practiced it: the real people these bigots were actually talking about. The focus would be on examining where their fears or misgivings about Muslims came from, and whether these held any merit.

I THOUGHT IT MIGHT BE VALUABLE TO HAVE A MUSLIM ENGAGING IN the kinds of conversations I was having with Mira and Mama as a creative approach to journalism. If I wanted to keep learning, maybe I could do it on camera, too. The benefit of approaching this project as a curious journalist rather than a preachy ideologue was clear. And who better to take it on than I—a young Muslim brimming with questions about his faith? Islam was the fastest-growing and perhaps the most misunderstood religion in North America, a paradox that fascinated me.

That fall, after Trump was elected, I pitched an episodic video series that would become *Who's Afraid of Aymann Ismail?* Each episode would delve into the broad apprehensions about Islam I frequently encountered, uncovering the political manipulations and narratives that fueled them. I could just be someone talking both to the people who believed Islamophobic tropes, and to the Muslims affected by those tropes. I would make the series about the people, as any good journalist would. In my eyes, the series would only succeed if it left viewers skeptical of the entire debate around Islam in America, on either side of the conversation.

THE FIRST EPISODE TACKLED HOMOPHOBIA, STARTING WITH AN INTER-view with Jim Hoft, a right-wing gay activist. He welcomed me, my *Slate* colleague and editor Jeffrey Bloomer, and an incredibly talented and overqualified freelance filmmaker, Oliver Lucian Anderson, into his St. Louis home.

As soon as we walked in, I noticed a statue of a Muslim man decapitating a Christian woman. "Want to tell me about this piece?" I asked, trying to mask my excitement.

"It's from the story of Saint Eurosia," Hoft explained, recounting a legend according to which a Muslim ruler executed a Christian woman for refusing to renounce her faith and marry him. His assistant hurriedly removed the statue after he was done explaining.

Jeff leaned in to whisper, "I don't think that was supposed to be out when we got here . . ."

WE SPENT HOURS TALKING ABOUT HIS VIEWS ON ISLAM, MOST OF which he admitted he had "read online." For a counterpoint, I turned to my cousin Mohamed Gamal, who is gay and much more religiously Muslim than I am. I knew that Mohamed had experienced some traumatic event with his mom, but I'd never heard the full story until I sat across from him in his bedroom, beneath a gay-pride flag. One time, after his mother discovered he was gay, he woke from a sleep to find she was pouring a liquid on him. "It was gasoline," he recalled. He had to jump out of the window to escape.

I asked him if he thought the presence of more Muslims in the country would lead to more homophobia. "I'm Muslim," he responded, with quiet defiance. "I pray five times a day. I fast for Ramadan. My mom's mentality doesn't define Islam. As long as there are Muslims like us, it won't."

Despite the praise the series received from *Slate*'s editor-in-chief, posting it wasn't without consequences. I received a flood of hate messages online, and one bizarre, hand-scribbled letter filled with racist insults.

And Mama confronted me again. "You can't say it's okay in Islam to be gay!" she protested.

I tried to explain that my cousin Mohamed's story was entirely real and that, even as Muslims, we ought to be much more upset about threatening murder than about someone's sexual preferences. Islam, she had always taught me, values life above all else, and murder is one of the gravest sins. Sexual preferences, on the other hand, are a private matter between an individual and Allah—it's not anyone else's business. If other Muslims are offended or disagree, they would be better off focusing on their own choices rather than scrutinizing the lives of others, especially for something Allah will not hold them personally accountable for.

Mama appeared empathetic to that line of reasoning, though she remained upset. "You should be showing the good things Muslims do, not exposing things like that."

IT WOULD GET WORSE BETWEEN MAMA AND ME AFTER SHE SAW THE episode in which she was featured. That episode was about the hijab, and it was personal—not just because I'd spent my whole life observing the women in my family wear it, but because I'd asked my older sister, Hebah, difficult questions about it.

In the episode, Hebah vulnerably expressed her personal doubts and explained that she wondered whether she veiled as an act of faith or because it had been imposed on her by Mama's expectations.

Mama appeared in the episode, to share her personal relationship with hijab, as well as her expectations for her daughter. I asked her, "What would you do if Hebah decided not to wear the hijab anymore?" And Mama cried just thinking about it.

This footage made it into the final cut, and though it felt like an honest portrayal of our family's relationship with hijab, it also felt like a betrayal of her trust. I was caught between wanting to be a good journalist and a good son. I hoped Mama would forgive me, but there was no escaping her vehemence.

"I only said yes because I wanted to help you. I didn't think you'd show me crying like that."

I tried to explain that her raw emotional response brought a humanizing perspective to a subject discussed rhetorically in the media. The episode showed the complexity of the choice—how, for some, the hijab is a symbol of faith, but others may struggle with the weight of that responsibility.

Mama didn't see it that way. "Why don't you do one about Muslims giving charity, helping people? Why focus on these things that make us look bad?" she argued.

———

THE CONVERSATION LEFT A RIFT BETWEEN US, ONE THAT DEEPENED the more I pushed boundaries in my work. It wasn't just about the hijab—it was about how she saw the country at war with our religion, and our roles as sentries representing Islam.

Still, I continued to make the series until it was cut because of *Slate*'s budget constraints. After producing fifteen episodes, I was proud of the work, and also exhausted. The series pushed me to start a podcast with *Slate* focusing on modern masculinity, which allowed me to continue exploring identity without breaking the bank.

BY THE END OF THE SERIES, THE INITIAL ANGER MAMA FELT HAD softened; she realized the impact it had had on Muslims who felt absent from the discourse about Islam in America. She had feared that her tears would be a source of embarrassment, but the people she knew saw them as a genuine expression of her deep love for her family and her faith.

"One of the teachers at school said she felt it helps young people to see Muslims asking hard questions. She's right. It's not always easy, even when you believe in it," Mama ventured.

There was a new tenderness in her voice, an acceptance that what she had shared wasn't a betrayal, but an honest reflection of her complex relationship with Islam. It made me feel safer to acknowledge my own conflicts.

"I still don't like seeing myself cry on camera," she admitted, "but I understand why you kept it in." She paused, searching for the right words. "It made people think, helped them see that the hijab isn't just a piece of cloth—it's about Allah." Her change of heart represented a shallow crack in the walls that had come up between us. For the first time, I felt that she didn't just see me as her rebellious son, but as someone who had a meaningful interest in becoming a better Muslim, even if my process was difficult for both of us.

———

A FEW MONTHS AFTER THE SERIES AIRED, HEBAH ARRIVED AT A FAMILY dinner without her hijab. The room fell silent. Hebah, sensing the tension, tried to put me at ease.

"This isn't because of the video," she said, her voice steady but soft. "I've been thinking about it for a long time. I wore it for Mama, not for Allah. So I figured, what's the point anyways if I'm not doing it for the right reasons?"

Mama's face was tight; her lips were pressed into a thin line. She didn't say anything at first, but I could sense the volcanic eruptions developing behind her eyes.

LATER, WHEN HEBAH STEPPED AWAY, MAMA PULLED ME ASIDE, HER voice dense with emotion.

"What did I do wrong?" she asked, her eyes filling.

"It's not about you," I tried to explain gently. "Hebah's finding her own way."

Hebah's decision was something I admired. Nobody in our family had been more afraid of disappointing others than Hebah. She was the one who kept the peace, always making concessions in the service of avoiding familial conflict. When she stepped into her autonomy, choosing something that went against our parents' expectations, I saw it as a brave act of self-realization. She was finally taking control of her life, and I couldn't have been prouder of her.

We connected in a whole new way, especially when she started experimenting with her hair—something she had never had the freedom to do before.

Mira was even more proud. She had worn the hijab since high school and throughout college, and experienced similar familial pressure before deciding the hijab had lost its tether to religion—she often felt it attracted more attention than it repelled. But she was sure that, as a personal decision, *making* the choice was the point.

Mama struggled. For weeks afterward, she seemed lost in thought. One evening, she finally broke the silence. "I just don't understand how something so important could be . . . lost," she said quietly in

Arabic. I could see her slowly trying to make sense of it. She watched as Hebah, with her uncovered hair, continued to pray, fast during Ramadan, and engage with her faith in her own way. It wasn't the same as Mama's journey, but it was hers. Gradually, Mama began to understand that Hebah's faith hadn't disappeared—it had simply evolved.

Mira and I are ambushed by rose petals as we arrive at our wedding ceremony on a yacht on the Hudson River, 2017.

Chapter 9

An Anomaly

MIRA AND I LOVED LIVING TOGETHER. OUR MODEST TWO-BEDROOM home quickly became a hangout spot, with a revolving door for friends, the scene of parties that would wind down into relaxed smoke sessions as the nights wore on.

One chilly October morning in 2018, just a year after we'd moved in together and right around Mira's birthday, we were in bed fighting for a few more minutes of shallow sleep as the sun slipped through the cracks in the window shades.

I felt her get up, but I lay still with my eyes closed, pretending to sleep, as she spent several minutes rummaging through the nightstand. Normally, Mira would just take a minute to wash up before heading down to brew some coffee. This morning was different.

Quiet fell on the room as she found what she was looking for. I watched out of the corner of my half-closed eyes as she withdrew something from the nightstand drawer and then hurried into the bathroom.

I rolled around in the bed, trying to find a warm patch to trick my body into going back to sleep.

"Are you awake? Or still pretending?" Mira asked in a hushed tone.

"Still pretending," I mumbled out of the side of my mouth. Using both hands, she practically tore the blinds off the window and threw all her weight onto the bed so hard I nearly bounced out of it. When I looked up, I saw a mischievous, excited smile.

"What are you hiding?" I asked, struggling to sit up.

"This," she said, extending her arm and opening her hand to reveal a pregnancy test. Her face betrayed a mix of uncertainty and concern.

"That's not a thermometer, is it?" I joked, trying to buy some time to disguise my nervousness.

Mira shot me an incredulous look, edging the thing closer to my face.

"If that's what I think it is, and I'm pretty sure that is what I think it is . . ."

Mira cut me off. "It's a pregnancy test," she said in a tired voice.

"Okay! Okay! I'm sorry. I'm so excited! Wallahi. This is the best news ever!" I exclaimed.

"Really?" she asked anxiously. I opened my mouth and ran my tongue back and forth, letting out a loud and loose zaghroota: "Lulu-lulululululululululueeeee!!!!" Mira came in for a warm hug. Already, she seemed like an entirely different person: she wasn't just Mira anymore.

"But we can still have fun, can't we?" I asked, dubiously.

"The fun's just getting started!" she assured. "It's just . . . it's a lot to take in, you know?"

"We'll figure it out," I said.

"Inshallah," Mira responded.

We regrouped in the kitchen for our morning routines. Mira poured us both cups of coffee, and as the steam rose, so did our excitement about the new life growing within her.

"Are you sure you're supposed to be drinking coffee right now?" I asked her suspiciously.

She placed the coffee cup up to her nose and stared down into the steamy pool of dark, opaque liquid. "Yes. Yes, I am."

I quietly withdrew my phone from my pocket and held it under the kitchen table as I googled the phrase *Coffee pregnant*.

"This pediatrics org says you shouldn't! Spit it out!" I darted toward her.

"What the hell, Aymann! Have you lost your mind?"

Confused, I held my phone out to show her the warning about possible complications.

"What website even is this?" she questioned.

"The American College of Obstetricians and Gynecologists!"

"It says *limit* coffee. One cup is okay," Mira said. "How about a compromise? If I can't drink coffee, then neither can you!" She reached to grab the mug out of my hand. Going without coffee would ruin me, I thought. I recoiled and gripped my cup.

"Yeah, that's what I thought," she said, and continued to sip.

With shaky hands, I returned my attention to my phone to google other tips and advice on how to handle a pregnancy.

"It says here that you should be walking around a lot. Want to do laps at the park or something? Or go up and down the stairs here at home?"

"We haven't even confirmed the pregnancy and you're already trying to ruin it," she shot back.

Ruin? I was sure I was helping, but she recoiled when I advanced for a hug to try to smooth things over. I felt ashamed. I seemed to be draining all the excitement out of Mira. I apologized and rubbed her shoulders. "Look, I get it. We're in this together," I assured her.

It was too late. Mira wanted to be left alone.

After a simple breakfast of toast with jam, Mira and I got in her white Nissan. It was Sunday, a day we reserved each week for dinner at my older brother Mohamed's house. The prospect of spending time with Mohamed's kids had just become a lot more exciting.

ABOUT A YEAR AND A HALF EARLIER, MOHAMED AND HIS WIFE, Kholoud, had had twin boys, Adam and Ali. Their first year as parents was miserable, because his boys had seemed to come out with opposite schedules. One stayed up all night, and the other was awake all day. It was torturous, particularly for Kholoud.

Now that the twins were mostly sleeping through the night, Mohamed and Kholoud seemed to be finding their rhythm. The experience had humbled Mohamed. He was calmer and gentler with me, and, for a change, we were having normal conversations—just talking about how we were doing or what we were excited about, in stark

contrast to our former dynamic, in which I'd whine as he offered his
tough-to-swallow advice.

I was surprised that I was most excited about telling Mohamed that
I might be joining the fatherhood club. The chance to have something
so important in common with the older brother I'd never quite seen
eye to eye with was thrilling.

WE GOT ON THE HIGHWAY TO EDISON, WHERE MY BROTHER LIVED, HUGE
smiles plastered on both our faces.

"Are we going to move, or what?" I asked.

"We just got here!" Mira answered, shocked.

I brought up all the problems with where we lived: the pollution,
the population density, the crime rate, the parking, and the worst
schools in the state.

"Well, you went to those schools, so it can't be that bad," she said.

"They *are* that bad," I said. "I know precisely because I *did* go to
them."

But Mira had a quick fix to suggest. "What about Islamic school?
How cute would that be?"

"I went to those schools, too . . ."

Mira seemed unbothered. "Yeah, but they'd have us for parents.
They can learn the basics in school, and we'll teach them what to do
with it," she said.

Islamic school ultimately pushed me away from Islam, not closer
to it. I was afraid of subjecting my kids to the same problems, but
Mira didn't seem worried about that prospect.

I began to see her point. "They'll have American parents in America, teaching them about Islam. That's so different from what we
had," I said, feeling both hope and a muted sense of panic.

"How can you think that and not get excited?" Mira answered.

AT MY BROTHER'S HOUSE, WE FOUND THAT THE TWINS HAD JUST
started to learn to walk, which made visiting them even more fun.
Mira and I sat on the floor at opposite ends as the boys took turns

waddling and then falling into our arms. We also exchanged secret knowing glances about what we imagined was on the horizon for us.

A FEW WEEKS LATER, MIRA AND I MADE OUR WAY TO HER FIRST appointment with the obstetrician. When the nurse called us in, she asked Mira to sit on the exam table and reclined her so she could slather her lower abdomen with jelly. As the nurse waved the transducer of the ultrasound machine back and forth, pressing down and digging, Mira's and my attention remained fixed on the monitor, trying to make sense of the black-and-white blobs. I squeezed Mira's hand in excitement.

"That what I think it is?" I joked to Mira. But she didn't even seem to hear me, in a trance as she stared at the screen. The image didn't look like much: amorphous circles that moved in and out of view as the nurse waved the transducer.

Slowly, the image on the monitor began to take on more definition.

"Is that the head?" I asked the nurse in excitement, but she only offered a quick "m-hm." Mira pointed at the monitor and shouted.

"That's the arms! Or the legs! Or whatever! It's something!" I strained my eyes to try to see what she was talking about, but all I saw was a blob wriggling from the motion of the transducer.

The moment was anticlimactic. The nurse's silence felt odd. Rather than celebrate the moment, her attitude was sucking the enthusiasm out of the room.

"That's our baby!" Mira said, lovingly.

The technician remained quiet.

After a little while, she pulled the transducer away and wiped the jelly off Mira's tummy. Without saying a word, she left the room.

Close to an hour later, the door to the ultrasound room was flung open without warning. The doctor seemed rushed.

"Everything looks normal," she said warmly.

"Oh, good!" Mira sighed. "We don't really know what normal is, so we really appreciate that validation right now," Mira said.

The doctor quickly yanked at the ultrasound machine to bring it closer, applied more jelly, and aggressively waved the transducer against Mira's tummy again. She was much rougher than the tech, and I had to stop myself from lunging to peel her arm away. The whole situation felt incredibly off to both of us.

"It looks like you're about eight weeks pregnant; everything looks normal, everything looks great. Their heartbeats are normal; this is exactly what we want to see at this point," she recited to us.

She took some more measurements, clicking and printing pictures from the ultrasound machine.

"They look really good. Here is Baby A. And here is Baby B. They're facing each other, which is what we want to see," she hurried on, pointing at the ultrasound screen.

Mira and I looked at each other in bewilderment. Neither of us had fully absorbed what we had just heard.

"Wait. What?" Mira interjected. "Baby A and Baby B? There's two?"

The doctor scrunched her brows. "Yes. Two. Look," she replied quickly, as she presented us with the printouts.

Mira and I exchanged stunned glances. Only then did the doctor realize that we had no idea we were having twins. But how could she not? This was our first scan!

BEFORE THAT TRIP TO THE CLINIC, I HAD ALREADY OBSESSIVELY RUN numbers on a spreadsheet to figure out exactly how much it'd cost to balance a family budget for one baby. That alone would have been tight, but now the burden had doubled.

I thought about how often my parents fought over money. I could tell that Mira was also tense on our drive home.

"Double the kids means double the love," I said.

"This was only the first scan, and they found two! How many are they going to find at the next one? *Four?!*" Mira exclaimed. Our laughter filled the car and dispelled some of the tension, though I could tell she was still anxious.

————

WHEN WE GOT HOME, I OPENED MY LAPTOP TO EXAMINE MY BUDGET spreadsheet—just as Mira announced she finally had a job prospect. Her master's degree in religion had seemed an uncertain path to employment, but after a full year of searching, she'd finally made some progress.

"The babies are already bringing baraka"—blessings—she said. "Once I'm certified to work as a chaplain, I'll be working for real, Inshallah!"

I hadn't intended on Mira's helping out financially. As I understood the Quran, it was my responsibility to use all my income for our family. I knew she'd been waiting for the right opportunity to put her education to use, but I didn't want her to feel she *had* to. I hoped to shield her from the stress I was experiencing, not look to her to be the solution. I already felt religiously inadequate.

As I scanned the spreadsheet, I moved some numbers around, reducing my "fun" budget category to zero, and assured Mira I could do it on my own. She placed her arms around me.

"You handle the family expenses, and I'll pay for the fun stuff," she said lovingly.

I'd worried about getting into arguments like my parents did, but it seemed that just wasn't going to happen with Mira.

WE SHARED THE NEWS WITH FAMILY OVER THE NEXT WEEKEND gathering. On the drive to my brother Mohamed's house, we tried to come up with a plan, but when the moment came, we both just knew. As soon as everyone took their seats around the dinner table, I asked Mira, "Are you ready to tell them?," loud enough for everyone to hear. Mira nodded, grinning.

"Tell us what?" Mama's eyes perked up. She'd been waiting for this forever. It was as if she already knew.

"We're expecting not one, but *two* babies!" Mira announced. She reached into her purse and unrolled the strip of ultrasound images. Mama rushed to embrace her.

Mohamed, already a father of twins, let out a maniacal laugh.

"Twins? Oh boy. You'll need double the patience . . . double the caffeine . . . Everything is double!" he advised.

I could tell that Mohamed was excited at the prospect of relating to me as a baba, and I didn't even realize how badly I wanted that connection with him until I grasped how grateful I was finally to have it.

When the dinner was over, the evening's festivities were winding down, and Mohamed was wrangling his boys for their evening bath, it had gotten quiet downstairs, and Mama decided it was time for a heart-to-heart. I braced myself for her advice, but she was focused on Mira.

"Aymann, habibi, your responsibilities as a Muslim are more important than ever," she began, her voice soft but firm. "God will also ask you about your wife."

I rolled my eyes, disapproving of her insinuation. She had often made small comments about how pretty Mira would look with her hair covered in a hijab. As we stood there, with the sound of clinking silverware echoing around the dining room while Kholoud and Mira cleaned up, I tried to steer the conversation gently back to the celebration. "Mama, now's not the time," I implored.

But she persisted, her voice laced with urgency. "Aymann, children learn religion first at home. They look to you as an example. If you, as their father, accept something that's wrong, they will, too. It's not me asking you to do something; it's Allah instructing us to follow his commandments."

I took a deep breath, searching for the right words. "Mama, you taught me that Allah will judge each of us individually, and we'll be held accountable by the limits of our own understanding, right?"

"Yes, but, Aymann, I—"

"Then that's it, Mama. Let's leave it at that." This was the rudest thing I'd ever said to her as an adult.

"Aymann, we must do our best, but we also have to follow his commandments. We can't just do whatever and say that we did our best." Her hands clasping mine, she was desperate for me to comprehend.

I sighed, feeling the weight of her concern. "I understand, Mama. But I can't force anyone to do anything."

Mama looked around at the joyous faces of Mira and Kholoud as they joked and laughed, but her expression was a mix of sadness and resignation.

"I just want what's best for you, Aymann," she whispered.

"I know, Mama. And I love you for it," I replied, enveloping her in a warm embrace.

I could sense that she felt she'd made her point. Ultimately, that was all she wanted. We didn't speak to each other after that except to say goodbye.

In the car ride home, I thought about telling Mira about what happened, but I kept it to myself, and tried my best to forget that it had happened at all. But that wouldn't be the last time Mira's personal relationship and outlook on religion would be challenged.

LATER THAT MONTH, MIRA RECEIVED A PHONE CALL FROM THE GOV-erning body responsible for certifying chaplains. After a series of interviews that were overwhelmingly positive, she'd expected the call to be a congratulatory one, welcoming her into the fold of the institutionalized Muslim American organization.

But Mira was furious after the call. The man she spoke with asked her if she wore hijab. She said no. And then he said they couldn't possibly certify her, because they've never endorsed a woman without hijab before, and that her values didn't align with their institution's.

Mira already had a job in a New York hospital lined up. All she'd needed was the certification to begin work, and now she would have to consider turning it down.

"What am I supposed to tell them? 'Oops, sorry. I don't wear a scarf on my head'? What the fuck?" she said, her anger overflowing. "I can graduate with a master's in religion, do all my prerequisite training, and at the last second, one guy can just say no and that's it? He literally said that if I were a man there would be no issue." Her voice cracked with emotion, and my heart ached for her.

I knew that this was just the latest iteration of the same tiresome story: reducing a woman's relationship with Allah to whether she chooses to cover her hair. And though it often felt like a relic from the last generation, it insisted on coming back in embarrassing ways.

As we stood there, Mira's frustration and hurt filled the bedroom. I could make an entire video series examining Islam in America and receive support from our community. Meanwhile, Mira, an actual expert in Islam, garnered only criticism for her personal decisions. I asked her what she intended to do.

"Fight," she replied.

OVER THE NEXT FEW DAYS, I HARDLY SAW MIRA, EXCEPT FOR AN OCCA-sional glimpse of her figure seated cross-legged on the couch in our living room, her laptop perched on her knees as she typed. An open Quran lay on the coffee table before her, along with several books of hadith, the sayings attributed to the Prophet Muhammad. I saw a tempest brewing in her eyes. She felt wronged, and she craved justice.

A FEW MONTHS PASSED BEFORE MIRA HEARD BACK.

"They're going to endorse me," she replied, so calmly it sent shivers down my spine.

Her letter examined the question of hijab academically and criticized institutional understandings of the commandment. "The obsession with this subject has prevented deeper reflections on these miraculous verses and has indeed made heavier the Muslim woman's burden to bear," Mira noted.

They would have needed to craft a rebuttal that matched the profound analysis Mira presented in her six-page masterpiece, complete with citations from the Quran and hadith. They must have assumed she was simply making up her own rules, choosing not to wear hijab on a whim or as an act of defiance against God. But this letter—and the organization's subsequent endorsement—proved that her faith and understanding of Islam were grounded not only in belief but in scholarship. She became the first unveiled Muslim woman endorsed by this organization in American history. From that point forward, every unveiled Muslim woman who faced similar judgments from Islamic institutions in North America would have a precedent on which to stand.

"They just admitted they had no real argument in the first place," I said admiringly. Though she flashed me a triumphant grin, she was far less celebratory than I was. "It was never about proving them wrong, Aymann."

WHEN THE TIME CAME FOR THE SIXTEEN-WEEK SCAN, MIRA AND I climbed into our car and made our way to a new doctor's office, one better equipped for special, high-risk cases like ours. We were dying to see the growth and progress of our twins, to find out their sex; this was the threshold after which the babies' vitality would shoot up tenfold.

As the technician applied the chilly gel and maneuvered the transducer across Mira's belly, her cheerful demeanor shifted. She fell silent as she waved the transducer back and forth. She dug it deeper and deeper, and checked the computer again and again.

"Is everything okay?" I ventured cautiously. The technician continued to move the transducer with purpose.

"I'm going to call the doctor in," she answered. Normally, we would get to hear the heartbeat, and the technician would take various measurements, but not this time. The atmosphere had changed, and we were left to sit and wait.

THE DOCTOR ENTERED THE ROOM BRISKLY, HER EXPRESSION UNREADable.

"Sometimes these machines can be faulty, so we're going to move you to another room and take a look with better equipment," she informed us.

In the new room, she pressed the transducer against Mira's abdomen, searched for the babies, and took their measurements. Then she let out a heavy sigh, removed her gloves, and faced us.

"It appears that your twins have stopped growing, and I can't find any signs of life," she said softly.

Mira's grip on my hand tightened, and I felt her body quiver. I was at a loss for words, devastated beyond belief. Tears welled up and streamed down Mira's face, but her expression remained unchanged.

The doctor shook her head, stood up, and began to head slowly toward the exit.

"Wait, that's it?" I asked. The doctor's stride stopped abruptly and she turned, as if she had to force herself to respond.

"We understand this is difficult. We're going to give you some time," she said.

I reached out to Mira, still on the examination table with her belly exposed and covered in gel. I couldn't even begin to comprehend what she must have been experiencing, but I did the only thing I could think of: I held her tightly and promised her that everything was going to be okay. Mira cried harder than I'd ever seen her cry. The kind of mournful tears that we'd been lucky enough not to need to shed. All our hopes had been cast out and replaced with dread, and we were both powerless to do anything about it.

The doctor and technician re-entered the room.

"What happens now?" Mira asked. "What happens to the babies inside my body? They're still there, just not alive, right?"

"You need to schedule a D and C, a dilation-and-curettage procedure," the doctor explained.

Mira sought a simpler explanation. "Can we do that here?" she asked.

"This isn't considered to be life-threatening at the moment, so it'd be classified as an elective surgery. And your insurance doesn't cover that," she explained.

"So what do we do?" Mira pleaded.

"You could go to a women's health clinic," the doctor stated matter-of-factly.

"I have to make an appointment somewhere else? What do I tell them? That I have dead babies inside me?" I held her close to comfort her, though I, too, was distraught. "This is insane," Mira declared.

"Stay as long as you need," the doctor offered. Then she was gone.

WE REMAINED SILENT THE ENTIRE DRIVE HOME, EACH LOST IN GRIEF. I discreetly wiped away tears as I accelerated down the highway. Mira gazed out the window, her eyes vacant. It seemed like an eternity before we got home. Both of us collapsed into bed fully clothed, and shivered under the weight of our misery. Though we found some solace in each other's arms, neither of us was in any shape to comfort the other.

After what felt like hours, Mira mustered enough will to schedule the procedure at the only clinic with appointments available, about an hour and a half south from where we lived.

It was surreal to hear her mutter the words into the phone: "Hello. We just found out our babies didn't make it, and I need to have them removed."

The earliest appointment was in four days. Mira shuddered at the thought of remaining pregnant with the lifeless twins we had been so thrilled about just a few hours ago. During those four days, we both withdrew entirely from the world around us. We took sick days off from work, and Mira prayed nonstop. I joined her when I could.

I'VE OFTEN HEARD THAT PRAYER IN ISLAM IS LIKE HAVING A DIA-logue with God. It's why there are certain cleanliness prerequisites, a ritual that involves cleaning yourself from head to toe. In sujood, the low-bowing position, I tried to make a direct appeal to Allah for the first time in my life. With my forehead pressed firmly against the ground and tears threatening to fall, I repeated the customary man-tra: سُبْحَانَ رَبِّيَ الأَعْلَى —"Subhana Rabbi Al-A'la"—Glory be to my Lord, the most high. In my head, I questioned how it could be possible that Allah would take this joy away from us.

———

AFTERWARD, MIRA SURPRISED ME WITH AN IMPOSSIBLE QUESTION.

"Do you think we'll meet them in the afterlife?" she asked quietly.

"You know the verse from the Quran, إِنَّا لِلَّهِ وَإِنَّا إِلَيْهِ رَجِعُونَ—Inna lil-lahi wa inna ilayhi raji'un—'We belong to Allah and to Allah we shall return'?" I asked. Mira nodded. "So we belong to God, right? And so do our babies. In that sense, nothing was taken away from us, because they were never ours in the first place."

Mira smiled softly, with a warmth I hadn't seen since that ultra-sound appointment.

"They came from God, like everything else in this world," she affirmed. "It just wasn't written for us to enjoy them in this life."

In that moment, our grief transformed into something else—not quite relief, but not tragedy, either. We hovered somewhere in between, both of us closer to our own understanding of Islam's answer for why pain and loss exist.

"We weren't owed the joy of becoming parents," Mira said, and I nodded. "We're here to embrace and accept what's given, and that's it. Though they were never born, they've taught us to show gratitude."

"So it was always part of God's plan for us not to have them," I continued. "And that excitement, that love—it was a *gift* from God, just as meaningful and generous as anything else good that comes from him."

"I see it that way, too," she said. "For me, this has been about spiritual growth. I think a lot about how we cried together, how we found comfort and support in each other . . . I think that was the gift from God."

AS THE DAYS PASSED, THE WEIGHT OF OUR GRIEF BEGAN TO LIFT IN the slightest increments. Slowly, speaking of our lost twins became easier, and we found a new sense of hope.

We also felt fortunate that not too many people had known of the pregnancy, sparing us the pain of having to recount our story over and over again. My mama surprised me when she opened up to Mira about her own miscarriages and explained that they were much more common than women often realized. Mira's father immediately booked a flight from Kentucky to comfort her. She seemed nearly healed after that. But we still faced another challenge: removing the babies from Mira's body.

Mira and I were joined by my parents and her father at the clinic in Cherry Hill. When we drove into the parking lot, we passed a group of Christian protesters camped outside and hurling hateful accusations. They bore posters of bloody and gruesome scenes supposedly depicting the aftermath of an abortion. One man leaned in toward our car window and shouted, "Jesus will not save you if you kill your baby!"

Mira scoffed to herself, keeping her eyes forward. But I was so upset I nearly crashed our car. "Those idiots are going to be really shocked when they find themselves being the ones sent to hell." Mira didn't respond, just looked stone-faced, focused on the procedure ahead. It hurt me so much to see her that way. The protesters were oblivious to our story, and the stories of any of the women they mindlessly berated.

The women at the clinic were the real saints. They saw Mira almost immediately and treated her with empathetic understanding. They met her where she was, and were delicate as they guided her inside, leaving us to wait for everything to be over.

While Mira was inside the operating room, her father invited my parents and me to pray at a local mosque a few minutes away. I rode in the front seat next to Mira's father; en route, he asked a Mira-esque question, as if he was resuming the conversation we had been having in private after prayers at home. "Aymann, do you know what God wants us to do on this Earth?" he asked me.

"Be good Muslims?" I asked.

"No," he answered. "Just be our best." As we drove, he continued, "Before every surah in the Quran, God declares that He is Rahman and Raheem. Do you know what that means?"

"The Most Merciful, the Most Gracious," I answered.

"Good," he said. "And do you know the root of those words, *raham?*"

I shook my head.

"It means 'womb,'" he said.

I was struck by how quickly the conversation deepened. "God's mercy isn't just kindness. It's expansive, unconditional, like a mother's love for her child. His mercy extends not just to people, but to plants, to mountains, even to those fools outside the clinic." He exhaled sharply, shaking his head. "And did you know that if you divided Allah's mercy into a hundred parts, only one is given to this world? The other ninety-nine are saved for when we need it most, after we die."

I sat with his words, floored, quietly absorbing the moment, feeling their weight like something sacrosanct.

When we arrived at the mosque, we exchanged a smile, prayed with the other Muslims who had gathered, then went to pick up Mira and go home.

AS MORE DAYS PASSED, THINGS STARTED TO INCH BACK TO NORMAL. Then, in a flash, a year had passed. By 2020, Mira and I had moved into a bigger home in anticipation of the twins that never came, which felt like another blessing they brought us in their short lives. Perhaps because we were getting older, or because we moved in when we were still grieving, this home was more of a sanctuary for the two of us. We didn't throw parties, and we rarely had friends over. We welcomed the isolation that came with the pandemic. The seclusion forced us to mature quickly, as if we had become parents without children. During the quiet, intimate moments we shared, the desire to try for a baby vanished.

Then, one morning, just like before, Mira got out of bed and hurried to the bathroom without a word. I could sense it, somehow—I knew what was coming before she even said anything. When she returned to the bedroom, her eyes shining with hope, she confirmed what I already knew: she was pregnant again.

This time, our joy was tempered with caution. We knew that it could end the same way as before, but we chose to embrace the possibility of parenthood as a gift, and we were ready to face it together.

Chapter 10

Alhamdulillah

SHE OFTEN FOUND IT AMUSING THAT SHE HAD BEEN HIRED THERE AS the youngest member on the team, surrounded by colleagues who had children older than she was. But Mira understood the value she provided, offering a unique perspective in her approach to spiritual care.

Her job was to meet the sickest people in their worst moments for unhurried conversations in between visits from overworked healthcare providers. Most of her patients were experiencing terminal cancer, and Mira seemed to genuinely enjoy surprising them with a knock at their door and asking them if they were interested in having a chat.

"No one sees the truth quite like those staring death in the eyes," she once confided in me. It gave me the chills, but Mira seemed thrilled by it.

As Mira's pregnancy progressed, she poured more and more of her soul into her conversations with patients, often returning home exhausted but fulfilled. If she had dark thoughts creeping beneath the surface, they never came up.

One early evening, when she got back from work, Mira invited me to enjoy the soup she'd made for us on the stoop in front of our house, so we could watch the final light ebb from the sky. I had read that speaking to the baby could stimulate a developing brain, and on impulse I pressed my head against Mira's belly, my lips grazing the surface. "You know, your mom is a superhero," I murmured to our unborn child. Mira looked down at me with a radiant smile.

Mira holding a homegrown zucchini,
the first fruit of my gardening efforts, 2020.

But when I asked about her day at work, her expression changed. She waited a moment to gather her thoughts. "When someone is at end of life, the first thing to die is their ego," Mira explained. "And in that sacred space, silence can be like magic. The silence creates a safe space for the other person to express what they need to say, or simply find solace within the stillness."

We both sat staring at the pink sky. I struggled with the silence. In a world silenced metaphorically by the pandemic, I was coming to realize how distracted and entangled I was, especially in the city of Newark.

"Accepting any truth is a journey in itself," she said, her voice contemplative. "A truth like accepting that one's life is coming to an end doesn't have to diminish the depth of knowledge one has accumulated through their lived experiences, which of course they cherish. If one accepts that they cherish their knowledge, then they can begin to understand what frightens them about death, which is necessary for accepting its inevitability," she explained.

"What do you tell someone who doesn't want to let go of that knowledge?" I questioned.

"Nothing," she said. "We sit in silence, and eventually they come to their own understanding."

I could hear birds cutting through the bustle of the heavy trucks and police sirens that seemed omnipresent in the city. It was like I caught a glimpse of life through Mira's eyes, for only a fleeting moment, and it was as beautiful as she was.

I longed to create a space for our child to feel challenged and to learn to trust themselves. Maybe, I thought, they'd need me to take several steps back so they could answer questions on their own, the way Mira helped her patients to do in the hospital.

I also pondered how they'd experience the death of their parents. But when the questions I wondered about got to feel too overwhelming, I broke the silence. "All right, I'm out of here. Thanks for the soup!" I said as I retreated inside. Mira didn't move or ask me to stay.

She was happy to sit and watch the rest of the sunset, alone and content.

I couldn't stop thinking about the ways in which Mira's and my professions overlapped; as a journalist, I, too, talked to people in their most difficult moments, asking questions only to help guide them in revealing their inner monologues.

MY NEXT BIG *SLATE* ASSIGNMENT WAS IN MINNEAPOLIS, IN THE LATE summer of 2020, where I sought to write a story about the aftermath of the police killing of George Floyd. A store accused him of trying to spend counterfeit money and called the police; a policeman was caught on camera kneeling on his neck as he pleaded for his life until he died. I spent several days walking around the area, speaking to as many people as I could, trying to imagine myself in their place.

This time, I tried to apply the lesson Mira had just given me and deploy silence, giving people the time and space to express their emotions rather than trying to extract their stories with a flurry of questions.

Inside the store, I spoke with each of the four brothers who owned and managed it. I stood by, keeping quiet as they delved into their memories and revealed truths beyond the rehearsed sound bites they had given other reporters.

By the end of the interviews, they trusted me enough to give me an exclusive, and to introduce me to the young man who had made the fateful 911 call. He was just a teenager, new to the United States from West Africa, and barely spoke English. The guilt hung on him; he told me he wished he had died. He was in so much pain, and I wished Mira was there to offer the support this kid badly needed.

As I worked out the story, I began to understand Mira's passion more clearly. She lived for the chance to connect with people, to learn from their struggles, and to offer compassion when they needed it most.

AS THE BABY'S DUE DATE DREW CLOSER, MY BEST FRIEND MIKE MOLINA shared devastating news. His father had been diagnosed with cancer.

I knew his dad well. He worked in construction, specifically with hazardous toxins like asbestos, which required he wear a hazmat suit. When we were kids and Mike's family was moving, we both watched in awe as his father carried an entire full-sized refrigerator down the stairs by himself. The diagnosis was crushing news, but Mike didn't seem nearly as affected as I was.

One evening, he invited me out to take a walk along the renovated boardwalk by the Passaic River. The air was thick with the scent of damp wood. We walked side by side, our hands in our pockets.

"He won't stop smoking," Mike said in frustration. "It's like he doesn't care. He's still working construction, too. He won't even take COVID seriously."

His voice remained steady, almost detached. I nodded, expecting more emotion, something to crack through his calm exterior.

He went on, railing against what he called his father's "overly aggressive masculine ego," describing his refusal to stop working with asbestos even as it killed him as a way of showing his stoicism. Mike had spent his teenage years rejecting that kind of masculinity, determined never to be like his father. That's how I always knew him—tough, but long exhausted by the act of performing it. So when his dad kept exposing himself to toxic chemicals despite the diagnosis, he finally admitted something that startled me. Part of him had been waiting for his father to learn, too late, that he wasn't invincible. "At this point, I'm just waiting for him to die. He doesn't care, so why should we?"

I couldn't bring myself to say anything. I kept my eyes on the water, my body stiff. He stared out at the water, his face expressionless, as if the situation had drained him.

His words landed like a slab, but his tone barely shifted. He was stating it like he'd already made peace with it. I thought maybe he'd crack a joke, make his grief funny like we always did, but he didn't. He was vulnerable without asking for comfort, just stating reality. And I didn't know how to meet him there. His impassiveness left me uncertain of my own role in this conversation.

I stiffened, staring out at the poisoned water beneath us, its surface glistening with green hues of oil. I wanted to acknowledge the weight of what he was sharing, but his detachment made any response feel unnecessary. Mike had always been good at getting real, but I wasn't. Outside of sharing nostalgia, intimacy felt foreign to me. My best friend was going through something huge, and I had no idea how to show up for him.

We walked a little longer. My mind scrambling for something meaningful to say, but it all sounded hollow. "I'm sorry, bro" was all I could offer.

I told Mike I was always here for him, that he could reach out anytime. He nodded, appreciative but knowing. "Mom has been home alone all day. I'ma go watch TV with her or something," he said. He climbed into his car and drove off.

Mike's resignation to his father's impending death was unexpected. And yet I felt echoes of that same attitude toward my own parents at times. His father's stoic nature mirrored my baba's. The gaps they left in their relationships with their sons had been in place throughout our lives, so why expect anything different when they were facing death?

I began thinking about the distance between Baba and me that had always been there. The more I thought, the more I realized that one thing had always defined him: his love for farming.

I could never forget his disappointment when I destroyed the old grapevine outside our first house. I was sure I'd now found what might be the only way to connect with Baba. It felt urgent to try: I didn't want to wait until the end to make things right.

The next day, I began work on my garden. I built a small garden bed and watched tutorial videos on how to care for vegetables and fruit. It was what my baba's family had done for centuries.

Growing up in Newark, I was acutely aware of how isolated I was from nature. Newark happens to be home to factories that produce steel, batteries, bricks, paint, and—for a stint during the Vietnam War—the bioweapon Agent Orange. Newark was and still is dogged by massive pollutants, such as a trash incinerator and an international airport just a few miles away from where I lived, but I was motivated by something powerful, a yearning to establish the kind of connection with my baba that I hoped to carry on with my own kid one day. As I dug my fingers into the soil and saw it beneath my fingernails, I imagined a kinship with him that I had never had.

After I began seeing some green, I dialed his number to tell him what I had done.

"Assalamualaykum! To what do I owe the surprise?" he asked in Arabic as he answered the phone.

Weighing my words, I asked him if he could lend his expertise and help me improve the garden. I knew that if I wanted his attention I had to give him an opportunity to feel needed and important.

"A garden? You?" he asked with hesitation. "Don't you live in Newark?"

"I built a little garden bed," I explained.

"The soil where you are is toxic," he told me.

"I know. I bought dirt from the store," I answered.

"You *bought* dirt? What are you growing?"

This conversation was already beginning to go deeper than any we'd had before. When I listed the array of plants in my garden—tomatoes, zucchini, broccoli, and a few other plants—Baba responded with caution. "That's too much variety. How do you expect to tend to their unique needs when they all require different care?" he asked in Arabic.

"I don't know, but maybe you can come and take a look? Come teach me?" The trap was set.

"When?" Baba asked, sounding reluctant. The prospect of his presence ignited a flicker of hope within me. It was the opportunity I wanted to get to know him better, not just as my baba, but as the man he'd been before he became a baba.

"Come now. Come whenever. It doesn't matter. I work from home now, so I'm pretty much always here," I told him.

A WEEK PASSED, AND WHEN BABA STILL HADN'T COME OVER, I THOUGHT I'd try once more. This time, I approached the conversation with more clarity and urgency. "How do you grow grapes from grape seed?" I asked him.

"Grapes require time and space. They wouldn't be feasible in a place like Newark," he asserted.

"But my neighbor has grapevines."

"Those grapes would be barely edible. They're only for show."

"They taste okay. I tried one the other day. It's sour, but still . . ."

"You ate from them? Did he give them to you?" Baba demanded.

"They've grown over onto my side of the wall," I admitted.

"That is haram!" He sounded frustrated. I listened to the rest of his lecture, which included a verse from the Quran that he recited from memory. "وَلَا تَأْكُلُوٓا أَمْوَٰلَكُم بَيْنَكُم بِٱلْبَٰطِلِ," Do not consume one another's wealth unjustly. I agreed not to pick any more grapes, and the conversation ended there.

I had always known my baba to hold tightly to his traditional values, but the realization that his mindset could derail my best efforts to connect with him was profoundly disappointing. I told myself I'd continue gardening and worry about this endeavor to bond with Baba another time.

ABOUT A MONTH AFTER THAT DISAPPOINTING CALL, I HEARD THE doorbell and a gentle knock. Baba had arrived unannounced.

My heart leaped with joy at the sight of him.

"Would you like some tea?" I offered, hoping to make him feel welcome.

"I need to pray first," he responded as he made his way toward the bathroom to perform wudu.

I joined him. Though I was again out of practice with praying, it felt like the right thing to do. After we finished, I asked him why he'd come.

"You told me you wanted me to come, so here I am," he replied to me in Arabic.

"Can I finally show you my garden?"

As soon as we stepped outside, I could sense Baba's disapproval from the pursing of his lips.

"You have a lemon tree in a pot?"

"Yeah, I read online that that would be fine."

Another disapproving grunt escaped him. "It may grow leaves, but it won't bear much fruit. And the fruit it does grow will be small and sour," he commented.

He stared at my herbs for a while, in a silence that I assumed was a sign of approval. Then, his gaze shifted toward my neighbor's thriving grapevine.

"This looks good. They know what they're doing," he commented.

"Yeah, it comes back stronger every year," I answered in Arabic.

After a brief pause, he finished his tea and retreated to a secluded spot to offer another prayer, this time alone. All I could do was bid him farewell.

"Salaam," he uttered.

"Salaam," I responded.

With that, he climbed back into his tow truck and drove away. That was it. The entire visit lasted about half an hour, and before I could even settle into what he was saying about my garden, he was gone.

Months rolled by, and the fruits of my labor materialized. I felt a swell of pride at what I had accomplished. One day, bursting with pride, I sent Baba a photo of an enormous zucchini I had just harvested. It stretched as long as my entire arm and was as thick as my neck. He didn't text me back.

WE WAITED A LONG TIME BEFORE WE LET MY PARENTS KNOW WE WERE expecting this time around. After Mira and I cleared the twenty-week anatomy scan, and fetus viability shot up, we presented my mama with a simple handmade card with an ultrasound picture inside.

"Mabrook!" she congratulated both of us, and got up to envelop us both in a group hug.

Baba, too, expressed his happiness for us. He was on the road working on his tow truck when I called him. "Baba, Mama just found out, so I wanted to let you know right away," I told him. Being the deeply religious man he is, he quietly uttered "Mashallah" repeatedly, showering humble blessings upon our unborn child.

"Baba! We're going to have a baby!" I exclaimed. He swiftly corrected me.

"Say 'Inshallah.'"

"Yes, Inshallah. But isn't it exciting?"

"Alhamdulillah," he responded.

"Of course. Yes. Alhamdulillah," I echoed, but a tinge of frustration was creeping into my voice. I had hoped this moment would bring us closer as a family, and religion seemed to be keeping us apart.

One reason I found it so difficult to connect with Baba was his habit of uttering things like "Alhamdulillah" when prompted to speak. In the Muslim faith, this common phrase translates to "Praise be to God" or "Thank God." I don't doubt that he's expressing genuine gratitude, but he says it so frequently that I can't help wondering if it's just a verbal tic, a useful religious platitude that he can use to avoid mutual connection. When he says "Alhamdulillah," is he saying anything at all?

AS I SAT IN MAMA'S KITCHEN, LISTENING TO HER AND MIRA CELE-brate, I was upset with myself for failing to connect with Baba as I had planned. Perhaps it was my fault. Had I taken him more seriously as a kid, would he take me seriously now? I regretted allowing our relationship to become so confined to transactional exchanges.

Chapter 11

Becoming Baba

MY EDITOR APPROVED THE IDEA, BUT THE IDEA OF GOING ALONE TO what I expected to be the last Trump rally was daunting. I called my former editor from *ANIMAL*, Bucky Turco.

"You look like a cop. Come be my bodyguard," I joked.

Bucky's response was immediate. "Team *ANIMAL* is back!"

WHEN WE ARRIVED IN D.C., THE STREETS WERE QUIET, BUT THE Ellipse, the park where Trump was to give his speech, crackled with energy. Parents gently pushed strollers, kids sat on shoulders, and the mood was festive. But amid the casual atmosphere were men in military-style gear, donning helmets, shields, and body armor. I snapped photographs of everything that caught my eye.

I approached a woman clutching a WOMEN FOR TRUMP sign as she walked past.

"Mind if I just hold you hostage for a quick sec to ask a few questions? I'm a journalist," I probed.

"I've got a gun in my bag. If you tried to hold me hostage, I'd shoot you." She punctuated her statement with a peculiar smile, gesturing to her fanny pack.

I told Bucky what had just happened. "You see any metal detectors out here?" he asked. The implication was obvious.

As I navigated the crowd, I interviewed a man distributing newspapers with the headline "TRUMP WINS!"

Baba embracing his children in a relaxed hug, 1990.

Bucky interrupted to say, "You spelled 'LOST' wrong! Trump lost!" The man smiled and handed Bucky a paper. Bucky accepted it.

"Great. A souvenir from the Twilight Zone. I'll keep this next to my Confederate flag in my drawer marked 'Losers.'"

At one point, a man I was interviewing accused me of celebrating 9/11, echoing Trump's infamous false claim. I explained how Muslims, too, had suffered that day. Bucky was less gentle.

"I'm a New Yorker! I was there on 9/11. I was a block away when the towers came down, and I breathed in all that crap. I almost died. Where the fuck were you?" he snapped.

I could have pulled Bucky back, but I didn't. Though I worried for a moment that his attitude might affect my reporting, I was also thankful. Bucky could say things I couldn't without worrying about how it might reflect on Muslims everywhere. Rather than risk validating the worst stereotypes about Muslims, I watched Bucky as he fought my battle.

Around noon, Trump took the stage, and the crowd surged. But before he even finished speaking, people began to move.

"We're going to the Capitol," Trump said, and that was all it took. Under banners proclaiming GOD, GUNS, GUTS & GLORY, the rallygoers— or were they protesters now?—marched, chanting *"Trump won!"*

The atmosphere had darkened. As the crowd frenzied, I wondered if they'd turn on me when they realized I was documenting their crimes—or if the cops would arrest me, thinking I was part of the mob. Still, I felt a quiet confidence born from years of navigating risky situations—in Newark, eyeing every corner; in New York, chasing graffiti writers down dark tunnels; in Egypt, reporting on a revolution from the front lines. The rule that always kept me safe was simple: show love, get love. If I stayed friendly and moved with grace, that energy would reflect back at me, even in the most volatile moments.

I kept taking photos as rioters scaled walls and smashed windows and doors to enter the Capitol. The police were overwhelmed. When Bucky and I entered the building, we observed the rioters milling about aimlessly in the rotunda. It was as if a museum had been taken over on Black Friday. People were smashing things, but most of those I saw smiled, took pictures, and hugged, oblivious to the crimes they were committing. It was obvious that this was history, so I focused on capturing as many angles as I could.

I'd been to Black Lives Matter protests where police used overwhelming force. I'd seen them crack batons over the heads of peaceful protesters and pile atop defenseless women like wild animals. Yet, here, the illusion of control was broken, and in that moment, my camera was more useful than their badges.

Bucky and I witnessed rioters using barricades as battering rams, while police deployed tear gas and pepper spray. Eventually, the cops pushed back and took the grounds by force. Rioters seemed confused. "We're on your side!" they shouted, as the police cleared them out.

We were making our way toward the exit when I saw a man pissing on the Capitol. Just as I snapped a photo, a riot cop shot him in the face with a PepperBall. I captured the moment of its explosion on his face. Bucky laughed when I showed him my picture.

Bucky and I made it out unscathed. When I regained cell reception, I saw frantic messages from my editor, Jeff, asking if I was safe. He told me to get out of D.C. and file a piece once I was somewhere secure. I told Bucky it was time to go, and we headed back to the car.

As we left, I heard the bang of a percussion grenade. The sun was setting on the Capitol, signaling the end of a day that would go down in history.

BY THE TIME I GOT BACK TO NEW JERSEY, MIRA'S NESTING HAD TRANS-formed the house. She had rearranged the furniture, and turned our spare bedroom into a nursery with a crib, a little changing table, a small dresser, and a futon. Mira had also sorted through the hand-me-down clothes from my older brothers, organizing them by size and packing away anything too large into boxes. I made my small contribution by setting up an air purifier near the crib. "This is genius," I told Mira proudly.

Mira nodded in approval, but was distracted by a pair of miniature

sneakers that had belonged to one of my nephews. Virtually everything in the room was a hand-me-down.

"Okay, now for the final touch," I said, and surprised her with a
framed T-shirt with Mira's face as a baby printed on its front. I hung
it near the crib. Mira couldn't contain her laughter when she saw it
on the wall.

"Stop! Each time you make me laugh it's like a roller-coaster ride
in there!" she exclaimed.

AS SUMMER APPROACHED, SO DID MIRA'S DUE DATE IN MID-JUNE. A
while back, Mira and I had made a deal: if we had a boy, I'd choose the
name, and if we had a girl, she would. Late one night, in our pajamas
ready for bed, the hospital called with the results of Mira's blood test.
I hurried over just in time to hear the voice on the other end announce
the sex. "It's a boy!"

Mira and I gasped.

"So I get to name him, right?" I asked, giving Mira a hopeful glance.

"I have veto power, remember?" she warned. "What's your plan?"

"I need my laptop," I said, already visualizing the spreadsheet I'd
assemble.

I started jotting down a few ideas in my phone's Notes app, but
soon built an entire ranking system. I wanted a name that honored
our cultural heritage but would be easy to pronounce and fit seamlessly in a non-Arab, non-Muslim country.

I created a scoring system, rating names with criteria like their
significance in the Quran and how easily my editor, Jeff, pronounced
them.

I added columns to fill in meanings, origins, and famous historical
figures for each name. After weeks of consideration, I finally settled
on the perfect name. When I was certain, I shared it with Mira.

"Musa," she repeated softly to herself. "It's perfect."

I showed her my spreadsheet, and she looked both amused and
horrified.

"'Musa' scored high in everything!" I said. "This is what it sounds like when a white guy says it." I played a recording of Jeff saying the name. Mira couldn't believe it.

Everything was falling into place. We were beginning to feel ready to become parents.

BY SUMMER, WE FELT OVERCOME WITH SUSPENSE, LIKE A WEDDING party, awkwardly waiting for the bride to arrive. The days passed, and Mira's due date came and went. Mira's mom, Maha, had bought an apartment back in her native Egypt, and was splitting her time each year between there and her home in Kentucky. She came back to the U.S. to support her daughter through the birth and to be the first to welcome her first grandchild into the world. But days turned into weeks, and our baby still refused to make an appearance. Finally, the night before we planned to induce labor, Mira started having contractions.

"Is it time?" I asked, my heart racing with excitement.

"No, go back to sleep," she replied.

When I woke up the next morning, she was lying beside me, focused on her breathing.

"Is it time?" I asked again, this time with more concern.

"It's been time," she admitted. "I just didn't want to go at night."

"So you're just holding it like you're holding a pee?" I teased.

WE HAD BEEN WAITING FOR THIS MOMENT FOR MONTHS, BUT IT WASN'T so easy. The birth took almost twenty-four hours.

The hours seemed to blur together, punctuated by the rhythmic beeping of machines and Mira's cries of pain. I used her mom as a barometer: if she seemed fine, I told myself I was fine, too. Mira sat on the hospital bed suffering, tears rolling down her cheeks as she gritted her teeth, and exhaustion evident on her face.

"I'm so tired," she whispered, her eyes closing momentarily.

When it seemed that the time for the final push had come, a nurse handed Mira a rope to tug on.

"Push! Push! You're doing so good! Push!" I yelled into Mira's face, trying to be encouraging. She paused for a moment and looked at me with a look of disgust. "Can you stop yelling at me?" she pleaded.

After what felt like an eternity, the moment arrived. The doctor was with another patient, and our baby flung himself out, past the hands of the nurse, through the air, and onto the bed. He literally *bounced*. I couldn't believe what I saw, but there was no time to take it in. The cries of our son filled the room, and the tension evaporated, replaced by relief.

The medical staff quickly cleaned him and wrapped him in a blanket before handing him to Mira. In amazement, I watched him settle on her chest, revealing his little face. Her exhaustion melted away as she held him for the first time.

"Musa," she whispered, her voice filled with love.

As the room settled into calm, I performed a ritual that fathers had done for their newborn babies for generations. I whispered the Muslim call to prayer into Musa's delicate ears:

$$\text{أَشْهَدُ أَنْ لاَ إِلَهَ إِلاَّ اللَّه وَأَشْهَدُ أَنَّ مُحَمَّدًا رَسُولُ اللَّه}$$

I testify that there is no God but Allah, and that Muhammad is the messenger of Allah.

When it was my turn to hold my son for the first time, I sat down, trying to find a comfortable position, though nothing about the moment felt comfortable. It was surreal and slightly overwhelming.

"Can someone bring him to me?" My voice was trembling with anxiety.

Tant Maha, hovering nearby, nodded and approached me with the alien creature bundled in her arms.

My heart raced. I'd never held a newborn before, not even one of my nephews. The thought of this tiny, fragile life in my hands was terrifying. I felt a wave of panic. His head seemed so small and delicate, as if it were held together by only a thread.

"Okay, support the head, support the head," I muttered, trying to remember the videos I'd watched in anticipation of this moment. My hands felt awkward and oversized, like they didn't belong to me.

"Hold him close," Tant Maha suggested.

"Look at you, being a dad," Mira said, as she gave me a tired but encouraging smile.

"Thanks," I said. Inside, I felt anything but natural. I'd expected to feel an overwhelming rush of emotion in these first moments. Instead, all I felt was a gnawing apprehension.

My arms were starting to ache, but I didn't dare shift my grip. My son made a small noise, and I froze, unsure of what it meant.

"Is he okay? Did I do something wrong?" I asked.

"Noises are good. You want noises," Tant Maha advised.

I looked down at his face, his eyes open and searching. There was a softness to his features that I found mesmerizing. Maybe the big feelings would come later, I thought. For now, it was enough just to hold him, to stay in this moment.

The longer I held him, the more comfortable I got. As the minutes passed, I gradually started to relax, my grip loosening slightly. Maybe it wasn't like the movies, but it was our beginning, and that was more than enough.

"Waaaaah!!!"

Musa sounded like a wounded sheep. I felt my blood turn with the shrieking. It was a rude awakening. If I had thought the hard part was over, I was devastatingly wrong.

THE NEXT DAY, MY PARENTS VISITED US IN THE HOSPITAL. MIRA LAY ON the hospital bed, still recovering, giving a smile and a wave as Mama approached to catch her first glimpse of Musa; she was eager to hold her newborn grandson.

When Mama had lifted Musa into her arms and effortlessly settled into a chair, Baba approached me with a faint smile. "Did you recite the Athan in his ear?" he asked in Arabic.

"Yes," I answered.

"Into his right ear?" he pressed.

"Yes," I repeated. "It was the first thing he heard."

Baba leaned down to Musa's ear and recited the Athan himself. He may have meant it as a sweet gesture, but I took offense; it felt like a show of his lack of confidence in me to be a competent Muslim father.

The nurse who had been attending to Mira and Musa knocked on the door and entered, to inquire about our plans for circumcision. I shared a look with Mira, confirming what we'd already discussed.

"Yes, we want to," Mira informed the nurse, but she sat up in bed with a concerned expression on her face. Circumcision was a Muslim tradition, one that my brothers and I had undergone when we were born. However, the thought of letting anyone approach my new son with a sharp object went against every protective instinct within me, and I could see that Mira felt the same.

Our apprehension must have been obvious, because Baba immediately picked up on it and cracked a joke. "Trust me, it's better to do this now. Someone from my village was circumcised later in life, and he had to walk around like this," Baba narrated, holding his hand with pinched fingers in front of himself, mimicking the act of holding out in front of him a galabiya, a traditional loose-fitting gown. He kicked his legs and pranced around the hospital room, miming the boy who had to protect his wound. It made me uncomfortable to watch. I looked over at Mira, sharing my disbelief. I'd never seen Baba this playful. Though he was trying his best, in his own way, I just wasn't in the mood.

Mira posed a question to everyone in the room: "Religiously, though, circumcision is more of a recommendation than an actual decree from God, right? It's not mentioned in the Quran."

"It's not optional; it's a significant part of our religion," Baba asserted. "Either you follow the whole religion and be Muslim, or you aren't." He began reciting Quranic verses from memory, as Mama nodded along in agreement.

"You can't just ignore parts of the religion you don't like," she added.

The discussion was cut short when we heard Musa's cries from the hallway. The nurse returned him to us, showing us his fresh wound and instructing us on how to care for it. Mama again reclaimed Musa and took him in her arms to soothe him, while Baba urged Mira to eat and rest.

ON THE FIRST DAY BACK FROM THE HOSPITAL, MIRA'S MILK HAD YET to fully come in, and Musa's crying seemed endless.

"Okay, according to this chart, Musa should be eating every two hours," I said, pointing to a colorful diagram in one of the baby books I had studied. Mira sighed, looking at me with her calm, steady eyes, and returned her attention to our helpless, crying baby.

"Aymann, babies don't follow schedules. You know that, right?" she said, rocking Musa in her arms.

"But doesn't it help to have a plan?"

Mira ignored me after that. To me, it seemed obvious that Musa was hungry—very hungry—and the more he cried, the harder it was for me to stay calm.

"Babies cry, Aymann. It's normal," Mira's mom assured me. But in my desperation to soothe him, I pushed Mira to consider feeding him formula until she could produce breast milk on her own.

"Maybe we should just give him a little bit, so he won't be *so* hungry. It could calm him down," I suggested, my voice beginning to shake with frustration.

"We agreed, formula would be a last resort, remember?" Mira replied, holding her ground.

"But he needs to eat!" I exclaimed, my voice rising. "He's not getting enough, Mira!"

Mira, understandably overwhelmed by my sudden outburst, struggled to stay calm. "Aymann, formula interferes with breastfeeding. If I give him the option, he'll choose formula over breast milk. It has to happen this way," she tried to explain, her voice barely cutting through the sounds of Musa's cries.

"He's literally starving!" I exclaimed.

Mira's eyes filled with tears. "If I don't form this connection through breastfeeding now, it might not happen at all. Don't you get that?" She retreated to the bathroom.

"حَسْبُنَا ٱللَّهُ وَنِعْمَ ٱلْوَكِيلُ," Hasbuna-Allah wa ni'mal wakeel, I chanted under my breath, a Quranic mantra of extreme duress—Allah is sufficient for us and is the best Protector. "This is sick. We have food, and we're just choosing not to feed it to him?"

Maha approached me cautiously. "I know you want to help, Aymann. But she's right. Breastfeeding is an emotional and physical bond between a mother and a baby. She needs to keep trying. And if he's hungry, that's even better. That means he will really try for the milk," she explained in English. Though she was calm, speaking to me in English was how I knew she was exasperated to the point that she was desperate for me to understand.

I was ready to fight with Mira, but never with her mom. In an instant, I realized I'd turned into someone else. Blinded by my obsession with instructions from baby books, I had become the opposite of the father I intended on being. I was ashamed. I needed to apologize.

I approached Mira in the bedroom slowly.

"I'm sorry, Mira."

"You're making this so much harder than it has to be," she shot back, her eyes welling with heavy tears.

"I know. I'm sorry. We're in this together, right? We need to trust each other's instincts," I conceded. But it was too late.

"I can't believe this is the father you've become. I'm literally trembling right now, not because of the baby, but because of you. If this is how you're going to be, I don't know how I'm going to get through this." Mira's voice shook, and she began to cry.

Her tears tore me apart. This was the last thing I wanted on the very first day of our lives as a family of three.

"Just get away from me," she muttered.

"Okay." I turned away and left the room, gently closing the door behind me. Maha shot me a look filled with pity as I laced up my sneakers and stepped outside to tend to my garden, which hadn't seen any water in the days since the lead-up to the birth.

I could hear Musa crying from outside, but gradually his cries subsided. I assumed Mira had figured out the breastfeeding situation without me. I had never felt worse, humiliated by the entire experience. Things continued this way for the next few weeks. My wife didn't want me around, and I was a depressed mess. It was nothing like I had planned.

IN THOSE EARLY DAYS, I TENDED MY GARDEN OBSESSIVELY INSTEAD. With my fingers deep in the dirt, pruning away dead leaves, I contemplated how I had always thought of myself as someone extremely calm and levelheaded. As a reporter, I had developed an appetite for stress, danger, and uncertainty. But nothing could have prepared me for the panic that set in when my son cried. This feeling was entirely foreign to me—a sudden and overwhelming fear and feebleness that seemed to come out of nowhere.

ONE AFTERNOON, MIRA STEPPED OUT TO RUN SOME ERRANDS, LEAVing me alone with the baby for the first time. As I sat there holding my newborn son, I felt my heart start to race and my palms grow clammy. I tried to calm myself down, but the feeling only intensified, as if all my fears and insecurities about fatherhood had come rushing to the surface at once. In that moment, I realized that I wasn't ready for any of this. The books, the research, the videos—all of it had given me a false sense of confidence. Clearly, I wasn't ready.

I knew that my son would cry, and that there would be sleepless nights and dirty diapers. But I had convinced myself that I could handle it all—that I could somehow keep the chaos at bay. Looking back, I see how foolish that mindset was.

The tears came easily after that as I grappled with the weight of my mistakes. I cried all the time. I had no idea how to fix the damage I had done, and I worried that my relationship with Mira was forever ruined. Worse, I felt like the best thing for my baby was for his father to disappear.

When I had read about depression after childbirth, it usually centered on new mothers. But what about new fathers? Was *I* in some kind of postpartum depression?

For me, the first few months after Musa's birth were a blur of sleepless nights, constant worry, and overwhelming responsibility. It was astounding to me how quickly my experience of being a baba rapidly shifted back and forth from "Does this joy know no bounds?" to "Will this hell ever end?" I was living in a fog, unable to connect with the world around me, experiencing a depth of isolation and despair that I had never touched before. I knew that my wife was going through physical and emotional struggles in the aftermath of childbirth, and I felt a deep guilt for not living up to my own expectations as a father.

After months of struggling, I finally decided to try therapy. Mira was excited by the idea. "It takes a lot of strength to seek it out," she said when I told her.

Before my first session, I sat in the empty, brightly lit waiting room, my mind racing. When my name was called, I took a deep breath and walked into the therapist's office. She was a kind-looking woman in her forties, but I was immediately sure I had wasted my time. There was no way she would be able to relate to my feelings as a new father, I thought.

"So where do you want to start?" she asked.

"I'm not really sure," I confessed.

"Well, we can start with what you want to get out of therapy. Why are you here?" she asked.

I took a deep breath and tried my best to explain that I felt constant pressure to be the perfect dad and partner, and that, even though I was obsessing over every little detail, things still weren't going my way.

"It sounds like you're putting a lot of pressure on yourself. Do you have any idea why you might be doing that?"

Her question made me feel uncomfortable, but I tried to answer it honestly. "I guess because I feel I know what perfect looks like," I answered hesitantly.

"And how has that been working out for you?" she asked.

"Generally, pretty good. It's just, sometimes, especially with my new son . . ." I faltered.

"One way to ease your anxiety is to find other areas where you can contribute. Are there some household tasks you could take on to help out?"

I thought for a moment. "Well, I could start clearing the table, emptying the dishwasher, or doing the laundry," I said.

"Those are great ideas," she said, still without cracking a smile. It seemed more like having a conversation with a moody bartender than with a trained therapist, but I did feel better after talking with her. "Focusing on other tasks can help make you feel more in control," she explained.

I STARTED IMPLEMENTING THE CHANGES AT HOME IMMEDIATELY. While Mira and her mom focused on the baby, I looked for other things to do. I vacuumed, washed the dishes, handled the trash, and whenever the baby needed a diaper or rocking, I was swift to volunteer.

Mira responded positively right away, smiling at me when she caught me folding Musa's miniature clothes. The constant knot of anxiety in my stomach had loosened, and I felt more present, useful, and engaged.

"Are you going to go to therapy again?" Mira asked one evening as she cradled Musa on the couch.

"Nah, I'm one and done," I answered, as we both laughed. "It's her fault. She was a little *too* good at her job. She should have drawn it out a bit more," I joked.

A FEW WEEKS LATER, TANT MAHA RETURNED TO KENTUCKY, AND MIRA and I geared up for our first night without any outside help. We took turns cradling Musa on the couch as we watched TV, nodding off.

"Ready for another all-night marathon?" I teased Mira. She nodded.

"I don't even sleep anymore. In between his napping and feeding, I'm just waiting." Mira loved her sleep. I could tell that the lack of it was starting to take a toll on her. "What do your stupid baby books say about when babies start sleeping through the night?" she asked.

I didn't remember, so I pulled out my phone to check. "No, this can't be right," I said as I stared into my phone.

"What does it say?"

"Six months!"

"We're not going to survive this," Mira muttered.

Cradling Musa with one arm,
showing off my confidence as a new father, 2021.

Chapter 12

Amo Mike

IN HINDSIGHT, I CAN'T HELP CRINGING AT A JOKE I ONCE TOLD IN elementary school just to get a laugh during lunch period:

"I'm gonna have enough kids to start my own basketball team," I declared. "A starting five, at least."

My best friend, Mike, raised an eyebrow. "You gonna stop at just five?" he asked, a knowing smirk on his lips. "What if they don't like basketball?"

"You're right. I'll need four more, just in case they prefer soccer," I answered. Mike chuckled.

Sarah gasped. "And who's going to give birth to all those kids? You?" she snarked.

"Who said they'd all have the same mom?" I replied, reveling in getting more laughter. "Of course, to all of you that sounds wild. But for Muslims . . . If I reach the maximum of four wives, that's only . . ."

"One and a half kids each!" Mike interjected.

Everyone burst into laughter except, notably, the girls in our friend group.

"How are you even going to remember their names?" asked Mike. "It's better to give them names like 'Goalie,' 'Striker,' 'Left-Back.'"

"'Left-Back' Ismail has a nice ring to it," I said, and cackled. Mike brought up that story when he came over for his first visit to meet my son, when Musa was still only a few weeks old.

"Mira didn't let you name him Left-Back?" he asked at the door, when he was taking in his first glimpse of the little guy.

I let out a big belly laugh. " 'Musa' is actually Arabic for 'Center-Forward,' " I joked.

WITH MY SON CRADLED IN MY ARMS, IT WAS MORE APPARENT THAN ever how much our paths had diverged. My reality was nothing but diapers and sleepless nights, while Mike was still living the bachelor life. His carefree demeanor contrasted sharply with the cautious, protective side of myself that had taken over lately.

Mike was wearing patched and paint-splattered purple suede pants with an embroidered poncho he had bought on one of his visits back to his ancestral homeland, Ecuador. His nails were painted in alternating black and purple, and his long black hair fell over the side of his half-shaved head. He looked like a rock star. In that moment, I realized just how much both of us had matured since we first became friends.

His eyes widened as he took in the sight of my son, but all Mike had to do was shoot me a cheesy grin to get us both chuckling. It wasn't the carefree laughter of our youth; it was tinged with the weight of what was happening. My childhood friend was meeting my child. It just felt otherworldly.

"I hope you don't mind that it smells like baby in here," I said, waving him in.

"I'm used to it," he said. "It was me and my mom taking care of my little brother, remember?" he assured me, carefully stepping inside. He instinctively kicked off his sneakers, a true sign of our long-lasting friendship.

When Mike settled onto the couch, I tiptoed toward him, being as careful as possible not to wake the sleeping baby.

"Want to hold him?" I asked softly.

"Huh? You want me to hold him?" he asked cautiously.

"I mean . . . the fact you're hesitating like this is making me feel like you're gonna fumble him," I said, mirroring his nervousness.

"Do you *want* me to hold him? I can give you a break if you need one," he said.

I scoffed and let out a laugh. "Never mind."

Mike's lips betrayed a slight grin. "Okay, okay. Come here, little man," Mike said, extending his arms toward Musa, slowly slipping his fingers into the space between the baby and my arms. He gently lifted Musa, cradled him sweetly, and brought him close to his chest. Musa's arms twitched, and his breathing briefly changed, but then it rose and fell to the melodic rhythm that signaled he'd continue sleeping.

I watched Mike interact with Musa.

"What's up, little homie?" he whispered, as he placed one finger in Musa's fragile palm.

As soon as Mike looked comfortable holding on to Musa, I stood up.

"All right, be right back," I said quickly, as I grabbed my shoes by the door and pretended to put them on.

"What do you think you're doing?!" Mike gasped.

"Just kidding!" I reassured him, a mischievous smile playing on my face.

In that moment, the air seemed to grow warmer, filled with the chaotic energy of our early school shenanigans. It was a welcome shift in my home, which had felt so stiff since Musa's arrival.

"Want to check out Musa's room?"

"You take him first. You got me worried I'll hear the door slam and your car starting," he joked.

I cradled Musa in one arm, like a football. With Mike around, I was keen to put on the front that parenthood came easily to me.

As we entered Musa's nursery, Mike looked astonished by the transformation. The last time he was in this room, it had still been a photography studio. Now it was the very essence of a nurturing haven.

We settled on the blue futon in the corner of the nursery. Mike's gaze drifted toward Musa's crib, snugly tucked into the corner beneath the window.

"I like the way you decorated. And what's that smell? Lavender?"

I sniffed, attempting to catch a whiff of it, only to be hit by the unmistakable scent of a fresh baby poop.

"That's not lavender," I grumbled. I got up and gently placed Musa on the changing station.

Mike leaned against the door frame, his eyes on Musa. A grin tugged at the corners of his lips as he watched me. I had changed poops before, but with Mike watching, the pressure was on.

"I appreciate you being here and showing love and all, but I'm five seconds away from tossing this baby at your head," I said. Mike doubled over with laughter, and his joy made me joyful, too, just as it always had, since we were kids.

Mira must have heard the laughter and joined Mike in the door-way. "Hi, boys."

Musa kicked, as if he recognized his mother's voice.

"Need a hand?" Mira offered, unaware that my ability to change this diaper had become tied to my ego.

"Almost done!" I assured her.

Mira approached to inspect. "He's been at this for an hour," Mike remarked, trying to stir up some drama for his amusement.

"I literally just started!" I assured her.

Mike chimed in again, lowering his voice, eager to fuel the feud: "He's literally been changing this diaper since I got here."

"Mira, tell him I've been changing diapers nonstop. This is diaper, what, one hundred?"

"He's been very helpful," Mira said, teasingly leaving it open to interpretation, joining in on the fun.

As I fumbled delicately with the diaper tabs, my hands suddenly felt clumsy. I let out an aggravated sigh; Mike continued chuckling in the corner, and Mira's eyebrows furrowed with concern. Part of me wanted to lash out, to yell, "Look around. Look at all I've contributed. Look at this house, the furniture, the lights are on, there's food in the fridge. You really think that isn't enough?" But I swallowed it down. I knew where that thought came from, the same place that had shaped my baba's understanding of what it meant to be a good dad, and I was terrified of turning into him. So I stayed quiet and pressed forward.

"One down, a million to go. You got this," Mike said, his voice softened with empathy.

Mira shook her head, walked over, and handed me a fresh onesie to dress Musa in. "Not finished yet, Baba," she asserted firmly.

"All right, another hour is about to pass while he does this. Start the clock," Mike mocked. It cracked me up, even though I gave him an indignant glare.

With Musa dressed and calm settling over the nursery, Mike unleashed an incredulous smile that I hadn't seen since we were kids. "A whole-ass dad . . ." he said in amazement.

Mira left the room and returned in an instant with a camera. "Keep changing him," she urged, her tone conveying urgency. I laid Musa down on the fuzzy carpet in his room and unzipped his onesie, just to zip it back up. As I maneuvered both of Musa's arms and legs into the loose onesie, she captured the moment, in my memory as well as on film.

"How does it look?" I inquired.

Mike approached and looked down at Musa, who was now on his back, wiggling his arms and legs in the air. "You're, like, the first of your kind. We're in uncharted territory," Mike said, and placed his arm around me.

"I was gonna say, sometimes it feels like I'm having to invent the wheel over here. Like I'm the first person to ever have a kid. It all feels so alien," I said.

He nodded. "Your dad was like my dad. They were at the door, waving to our moms, like, 'Y'all got this? I'm out. Peace!' You're a few weeks in, and you've already changed more diapers than the two of them combined," he shared.

We both laughed, but that laughter was enough to startle Musa, who began to cry.

Mira let out a sigh. "And here we go again," she said, preparing herself to try to feed him once more.

A sense of purpose surged through my veins as I put my extensive knowledge of soothing techniques into action. This time, I was brimming with confidence.

"Watch this," I announced, carefully cradling Musa. I turned him onto his side, facing outward, and swayed him gently up and down, mimicking the rhythmic motions I had practiced countless times, softly shushing into his ear. As I continued to sway and bounce, Musa's eyes slowly closed, and his breathing became calm and steady. The room was imbued with a serene stillness, interrupted only by the gentle hum of contentment emanating from Musa as he fell back asleep.

"That's the five 's's," I boasted to Mike.

"Damn! That worked perfectly," he acknowledged, his eyes reflecting his genuine happiness for me.

Mira couldn't resist a sarcastic remark. "Okay, so that's your job," she declared, a mischievous grin playing on her lips. "Whenever he cries, I'll just yell '*Baba!*' and put him right in your lap." I smiled, proudly accepting the responsibility.

"Careful what you wish for. Crying is pretty much all babies do," Mike said.

Mike began gathering his things, but before he headed for the door, I made sure we got a photo of him with Musa. "Amo Mike!" I said, using the Arabic word for "uncle," as I clicked the shutter.

"You always gave off dad vibes. Now it all makes sense," he remarked with a laugh. He was chuckling loudly as he stepped away and climbed into his car. When he turned on the ignition, loud reggaeton music blasted out, rattling his windows. I was overwhelmed with the hope that our friendship would endure another twenty years, and that Musa would come to know the joy of hanging with Amo Mike.

I ALSO COULDN'T WAIT FOR MY OLDEST BROTHER, MOHAMED, TO MEET Musa.

Having gone through fatherhood himself, Mohamed understood my emotions and needs and called me frequently after Musa's birth just to check on me, even though he was busy with his twins.

"What's up, Abu Musa?" he greeted me when I answered the phone.

He came to visit right after Mike had stopped by. I answered the door with Musa in my arms while Adam and Ali darted into the house.

"Shoes! Shoes!" Mohamed called after them, but his words fell on deaf ears.

"Give me the baby," Mohamed exclaimed as soon as he entered, his hands reaching out to take Musa.

"By all means," I said, and handed Musa over. Kholoud placed the shoes her boys had kicked off to the side neatly and immediately began making endearing sounds at the sight of my son.

"Don't we have enough boys?" she jokingly remarked. "I really thought you two would be the ones to bring us a girl." Mira heard that from down the hallway and joined us in the living room.

"Haram! He's perfect," she said. "But I know, right," she added chuckling.

With their wide eyes and shy smiles, the twin boys marveled at the presence of their baby cousin. They approached Musa with awe and gently reached out their hands to touch his delicate fingers.

"Did you know that Musa lived in Auntie Mira's belly just a little while ago?" Mohamed asked them. They shook their heads in disbelief.

Mira turned to Kholoud. "I know twins are different, but do you have any advice for us?"

"I don't know, what do you think, Mohamed?" Kholoud asked, amused by the magnitude of the question.

Mohamed leaned forward and matter-of-factly stated, "Let them tire themselves out so that you don't tire yourself out. It's all about conserving your energy."

"What about this stage?" I asked.

Mohamed chuckled in response, looking down at the peacefully cooing Musa in his arms. "Enjoy it as much as you can, because it only gets worse from here," he joked.

Mira and I exchanged a worried glance.

"Worse? It doesn't get worse!" Kholoud interjected. "Let's just say it gets . . . different," she clarified.

Mohamed's twins continued to explore the rest of the house. Mira and I smiled at the scene, imagining what it would be like when Musa was old enough to walk around on his own, explore, and play with his older cousins. But my attention was fixed on Mohamed, who seemed relaxed.

"You have a way with them," I remarked. Mohamed chuckled.

"Trust me, I wasn't always this calm." He turned to me. "The key is to find joy in the chaos. If you wait for things to calm down so you can start enjoying them, you'll be waiting forever," he said.

I nodded, absorbing his words. "Easier said than done," I replied. Mohamed laughed. "Watch this," he said.

He crouched down to the twins' level.

"Adam, Ali, can you show Amo Aymann how fast you are?" The boys immediately lined up against a wall.

"Ready? Three . . . two . . . one . . . Go!" he shouted. And, like a shot, the twins ran around full-speed, their little faces focused and determined. "See? It's a game to them. And if they tire themselves out, even better," he advised.

As the evening wore on and the twins' energy began to turn toward the fussy and destructive, Kholoud called them one by one to change into pajamas.

"Thanks for coming by," I said, genuinely grateful.

Mohamed smiled. "Anytime. Remember, find the joy," he said, giving me a knowing look, before heading out the door with a twin nestled against each of his shoulders.

Mira handed Musa back to me, and we sat together on the couch, soaking in the calm.

"You're getting the hang of this," she said.

She leaned her head on my shoulder, and for a moment, it felt like we were a real family.

———

THE DAYS TURNED INTO WEEKS, AND, SLOWLY, WE STARTED TO FIND our footing. The sleepless nights became a little more bearable, the crying a little more manageable, though not any less frequent. Most days followed a similar pattern. Diapers and house chores were my domain, and feedings and soothing were Mira's. And in moments of exhaustion and frustration, we also found pride in having survived so far.

NEXT TO VISIT WERE MY PARENTS. MAMA ENTERED WITH ONLY ONE sentence as a greeting:

"Where's Musa?" she briskly asked in Arabic, offloading a massive tray of food into my arms.

Baba followed closely behind, carrying a second tray, with a tired yet contented expression on his face.

"How are you?" Mama asked.

"Exhausted," I answered, hoping to initiate a conversation. Baba walked past me, gesturing for me to express gratitude to Allah for having a healthy baby.

After placing the food in the kitchen, Baba tugged at my arm. "Have you prayed yet?" he asked me.

"Not yet," I admitted.

"Have you been praying at all?" There was a hint of interrogation in his tone.

"Honestly, no, not since Musa was born." It had been much longer than that.

"Aymann, this is the most crucial time for prayer. Your son needs to witness you praying so that he can emulate you."

"You're right, let's pray," I acquiesced, opting for the path of least resistance.

As we prayed, I listened to my father recite the Quran from memory. With my eyes closed, it felt like my first break since Musa's birth, and I absorbed the significance of my expanded responsibilities as a father. Merely seeking a deeper connection with God for myself was no longer enough. I now had the added responsibility of instilling a love for God in my son. It was a profound realization; the fate of my son's soul depended on this.

After the prayer, my father extended his hand while continuing to murmur his own prayers under his breath.

"We're both babas now. How cool is that?"

"May Allah guide you in raising him into a good Muslim man, and invite you both into heaven," he said, and, with that, he retreated to the nursery.

I followed Baba, and watched as he reached for Musa, scooped him up, and whispered Islamic verses into his ear. I smiled, but I wondered if Baba was only doing this out of a devotion to Allah, not as a grandfather to a newborn baby boy. By the end of the evening, my urge for connection to Baba had turned into a painful resentment. Why couldn't he be as excited as everyone else for me? I wondered. Why couldn't he love me the way he loved being faithful?

I was glad when my parents left, so I could fall back into my exhausting routine. I was in a bad mood for a few days, but around Mira and Musa I swallowed those feelings, offering only smiles and joy. I had been so certain that once I became a baba I would understand mine better. Instead, I was sure Baba could have done more and had chosen not to.

BY SEPTEMBER, IT WAS TIME FOR MIRA TO RESUME HER SCHEDULE OF working part-time. She was excited to get back to work, but she was equally worried about being separated from her newborn baby. She looked back at me from the doorstep.

"What are you going to do all day?" she asked, trying to hide her worry behind a façade of casual curiosity.

"I guess we'll go for a walk, go to the park, maybe do some shopping, and then I'll FaceTime everyone in my phone book so I don't lose my mind," I said, the words tumbling out faster than I could think them through.

A laugh escaped Mira's lips as she nodded. "Good idea."

I grabbed one of Musa's arms and waved goodbye. As the door swung shut behind her, a sense of silent emptiness filled our little home. It was as if the walls were holding their breath, watching us. But the quiet didn't last long. Right on cue, as though he had been waiting for that precise moment, Musa began crying. The sound was piercing.

Mira had left a generous stockpile of her breast milk in the fridge for us to use. I warmed a bottle for him and held him tightly while he ate.

I flicked open my laptop to log in for work. With Baby Musa content and cozy in my lap, and my hands free to type, I breathed a sigh of relief. "This is going to be a breeze, actually," I murmured to myself.

MUSA SEEMED TO ENJOY NOTHING BETTER THAN EARLY-AUTUMN walks around Newark. The morning sun was bright but gentle, casting a golden hue over the neighborhood. Musa was snug in his stroller, and his wide eyes blinked up at me, full of curiosity and wonder.

"Ready for a walk?" We set off down the sidewalk toward Independence Park.

I had some strong associations with that park: it was across the street from East Side High School, and it was where a few of my friends had been robbed at gunpoint when I was younger. On cue as I thought of this, I noticed a group of rowdy men gathered around a bench, clearly still drunk from the night before. Normally, I would have felt I needed to be ready for action, but with Musa, I felt an unexpected sense of safety.

One of the guys, who was taller than me and wore a baseball cap, leaned down to get a better look at the baby, and waved. Musa gurgled in response, his little hands waving back. The group laughed, and any remaining tension melted away.

As we continued our walk, I began to think of Musa and the stroller as something of a force field. The stereotypes about who I had to be, both as a man and as an Arab, seemed to vanish. Women who might usually rush past me clutching their purses now smiled at us. A few even stopped to admire Musa.

"He's so handsome. What's his name?" asked one woman at the park, her eyes crinkling with a genuine smile.

"Musa," I replied, feeling a sense of camaraderie.

"Tchau, Musa," she responded.

Even a local police officer who stood just outside the park—usually a figure that evoked fear in me—waved at Musa as we passed. "Look, Musa, a police officer," I said, nodding toward him. I'd never said hi to a cop like that before. Now I was just a baba out with his son, and nobody, no matter how crazy, was going to mess with a dude rolling a stroller—not cops, not bozos, nobody. I'd expected I'd be the one who made Musa feel safe, but it was the other way around.

Spending time alone with Musa felt like discovering a softer version of myself, one I hadn't known was there. The world seemed to meet us with more warmth than I was used to, and I met it back in kind. I was still me, still carrying all the things that had shaped me, but with Musa, I felt like I had permission to move differently. I could let my guard down. I could smile more. A new version of myself reflected out into the world through Musa's wide, unfiltered eyes, and I liked the person I was becoming.

WHEN MIRA WALKED BACK THROUGH THE DOOR EACH DAY, THE fatigue was clear on her face. But her eyebrows raised in surprise as she scanned my face, looking for signs of exhaustion and not finding any.

"I've got an idea," I called out to her one evening while she set her belongings down and settled in. "How about you start working full-time, and I'll be a full-time dad! That'll really stick it to the patriarchy, right?"

She turned, giving me a stunned look. "Is Musa that behaved when I'm gone? You'll do the nighttime thing by yourself tonight, since it's so easy?" she asked, her tone challenging.

"If you take on the breadwinning, absolutely!" I declared, my voice full of playful determination.

She somehow knew that I was leading her on with a half-truth. I loved playing with Musa all day, but I wasn't getting to even a fraction of the work I used to do. Typically, I waited for Mira to come home from work before diving into my own work, though I rarely found the energy for it by then.

THE NEXT MORNING, I APPROACHED MIRA, READY TO ADMIT DEFEAT. "I think we need help," I admitted. "How the hell do working parents get it all done? It's like this country hates parents."

"Back home in North Africa, families lived together. New babies were a shared responsibility," she told me.

"I can't believe our parents left that behind for *this*," I said.

Just as I spoke, Musa's cries began to echo through the house. I rushed to change his diaper, helplessly feeling that we were drowning under the weight of our expectations of ourselves. I wanted to be both a present baba and a productive journalist. It seemed I needed to choose between the two.

THINGS CAME TO A HEAD WHEN, DURING ONE OF MUSA'S NIGHT FEEDings, I spilled a precious bottle of pumped milk.

"Do you realize how much effort it takes to make that bottle?" she demanded.

Instead of apologizing, I lashed out: "The bottle shouldn't have exploded when it hit the floor. Are you sure you screwed the cap on correctly?"

Exhaustion had worn us down, making it hard to communicate with empathy. We both anticipated the day's end, but when the night shift began, we yearned for day to break. Every day blended into the next, and finding moments of peace and purpose became a daily struggle. The vision I had for myself as the perfect baba never felt less possible. When Mira came home, I'd briskly hand Musa off to her at the door and escape.

BY THE TIME MUSA WAS ABOUT NINE MONTHS OLD, MIRA AND I SEEMED to have reached a new stage of our relationship. We settled into cautious truces, and when she seemed even the slightest bit annoyed,

I took it as my cue to give her some space. She had been quietly struggling with her milk production, and then the day came when it stopped entirely.

"This is it. He's going to be a formula baby," she stated, as she wiped away a splatter of powder left over after preparing a bottle for Musa. "I think he's probably ready for solid foods, anyways," she said.

"Oh, snap! Is it finally happening?" I exclaimed, repeating a headline about baby food that had caught my attention.

It was winter, and without a garden to tend to, I had been looking for something else to pour my energy into that wasn't directly baby-related. Making meals for Musa felt like the perfect thing to do.

AS THE LATE MORNING GAVE WAY TO THE EARLY AFTERNOON, MUSA sat upright in his high chair, eager for his first taste of solid food. Mira prepared an avocado, and, with steady hands, carefully scooped a small spoonful and brought it to his mouth. Her movements were slow, honoring the gravity of the moment. I watched through my camera lens, where I could see Musa's eyes widen with curiosity and excitement.

As the spoon touched his lips, his mouth opened slightly.

In the pictures, Musa's small puckered lips are faintly smeared with bits of green avocado—a clear sign that our experiment was a failure. He hadn't swallowed any of it. But Mira and I were content, and in that moment, our shared effort felt more important than the outcome. We were desperate for little wins.

ON AN EARLY MORNING, AFTER I'D FINISHED CHECKING WORK EMAILS, I found an easy recipe for mashed potatoes. As soon as Musa was down for his morning nap, I grabbed everything I thought I needed: a small pot, butter, cheese, salt, and, of course, potatoes.

"Okay, how do I do this?" I asked Mira.

She couldn't believe I didn't know how to peel a potato. With a sigh, she brushed me off and told me to call Mama for instructions.

"You can thank her for cooking all those meals your entire lazy, entitled life while you're at it," she added, giving me a playful bump with her hip before flopping onto the couch, exhausted.

I dialed Mama's number and put her on speakerphone. Hebah had mentioned how much she'd bonded with Mama over shared cooking tips, and I was eager to experience that connection.

"Salaam, habibi!" she greeted me cheerfully.

I eagerly explained my plan to Mama—I was going to make some mashed potatoes for Musa. But it didn't go as planned.

"And where is Mira?" she asked, her tone brisk.

I explained that Mira was taking a small break, not realizing the implication behind her question.

"Why isn't she helping you?" Mama pressed. That's when I realized I might have unintentionally thrown my wife under the bus. I scrambled to explain, but it was no use. Mama launched into a lecture on how proud parents should fulfill Allah's preordained roles with their children. As usual, her words went in one ear and out the other; I hadn't called for another lecture on Islam.

"So, if a father wants to be involved in feeding his child, that makes him a bad Muslim?" I snapped, too tired to hide my irritation.

Mama let out an exasperated sigh. She seemed frustrated, as though I wasn't taking her—or, worse, God—seriously. "Nobody can do it all. Believe me, habibi, I tried. It broke my body. Be fair to yourself, and don't let yourself be taken advantage of."

I could tell her words came from a place of hurt, but I was paralyzed by disappointment. "It's fine. I'll just look it up online," I replied curtly.

Mama's frustration soon gave way to the sad realization that she had inadvertently dampened my excitement. She asked me how work was going, and I offered her the default "Alhamdulillah."

The call ended soon after that. I watched a quick YouTube video on how to peel a potato instead, and, feeling deflated, made mashed potatoes.

Just as I finished, Musa's cries sounded throughout the house. Mira joined me in the kitchen with our cranky son. "Showtime!" she called out.

Musa opened his mouth eagerly, now more accustomed to solid food. Mira noticed the uneasy look on my face and asked how my conversation about peeling potatoes with Mama had gone. I told her it didn't go well, that Mama had instead given me a lecture on gender roles. Mira's eyes widened in shock.

"Oh no, Aymann. What exactly did you tell her I was doing?" Mira asked, panic creeping into her voice.

"I told her the truth, that you were taking a very, very, very short break," I replied, stretching the truth slightly in my favor.

"Great. Now your mom thinks I'm a deadbeat mother," she said, leaving me alone with Musa in the kitchen.

I could see things from her perspective. I understood that, as Musa's mother, Mira felt an added layer of pressure. My mama had always been very sweet and caring, but she was in the process of over-coming her instinct to correct and guide us. In my struggle to communicate with her, I had inadvertently created unnecessary drama—and, worse, a wedge between my mama and my wife.

I'd gotten used to giving Mira her space, but this time, with Musa in my arms, I followed her into our bedroom. I confessed that I felt like I was stumbling from one mistake to the next. She appreciated my vulnerability and reciprocated with her own. "I just don't understand why anyone would willingly believe something like Allah wanting men to be separate from their kids. Like, what?" she exclaimed. I nodded.

"If God really wanted all men to only focus on work, well, that would be very, very sad."

In the end, we laughed. I couldn't handle another ounce of stress. I just wanted to fast-forward to the part where we could laugh every time things felt shaky. I think Mira felt that way, too.

ABOUT A WEEK LATER, I WOKE UP NEXT TO MIRA FOR THE FIRST TIME in a long while without hearing the cries and wails of our baby. Mira was already awake. Part of me wanted to savor every bit of rest before Musa inevitably woke up, so I reached for my phone and mindlessly scrolled through my unread emails. When Mira emerged from the bathroom, I quickly put my phone down and pretended to be asleep.

"Don't even try that," she chuckled. "You can't steal my move and use it against me."

From under the sheets, I joked, "Let me guess. You're pregnant." Mira's silence said it all.

"Oh my God," I exclaimed, shooting out from under the sheets. Although I was outwardly expressing a surge of emotions, inside I felt numb. "Musa isn't even a year old yet. It's like you got pregnant the moment your body was ready. It's actually unbelievable."

"In nine months, Musa will only be a year and a half old. That's two babies under two," she noted. "Not how I would have planned it, but, ultimately, we're not really in control, right?"

"We are whatever the opposite of in control is," I replied.

Just then, Musa's cries echoed through the house.

"He knows he'll have to learn to share now," Mira joked, her laughter contagious.

After getting Musa ready, Mira held him and fed him a bottle. She looked at me thoughtfully. "Now my milk drying up actually makes sense," she said.

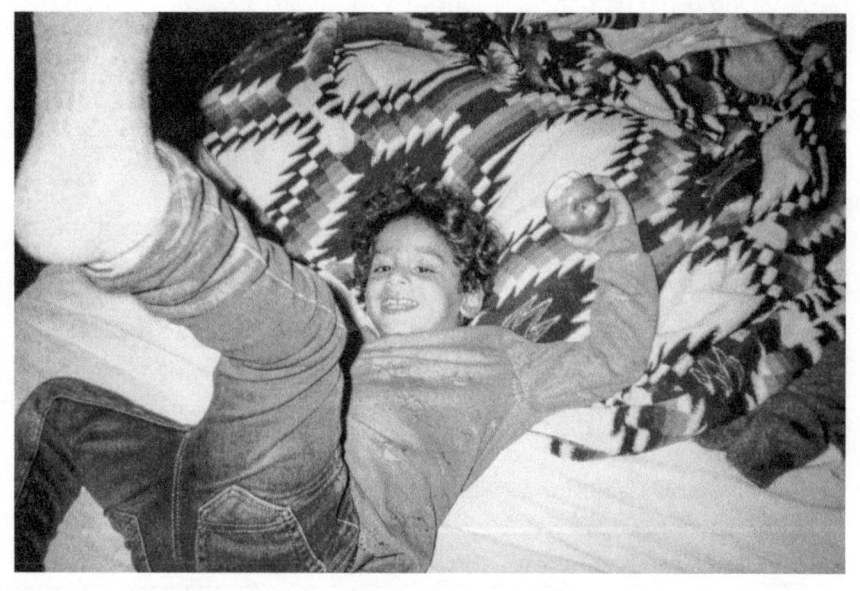

Musa clinging to an apple, 2024.

Chapter 13

Game of Tawla

IT WAS THE SUMMER OF 2022, AND WE HAD BIG PLANS. I WAS SET TO accompany my one-year-old son and pregnant wife halfway across the world to the country of our parents' origin. The morning of our flight, I turned to Mira. "You know what I'm most excited about? Taking pictures! Like the ones I have of me as a baby in Egypt—at the Pyramids, at the beach with my family."

Mira looked at me, puzzled. "That's what you're most excited about? Not that we're about to give his little palate a crash course in Egyptian food?" She rattled off all her favorite dishes. "Mulukheya, bamya, kushari, falafel, shawarma . . ."

"Shawarma?" I laughed. "I get wanting to get him to experience Egypt, but, Mira, he has no teeth."

"I'll chew it for him and feed it to him like a mama bird!" she joked.

Our goal was the same: to awaken Musa's inner Egyptian.

WHEN WE BOARDED THE PLANE, MUSA SEEMED HAPPY. HE LOOKED around with wide eyes, absorbing the new environment. The plane was full of babies, and almost immediately it seemed that each of them began wailing. Not just the crying Mira and I had grown used to with Musa. These kids all sounded like they were being cooked alive. Musa, miraculously, was not affected by the ambient shrieking.

I whispered to Mira, "I forgot this is how Egyptair rolls."

"You lost your right to complain about babies the second you brought one on the plane," she teased.

After what felt like an eternity, the plane landed in Cairo.

The second we stepped outside the air-conditioned sanctuary of the terminal, we were blasted with the scorching Egyptian heat. It was like swinging open the door of a preheated oven. I'd wondered if it was a good idea to come in the summer, but Mira hoped marking Musa's birthday in his ancestral homeland would make it worthwhile.

Just beyond the scrum of people, we were greeted by a familiar and comforting sight—Mira's mother, Tant Maha, waving her arms and jumping up and down, radiating excitement.

"How was the flight!?" Maha asked as she guided us toward her waiting car.

"We didn't sleep," Mira lamented to her mother.

Maha nodded sympathetically. "I know, I know. Believe me. I've done it many times, with four kids, not just one. And by myself, too," she said.

Mira's mother had her own apartment in a new development in Egypt called New Cairo—an upscale area in the desert designed to ease the city's congestion and offer a fresh urban space.

Maha turned to us. "So—what do you want to do first?"

Without hesitation, Mira exclaimed, "Falafel, please!"

I enthusiastically joined in: "Yes, and then sleep!"

Maha playfully dismissed our desire for rest. "You can sleep when you get back to America," she retorted, setting the tone for the trip.

THERE WAS NO ROOM FOR A CAR SEAT IN THE CAR, SO I HANDED MUSA off to Mira. She was taken aback by my willingness to let go of my usual insistence on safety precautions. "Wow, you're a completely different baba out here," she joked.

I couldn't resist teasing, "We're home! This is the real me!"

Even amid the honking horns and crowded streets, we felt a profound sense of peace. Everyone moving or driving seemed conscious of being tiny organisms in a vast ecosystem. I had been to Egypt before, but it was thrilling to see it through the eyes of a baba.

But as we drove through the city, I couldn't help noticing all the potential dangers. Entire families with infants even younger than Musa were perched on mopeds hurtling down the highway. Children sat on the trunks of cars or the beds of pickup trucks.

Mira enveloped Musa with her protective embrace, doing her best to at least give herself the illusion that she was keeping him safe. Our lives were out of our hands, and there was something beautiful about that. The chaos outside the car windows mirrored the tumultuous journey of becoming a baba. It's an unending challenge in accepting you're never in control.

"You know," I said, turning to Mira with a grin, "I think Musa is handling all this better than we are."

"He's just here, going with the flow. Enjoying the ride," she mused.

EACH TIME I RETURN TO EGYPT, I WONDER WHY MY PARENTS EVER left. The delicious foods, the melodious echoes of the Athan, and the comforting warmth of the Egyptian sun—I couldn't believe my parents chose to raise their children in New Jersey instead. With each turn, the streets of Egypt seamlessly blended ancient history with modern life. Donkey carts trotted alongside cars blaring mahragan music, and centuries-old architecture coexisted with majestic pyramids.

Eventually, we reached a café nestled up a narrow flight of stairs, on the second floor of an unassuming residential building. I had planned on resting after breakfast, but the irresistible scents of freshly brewed coffee enticed me. Maha led the way, sharing her enthusiasm.

"This place offers all the traditional Egyptian dishes. It's always my first stop when I arrive in Cairo," she explained in Arabic before ordering what felt like everything the café had to offer.

Soon, twelve small mezze dishes filled the table. We savored all of it: the besara, the fuul, the falafel, the torshi, the kofta, the ruz, the salata, the asal wa tahina, and more.

With the utmost care, we selected bite-sized portions and arranged them artfully on Musa's plate. We allowed him to reach out and dip his fingers into the food and delighted in watching his little fingers explore the textures. Mira guided a falafel to his lips and encouraged him to take a bite. Instantly, his expression transformed into a mask of surprise and joy. His lips smacked with pleasure as he savored the new experience.

"I think he likes it," I said, chuckling.

Maha exclaimed, "Of course he does! He's Egyptian!"

Afterward, we ventured east, leaving behind the ancient heart of Cairo. The roads gradually widened, creating a contrasting sense of spaciousness and calm. Many of the contemporary structures had been built within the past five years, and ongoing projects were visible everywhere. We encountered well-maintained gardens, lush patches of grass, and upscale shops and restaurants that exuded an atmosphere reminiscent of Dubai's new developments. New Cairo transported us to a world of opulence and grandeur, offering a glimpse into the future.

I wasn't immediately sold on it. In fact, a part of me hated it—it wasn't the Egypt I had always romanticized. When my parents spoke about Egypt, they reminisced about the warm hospitality of its people; the soul-stirring call to prayer from mosques so old their minarets have stood for many generations; the bustling shops; the unique twist on the Arabic language; and the rhythm of each day that began and ended with a hot drink. I longed to introduce Musa to that Egypt. The days spent in the air-conditioning, eating takeout before jumping into the pool, could wait.

As soon as our bags were dropped off, my plans to get some rest were overcome by my desire to explore. I exchanged messages with my cousins, who urged me to come over right away. Hamada, Yassir, and Osama had always treated me and my siblings like their own brothers and sister. And after our antics during the Egyptian revolution, Osama and I were bonded for life. They lived in a building that my grandfather Abouzid had built by hand.

"It's your house. The door will always be open for you," Osama texted. He added, in a voice note: "I'm at a café near the house right now. I'm sitting with our friends. Do you remember them? They also send their well wishes. Will you know how to get here? Or should I come get you?"

I took it as a challenge. "I'll see you soon," I wrote back. I extended an invite to Mira, though it was halfhearted. I was meeting male cousins at a café, and in a place like Egypt, societal norms dictated the facets of everyday life. Mira must have sensed that the invite was more of a courtesy: she casually declined.

I called an Uber, and as Musa and I settled into it, I leaned toward him and whispered, "Are you ready for the *real* Cairo?" I gave him enough space to observe the world passing by outside the window.

The journey lasted about an hour, but I didn't mind. The view beyond the window encapsulated everything I cherished about Egypt—the bright sun, the hazy veil of dust and sand, the surreal quality of cars rushing by.

When we reached the neighborhood where my paternal family lived, the driver asked if we could get out there instead of the street address, gesturing an entrance to the unpaved street.

I stepped out of the car with Musa in one arm and my backpack filled with diapers and other essentials in the other, and pressed forward down the narrow street, relying on a glimmer of faith that I would stumble upon a familiar landmark.

AT TIMES, SHUBRAH CAN FEEL UNSAFE. IT'S A POOR NEIGHBORHOOD, and there was no hiding that I was a foreigner, no matter how good my Arabic was. I passed packs of young men on every corner. One group was playing pool, and one of the larger of the teenage boys reached over and smacked another on the head, ripping the pool cue from his hand. They noticed me right away, but I felt safe holding Musa. Egyptian culture dictates a special respect for parents.

Eventually, I recognized the street café where my cousins and their friends always gathered, and where I had spent countless hours sipping coffee during previous visits.

I settled into one of the many empty white plastic chairs that lined the street. The café sprawled into the intersection with a simple out-door setup: about twenty plastic chairs scattered haphazardly, a few small side tables, and a lone TV nailed to the exterior wall of some-one's house. It felt like it operated solely by communal consent, with-out the kind of permits you'd expect back home in the United States. This café had become the neighborhood's outdoor living room, where individuals flowed in and out as they pleased.

One man operated the entire café and tended to all the customers from his apartment. He would emerge to take orders, then disap-pear back into his apartment to prepare coffee or tea or to grab ice and a soda. The chairs sprawled across the intersection, and when the occasional car ventured through Shubrah's dusty roads, nobody budged an inch, so it was left to the driver to navigate the intricate maze. Small wonder that the taxi that dropped me off had hoped to avoid the densely packed area.

Before I could spot anyone I knew, the café owner approached to take my order. I politely requested "A'hwa mazboot," a Turkish coffee with medium sugar. With my coffee finally in hand, I settled in and tried to savor the moment like other Egyptians who enjoyed these daily rituals. In America, any moment spent idling often felt unpro-ductive. In Cairo, particularly in Shubrah, it seemed like all we had was time. Time with friends and family was time well spent. Work and making money was a priority that fell further down the list; hang-ing out was the main objective of each day.

I texted Osama, who didn't respond right away, and placed Musa on my lap, then lifted him onto my shoulder to keep him entertained and gently bounced him up and down, recalling playful moments back home on our sofa.

Soon enough, Moawad, a family friend who often spent time with my cousins, spotted me and called out to me by a new name. "Abu Musa!" he yelled: Musa's father. A bit shorter than me, he walked with an exaggerated swing of his arms, dipping his shoulders up and down like a bodybuilder. He was well-groomed and sporting aviator sun-glasses, with a laptop bag slung casually over his shoulder—standing out in an environment filled with older men in loose-fitting galabiyas and kids in tight ripped jeans and flip-flops.

"Have you ordered already?"

I held up the empty cup in front of me, and he scoffed with genuine disappointment.

"If you wanted coffee, you should have told me. This coffee is okay. But it's not fit for a prince like you. Maybe I'll drink a cup here if I'm in a hurry. But for really good coffee? I go someplace else. Did you pay yet?" he asked briskly.

"Not yet. I'm waiting for the basha to come back," I said, chuckling from his description of me as a "prince."

"No problem," he said, tugging my arm as we walked down the street toward my family's house. As we passed by the café owner's door, Moawad loudly called out and banged his fist on the window awning. "Mohamed! We're in a hurry!" he yelled. "Don't charge this guy. He's our guest from America!" And we continued on our way.

Moawad snatched Musa out of my arms and placed him high up on his shoulders. "How are ya, Musa?" he greeted my son, eliciting a contagious grin as Musa bounced up and down. "Osama got pulled away for work and sends his regards. I just spoke with him. He made me promise that if you needed anything, anything at all, it's my responsibility. I told him, 'Are you crazy? Aymann, the prince? Aymann, habibi.' All you have to do is ask." He brought our brisk walk to a halt. "Tell me. What do you want to do while you're here?" he asked.

His kindness made me blush. My family is accommodating, but this felt like a whole new level.

"Nothing! I'm just here to see you all. I wanted to bring Musa, show him around, get him to meet the family, take some pictures, feed him some food, do whatever you guys are doing. Honestly, bringing him to Shubrah was really it," I explained in halting Egyptian Arabic.

Moawad smiled and nodded. "Of course! Osama is like a brother to me, and because he loves you like a brother, that makes us brothers, too. So, if you need anything at all, you call me first, okay?"

"Okay, then let's take a picture together," I suggested.

Moawad immediately spread Musa's arms like wings, which brought a wide smile to my son's face.

"Yalla. Say 'cheese'!" he exclaimed, excited to use the little English he knew.

We finally reached my family's house—a place that seemed frozen in the past. The slanted, weathered building bore the marks of age, its uneven and occasionally missing concrete steps inside whispering tales of a bygone era.

I couldn't help feeling immense pride whenever I came back to this house during my visits to Egypt. It had become my personal tradition to go from door to door, giving everyone in the apartments it contained a big hug and a warm hello. This time, as I embarked on my familiar ritual, my heart overflowed with joy to be visiting with my son.

But this time would also be different. The house's four modest apartments were no longer occupied solely by family. Time had scattered the family members like seeds all over Cairo. Some had moved to larger, more upscale residences in newer neighborhoods, or had chosen to rent out their portion of the house and downsize to live off the profits.

During this visit, I found two family members who had preserved their apartments—Osama and Yassir's mother, my father's cousin Um Hamada (named for her eldest son, Hamada), and my father's sister, Um Ulfat (named for her eldest daughter, Ulfat).

After delivering me to the doorstep, Moawad bade Musa and me farewell and retreated to his own apartment nearby. I climbed the stairs with Musa cradled in my arms, mindful of the loose and missing steps. Hamada, the oldest brother, opened the worn wood door at my knock, dressed in a thin white shirt and sweatpants, and welcomed me into the apartment, but I noticed that his voice lacked its former strength.

"I'm so happy to see you, Cousin. Mama is sick. But it's great that you came to visit. I'm sure seeing you will cheer her up," he murmured.

With heartfelt welcome in his tone, he called out into the apartment, "Mama! Aymann, Mohamed's son, is here!"

Um Hamada lay confined to her bed—the same bed that I vividly remembered her husband (my father's cousin) occupying shortly before his passing. A veil of fragility enveloped her, and her movements were scarce and punctuated by the occasional cough. I entered the room and presented her with Musa.

"Ahlan ya amiti," I greeted her tenderly: "Hi, auntie" in Arabic. "I brought my son, I want him to meet you," I explained softly.

"Aymann, habibi, come closer," she beckoned. She extended one frail hand toward her son Hamada. "Help me sit up." Her voice still carried an undeniable authority. With help, Um Hamada summoned the strength to sit upright.

"Hamada! Bring the freshly delivered fruits," she scolded, her tone tinged with embarrassment.

I was caught off guard: I hadn't come for a meal. "God bless your hands!" I said. "I know that every time I come over, you always insist on stuffing me full of food. But I promise you, this time I'm only here for a quick visit. I don't want to burden you," I explained in an attempt to decline politely. But it was no use.

Hamada returned with a tray full of a variety of fruits and sliced a piece of apricot for Musa to nibble on.

"Can you believe Musa hasn't had any fruit in Egypt yet?"

"Take care," Um Hamada cautioned. "Avoid giving him fruits with a lot of water in them, like grapes or watermelon. Our water isn't like your water. We don't want your son to get sick," she warned.

Hamada chimed in, echoing her sentiment, "And you shouldn't eat those fruits, either! Okay, Aymann? You have an American gut. You aren't built like us," he teased.

I added playfully, "But Musa isn't accustomed to anything yet. Maybe having it now will make him stronger later?"

Musa delighted in the juicy apricot, his narrow fingers gripping the fruit. He only had about four teeth, but he put them to work, leaving a trail of dribbles down his wrist.

Sensing Um Hamada's frailty, I expressed my concern: "I don't want to exhaust you. We will visit again soon, I promise. I'm here for a month. We will be back," I told her.

As I gathered Musa in my arms, Um Hamada extended her arm toward him.

"Let Musa stay. I'll keep an eye on him. Go out, and you can come back to pick him up whenever you wish," she offered. Even in her frail state, she had an irresistible desire to fulfill her role. I politely declined, but again promised I'd be back.

WHEN I RETURNED TO THE CAFÉ, I WAS MET WITH AN UNEXPECTED sight—eight friends, comrades of Yassir and Osama, gathered around a tawla (backgammon) board, engrossed in a spirited match. Ahmed, their closest friend, who lived near my family's house, seemed wholly fixated on the black-and-white checkers before him.

As I approached, one of the group, Islam, playfully chided me, "Moawad mentioned he saw you sitting here alone. Why didn't you come over and say hello!"

"I had no idea anyone was here!" Their laughter filled the air.

"How strange! He even said you were drinking coffee here! How can you tolerate the taste of it?" another friend quipped, joining in the amusement as if deliberately to chide the old man who operated the café.

"Don't all of you drink coffee here? I see everyone with a cup!" I countered.

"Yes, we *drink* it, but we don't like it. It tastes like river water!" The comment echoed loudly, fueling the jovial atmosphere.

I realized that I had encountered nearly every person within this lively group at some point in the past. It was as if Musa and I were surrounded by loving relatives.

Following his defeat in the game of tawla, Ahmed rose from his seat in frustration, venting his exasperation at the friend who had bested him. He joined me, enveloping me in a protective gesture.

"Give me Musa," he requested sternly, prying my drowsy son from my arms. Musa rested his head on Ahmed's shoulder and succumbed to his exhaustion. In a few minutes, Ahmed handed Musa over to another friend. Despite the animated conversations and boisterous laughter, Musa remained serene, as if tucked into the comfort of his own bedsheets.

"How is he still sleeping?" I commented to Ahmed, slightly bewildered.

"It's the heat. I have children of my own now, and all they seem to do is sleep. So lazy," he jokingly remarked. "So how does it feel to be back?" he asked me; I could see the curiosity in his eyes.

"Like I never left. I wanted to show Musa around so he can grow up feeling like an Egyptian," I explained.

Ahmed pulled my entire body toward him. "He's Egyptian because *you're* Egyptian. You came here to visit us, and when you come and brighten our little corner, that light you bring is what makes you Egyptian." This was a level of male intimacy that I don't usually experience in America, where expressions of male camaraderie are often given with a sense of caution and reservation. Even among friends I've had for what feels like my entire life, physical closeness can be uncomfortable or out of place. But in Egypt, Ahmed's embrace conveyed a warmth and acceptance that transcended words. There was no hesitation in his actions, no fear of judgment. The bond between us felt stronger, more genuine—nurtured by a culture that embraces emotional expression and physical touch between men.

At first glance, the many male-only spaces in Cairo felt antiquated, even sexist, to my American sensibilities. Back home, the idea of excluding women from certain social spheres would be a relic of a bygone era. As I spent more time in these spaces in Egypt, however, I began to sense a unique kinship and ease among male friends that just didn't exist in America.

Here was a space where men could express themselves freely,

unburdened by societal expectations or judgments, and relieved of the pressure to perform masculinity in front of women. These environments emphasized brotherhood; advice and support were given freely.

Ahmed added, "But next time, leave your son with his mother, so we can go out and have some fun."

I protested immediately: "What? I wouldn't want to leave Musa behind."

Sensing my devotion, Ahmed continued: "There's nothing wrong with loving your child. But taking care of them this way when they're so young is usually left to the women. You should enjoy your time before they grow older, because then you will have to bring them everywhere," he advised.

I hadn't even noticed that one of the friends in the group had quietly passed Musa to yet another person. I leaned back in my chair and accepted that I wasn't in charge of Musa now, but I could rest easy: he was with family, even if I hadn't seen these folks for years.

Just then, the melodic call to prayer, the Athan, echoed through the air. Although a part of me felt drawn to stand up and head to the mosque, I observed that the guys hanging out didn't budge. In that moment, I realized it was time to bring Musa back home and let him drift off to sleep for the night.

I CALLED AN UBER, SCOOPED MUSA FROM THE SHOULDER OF ONE OF my friends, and bade the group farewell. Ahmed insisted on accompanying me, and sent me off with a final hug before insisting on a selfie together. With his help, I climbed into the car.

"This is our brother! He is visiting from America. Take care of him and his son! They're our family, all right?" he told the driver.

The driver nodded earnestly. "Of course. He is my brother, too."

We arrived back in the affluent New Cairo quite late. Mira, utterly exhausted from a long day spent frolicking in the pool, gave me a massive hug.

"We wished Musa could join us for a swim!" she said, disappointed.

I chuckled. "Yeah, instead I dragged him to the hood and huddled around a small table with a bunch of men getting their feelings hurt over tawla," I replied.

Mira's smile of satisfaction mirrored my own. "I want to come next time!"

"You absolutely have to come. Everyone was asking about you." Despite what the guys had said to me, bringing Mira to see Um Hamada and Um Ulfat was much more important and meaningful than seeing friends at a café. Mira was my world, and I wanted nothing more than to share everything that excited me with her, even Shubrah.

"It's your family, too, you know?" I added.

MIRA'S MOM HAD BOOKED A PRIVATE TOUR WITH A GUIDE WHO LED us to some of Cairo's most famous sites, including ancient mosques, churches, and of course, the Pyramids. When the bus rolled to a stop and the doors opened, the structures came into view, bathed in the sun's glow. COVID had cleared the usual crowds; it was like we had the entire ancient complex to ourselves.

Our tour guide, Layla, rattled off countless facts about the Pyramids, but my focus was on getting photos of Musa. Mira and I took turns holding him and tried to get closer to the section where you're allowed to climb the Pyramids.

"Want to ride a camel?" I asked Mira. She laughed and subtly reminded me of her "condition."

Layla called for our attention, but I was busy positioning Musa for a photo. He hadn't begun walking yet and could just barely stand a few seconds without falling. Mira anxiously kept her arms up around him while I snapped some pictures. He looked up at me with wide eyes, oblivious to the ancient stones beneath him.

"Perfect!" I called. Musa gurgled happily, excited that he could stand at all, never mind that it was on a block of stone that had been there for thousands of years.

Just then, an Egyptian police officer blew his whistle, warning us to bring Musa down before he fell. My mission was complete. That photo of Musa on the Pyramid would, I knew, be a timeless treasure.

As we headed back to the bus, I felt a profound sense of fulfillment. The day had been for me a bridge between past, present, and future—a way to connect our beginning with Musa's world.

"These pictures are for when he's older, when he starts searching for his place in it all," I said to Mira as we went through the bounty of images I had collected.

Her eyes filled with understanding. "And maybe for when you need to remind yourself, too," she said.

As the sun set, casting a golden glow over the Pyramids, I glanced at Musa, who had fallen asleep. I hoped one day that I'd get to tell him about how we trekked to the Pyramids just for him to fall asleep. The thought made me smile.

THOUGH I WAS BORN IN AMERICA, MY PARENTS HAD IMPARTED A sense of our belonging to another culture, which afforded me a pride in being both American and Egyptian. But my connection to Egypt was different from what my parents knew. For them, it was the idyllic homeland they had left behind, where their religion, culture, and identities were deeply rooted. For me, Egypt was more abstract—a mosaic of family visits, nostalgic movies and songs, and cultural practices that felt both familiar and distant.

Their success as parents seemed tied to how strongly we identified as Muslims, and Egypt, to me, represented an alternate reality. I imagined that had I grown up there, my parents might have been different—less anxious, less worried about external influences threatening to dilute or corrupt their children's faith. Egypt seemed like a place where we could simply exist, where Islam was seamlessly woven into daily life rather than being something to constantly protect. It wasn't just the origin of our family heritage; it was a sanctuary of relief and a way of being that I often found myself longing for.

As I sought to pass this connection on to my son, whom I also hoped to raise with strong ties to Islam, I had to accept that his bond with Egypt might be even more strained than mine. He would be two generations removed from that land, and his parents had grown up in the same country where he was now being raised. If he developed any relationship to Egypt at all, it would be his own unique bond. And if I wanted him to feel even a hint of what Egypt meant to me, all I could do was leave a trail of breadcrumbs—photos of him as a baby in the arms of his relatives, or standing atop the Pyramids—hoping that one day he'd follow them back.

On the day before our journey back home, I made one final trip to Shubrah to say goodbye to my family there. Mira and Musa had joined me on one of my many visits to Shubrah, but on this particular visit, I went alone. I had something else on my mind, too—I asked Moawad to take me to that coffee place he had insisted was "fit for a prince." I hadn't forgotten.

To my surprise, instead of leading me to a café, he guided me to a small kiosk, a modest vendor stall selling chips, chocolates, random spare smartphone parts, and a few pharmacy items like soap and toothpaste. On the counter was an electronic coffee machine. Moawad dropped a few coins on the counter and pressed a button; the machine buzzed to life, lights flickering, and dispensed a shot of hot Turkish coffee into a thin paper cup. I had to use the tips of my fingers to handle it. Moawad's eyes sparkled as he watched me take my first sip. The coffee tasted fine, though I couldn't quite understand why he'd made such a big deal about it.

"This really is worthy of a prince," I said, playing along.

"You see? I told you!" He beamed as he locked arms with me again and took me for one last walk around the neighborhood.

Mimi (left), mother of Maha (right), mother of Mira (top),
mother of Noon (center)—four generations of Egyptian women.

Chapter 14

By the Pen

ONCE WE GOT BACK FROM EGYPT, WE WORKED DILIGENTLY TO SECURE a daycare spot for Musa. We had hoped to hold off as long as possible, but with my work demands increasing, and Mira still working while managing the fatigue of her pregnancy, it felt like our only option. One August morning, we drove to a daycare for Musa's first day. My mind buzzed with worries, but, to be honest, they barely contended with my anticipation of focusing on something other than being a baba for a change.

In the car, Mira seemed excited. "Were you up late googling everything that could go wrong at daycare?" she teased.

"I know, I know." She was right—I worried about all the little moments I might miss. I'd been there when he first crawled, and when he took his first steps in Egypt. I didn't want to miss those kinds of milestones.

At a red light, I turned to her. "I'm prioritizing work, which sucks. I don't want to be that kind of baba, but it's the truth," I lamented. "I wanted to be the kind of baba who made spending time with his kids a top priority. And now I'm dropping him off so I can—what?—sit at a computer? It doesn't feel right."

Mira nodded in understanding. "Is that why, earlier, you were saying it was too expensive?" she teased.

"It's like your entire paycheck, isn't it?" I answered, but in a less playful tone.

Immediately Mira's face darkened. "More like half," she corrected, clearly hurt.

The light turned green, and I accelerated. I had clumsily touched a sore spot. When discussing our options, I'd suggested weighing the cost of daycare against Mira's part-time income. Since it seemed to cancel out, I thought it would be beneficial if Mira put work on hold to stay with Musa until he was old enough for school. But to her it felt like an attack on her values. The thought of giving up her career, especially after she'd earned her master's degree, made her feel pressured into the stay-at-home-mom role.

While we had discussed the steep cost of daycare before, I always hesitated to push the issue with Mira. I told myself I needed to be sensitive, but that morning the words tumbled out. "I just want us to be realistic."

Mira retreated deeper into her seat, her body language shifting. It was clear we were no longer having a conversation. She stayed quiet as we neared the daycare.

We'd signed Musa up for a part-time schedule to match Mira's, but saying goodbye still felt strange. The teacher who opened the door took charge right away.

"Welcome, Musa!" she said warmly, taking his hand, and guided him inside. It was endearing to see him accept her hand so readily, likely enchanted by the colorful décor and the sight of toys scattered everywhere. And, just like that, the door closed, and the moment was over.

BACK IN THE CAR, MIRA AND I SETTLED INTO A SILENCE THAT WE HAD forgotten was possible.

"I guess I imagined it differently," I confessed.

"Yeah. I expected him to at least look at us," she said.

"Yeah. That felt way too much like an Uber Eats delivery," I joked.

"So—what now?" Mira asked, her voice filled with affection as she held on to my arm.

"A relaxed, baby-free breakfast?"

"Sounds divine," she said, a wide smile spreading across her face.

WE TRIED A NEW NEIGHBORHOOD CAFÉ CALLED SIHANA, WHERE we indulged in coffee and way too much food. With its lattes, crois-sants, and stylish Newark-branded merch, this café felt like a milestone for our neighborhood, a sign that the area was getting trendier and safer. I gazed out the window at people enjoying the crisp fall morn-ing, exploring the shops and eateries along Ferry Street.

As we sat in the café, we found the absence of Musa's cries surreal. And it wasn't just the quiet around us; it was a rare, internal stillness I hadn't felt in months, as if time had slowed, allowing us to hear every small sound—the clink of a coffee cup, the murmur of distant conversations. Without the constant pull of parenthood, the quiet was strange and unfamiliar, an empty space that made room for forgot-ten parts of ourselves. For a brief moment, it felt like stepping back into the people we'd been before Musa, but with the deep, unspoken understanding that we could never fully go back.

"It's wild to think I'm raising my kid where I grew up," I said, eager to break the silence.

Mira smiled. "I don't really have one place I'm from. I was born in Nashville, went to elementary school in Kentucky, high school in Saudi Arabia, and then college in Jersey. I don't think I can claim any of those places as 'my neighborhood,' like you do with Newark."

"That's the charm of the Ironbound," I replied. "No one's from just here. Everyone is from somewhere."

Mira nodded. "Not Musa, though. He's second-generation."

"That's the weird part, right? Both our parents flew thousands of miles to get here. Staying put is like going against our instincts."

Mira sipped her coffee thoughtfully. "Musa might leave one day, too."

"That would break my heart," I admitted.

"Let him be. Just love him. It can be that simple if you let it," she reminded me gently.

I grinned, allowing a silence to linger, before teasing her: "We're raising a man. Doesn't that scare you?"

Mira rolled her eyes. "Trying to decide their fate before it happens is just paving a road to disappointment."

As I pondered her words, Mira stood up, too restless to sit after all that caffeine. "That said, follow your instincts if you feel he needs guidance," she added. "You could be part of Allah's plan. But never for a moment think you control Musa's destiny. He deserves more than a disappointed father."

Her words sank in as we made our way home, savoring the freedom of walking without a stroller. I couldn't help marveling at how she could drop so many wise gems, effortlessly. How lucky I was to have her as my partner on this crazy journey.

"Baby Number Two is definitely different," Mira said. "When I was pregnant with Musa, you treated me like a princess—foot rubs, back rubs, running out to get me chocolate whenever I wanted." She shot me a sideways glance.

She was right: this pregnancy felt less ceremonious. Even finding out the baby was a girl seemed to happen in passing. I tried to give Mira breaks whenever I could, but balancing work and taking care of Musa felt impossible without her help. And before we knew it, it was time for our second baby to join the family. It all happened so fast.

MIRA TOOK CHARGE OF NAMING THIS ONE, AND, AS ALWAYS, SHE WAS calm and thoughtful about it. When I asked her what names she liked, she only had two.

"I really like 'Hawa,'" she said.

"'Hawa'? Like 'wind' in Arabic?" I asked, a bit surprised.

"And 'Noon,'" she said with a warm smile. "I love how it sounds. It's so satisfying to say. Plus, I've never met anyone named Noon before."

"Aren't you worried people will think it's just a typo for 'Noor'?" I asked, thinking of the more common name.

Mira grinned. "Yeah, but then Noon will be all, like, 'It's *Noon*! Get with it!' It's a noun in the Quran. It's indisputably an Islamic name."

MIRA RECITED THE PASSAGE FROM MEMORY, MAKING HER POINT UN-mistakably clear.

$$ ن ۤ وَالْقَلَمِ وَمَا يَسْطُرُونَ (١) $$

Noon. By the pen and what they inscribe!

$$ مَآ أَنتَ بِنِعْمَةِ رَبِّكَ بِمَجْنُونٍ (٢) $$
$$ وَإِنَّ لَكَ لَأَجْرًا غَيْرَ مَمْنُونٍ (٣) $$
$$ وَإِنَّكَ لَعَلَىٰ خُلُقٍ عَظِيمٍ (٤) $$
$$ فَسَتُبْصِرُ وَيُبْصِرُونَ (٥) $$
$$ بِأَييِّكُمُ الْمَفْتُونُ (٦) $$

Your Lord's grace does not make you [Prophet] a madman:
you will have a never-ending reward
truly you have a strong character
and soon you will see, as will they,
which of you is mad.

I felt chills down my spine. "Like 'Alif Lam Mim,' those letters that set the rhythmic tone for the verses that follow it?" I asked, astonished at how much I suddenly loved the name.

"Exactly. And when people ask her what it means, she can say only God knows," Mira replied, referencing the mystery behind the letters.

"I don't want to rule out 'Hawa,' though," she added.

I gave her a look that implied it was pointless to keep debating, and she just shrugged. Though neither of us said it outright, we both had our hearts set on the name Noon.

WITH MUSA, IT HAD FELT LIKE EVERYTHING IN THE UNIVERSE WAS guiding us toward his birth. This time, Mira's due date seemed to sneak up on us. I realized that the sense of urgency we'd felt before was mostly self-imposed.

While Mira focused on preparing her body for the birth, practicing her breathing and going for walks, I focused on preparing Musa to be an older brother. We rehearsed having a tender touch with the plants around the house and with his toys, repeating "Show me gentle," like a mantra, and showering him with praise when he obliged.

Tant Maha came back to stay with us until the baby was born, just as she had for Musa, and, that winter, almost exactly one and a half years after the first birth, it was time for our second baby to arrive.

LATE ON THE NIGHT OF DECEMBER 11, 2022, WE LEFT MUSA AT HOME with Maha and drove to the hospital. The streets seemed surreal and empty as a light snow fell.

In a moment of inspiration, I played the Quran on the car stereo. Mira and I soaked in the moment.

$$ن وَٱلْقَلَمِ وَمَا يَسْطُرُونَ (١)$$

Noon. Walqalami wama yasturoon.
Noon. By the pen and what they inscribe.

Mira and I shared a loving glance. Without saying a word, we confirmed her name.

THIS BIRTH WAS MUCH EASIER THAN THE FIRST. THE DOCTOR WAS present this time, and the epidural worked wonders, leaving Mira with virtually no pain. As she pushed the baby out, Mira leaned forward with a huge smile, eagerly watching the miracle unfold at her feet. In that moment, the prophetic saying "Heaven lies beneath the feet of your mother" took on a literal meaning.

ON DECEMBER 12, AFTER TWELVE HOURS OF LABOR, NOON WAS BORN, and her name felt destined.

"Looks like we've got a singer," one of the nurses remarked

on hearing Noon's powerful wails. She was a big baby, nearly nine pounds, taller and heavier than Musa at birth. But everything about Noon's arrival was more relaxed. Mira and I took turns holding her. With her long hair, light-gray eyes, and wrinkled skin, she looked like a little creature from outer space. I cradled her with one arm, feeling confident—a seasoned baba ready to take on this new challenge.

Later that day, Hebah arrived with Musa in tow to meet his new sister. But he barely noticed Noon, instead running straight to his mama to give her a big hug. Mira lay in the bed, pale but radiant, cradling Noon in her arms. I couldn't help overhearing her conversation with her mother.

"I need to love Noon extra-hard, because she won't get the love Musa got when he was born," Mira said. "Not because she's the second baby, but because she's a girl."

Tant Maha shook her head in disbelief. But Hebah's eyes softened with empathy. "It's not enough that she's the second child. Being a girl adds a whole other layer," she agreed.

Mira sighed, looking down at her newborn, who remained sleeping in her arms.

Their words left me feeling guilty, as though they were talking about my attitude. I wanted to say something, but I knew it was better simply to listen.

Maha reached over and placed a comforting hand on her daughter's arm. "Mira, every child is different. Noon will get the attention she needs. It may not look the same as it did with Musa, but that doesn't mean it's any less," she explained in Arabic.

Noon shifted in Mira's arms and cooed softly. Musa noticed and moved over to the bed, to peer curiously at his new sister. I lifted him up so he could see her better, and he giggled, reaching out gently.

"See, Musa already loves her plenty," I said.

But just as we all began to relax, Musa swatted at Noon's face, narrowly missing poking her eye.

Hebah laughed. "See? That's the perfect metaphor for the patriarchy right there."

When we got home, Musa became obsessed with Noon. Without prompting, he approached her and gently touched her bare legs. He couldn't yet speak, but his expression seemed to convey a quiet understanding of who she was. I found myself imagining them older, playing and laughing together.

For the next two months, we hunkered down, focusing only on the rapid routine of feedings and diapers. And with a toddler in tow, it felt impossible to come to each moment with the patience our toddler and baby deserved. But rather than isolate like we had with Musa, who was born when we were still taking COVID lockdown precautions, for Noon, we tried to be in company as frequently as possible.

On our way to my brother Mohamed's house for family dinner with our new baby, I glanced at Mira through the rearview mirror. She had discovered that, if she contorted herself just right, twisting sideways, she could fit between Musa's and Noon's car seats in the back. Noon still needed her bottle, and the only way to avoid an en-route cry-fest was for Mira to be back there, ready to help.

Neither of us could wait to reach Mohamed's house. I'm not embarrassed to admit that nothing made me happier than arriving and watching him or Kholoud reach out for our babies. When you're starving for sleep because your newborn is louder than an air-raid siren and your toddler is at peak demand and clumsiness, the only relief is in handing them off and hiding in the bathroom. Who knew that pretending to poop for fifteen minutes could feel like a beach vacation?

WE KNOCKED ON THE BACK DOOR, AT THE EDGE OF MOHAMED'S YARD. His twin boys were too busy to say hello, sitting in his driveway in pajama pants and winter coats, wielding hammers and shovels as they pulverized bricks and stones into dust. Just as we'd hoped, Kholoud's voice rang out: "Is that Noon? Can I hold her?"

I could hear the relief in Mira's voice as she replied, "Yes, please!" Mira hobbled over and handed the entire car seat to Kholoud.

Mohamed greeted me before turning to check on the Bluetooth-enabled smoker and grill he had snagged at a discount off-season. The cold weather didn't faze him; nothing was going to stop him from playing with his new toy. Casting a quick glance at our exhausted faces, he smirked. "Kids kicking your asses that bad?"

"We're good." I replied, "Musa is talking more and crying less, which helps a lot." The last thing I wanted was to bring him down—he had enough on his plate with twin boys.

With a playful nudge and a mischievous wink, sporting a sly grin, Mohamed pulled me aside. He flipped open the grill and murmured, "Check this out." My eyes widened as I caught a glimpse of salmon sizzling to perfection.

Mohamed's boys, Adam and Ali, rushed over, eager to see the grill. "Be careful, it's super-hot!" he called, nudging them back. Normally, I'd coax a handshake or a high-five from them, but this time, I just nodded, keeping my gaze on the fish. At least the salmon didn't require emotional energy from me.

Mohamed seemed empathic. He leaned back, his posture relaxed, and his expression softened as he watched me zone out. "If you need to lie down, go lie down," he suggested.

"And leave Mira to take care of Musa and Noon all by herself? No way."

"Don't be a fool! She's not alone!" he countered, amusement in his voice. There was a calm assurance in the way he said it, a recognition that we were both in the same boat now.

Mohamed and I had always had a complex relationship. Growing up, he'd felt the pressure to fill the void left by Baba's absence, taking on the role of raising me himself. But now, something had shifted. Since I became a father of two, it was as if he finally saw me as an equal, someone who understood the weight of the responsibility he had carried for so long. In that moment, I felt the unspoken bond between us—two brothers navigating fatherhood. If he was offering me advice, maybe I should take it.

I retreated into his house, where the couch seemed to beckon. I sank into it, letting the weight of the day pull me under. I didn't want to "be a fool," as he liked to say. I didn't plan on sleeping, but after just a moment on the couch, it was like I'd teleported into the future. Though I hadn't dreamed and didn't feel rested, it was suddenly two hours later, and Musa's cries were snapping me back to reality.

After a quick dinner, Mira tapped me on the shoulder and gave me a thousand-yard stare. I knew exactly what it meant.

"I think we're going to head out now," I announced to the family. Mira smiled, glad I understood what she needed from me in that moment.

WE TRIED TO RE-CREATE THE SAME SETUP FOR NOON THAT WE'D HAD with Musa, sleeping in the room with her and taking turns with feedings. But since Mira was having more success breastfeeding this time, there wasn't much I could do to help, and whenever Musa woke up, the whole family was miserable.

To solve this, I set up a makeshift bed on the floor of my home office. For the next several months, Mira and Noon shared a bed, while I slept alone. During the day, I took on cooking, cleaning, and caring for Musa. When Mira emerged from the bedroom with Noon, she'd juggle both kids, giving me space to work, though I felt guilty, handing over the responsibility to her clearly exhausted arms.

This division of labor was a mixed blessing. Family time, when we could all just be together, became rare. The joy of parenting was replaced by sheer exhaustion. Our small home turned into a pressure cooker, with a newborn demanding constant attention and a toddler often on the brink of a meltdown.

IT FELT LIKE MUSA HAD BECOME MY KID AND NOON HAD BECOME Mira's. Our alternating shifts made Mira feel more like a co-worker. One morning, trying to reconnect, I gave her a hug and asked how she was feeling. Not good, apparently.

"Noon was fussy all night. She wouldn't sleep," she whined.

I felt I had stranded Mira with the newborn. I could see that she missed Musa and the time we used to spend together as a family. We'd only just started to find our rhythm before Noon was born, and now everything was out of balance again.

THAT SUMMER, AS NOON APPROACHED SIX MONTHS OLD, AND MUSA'S second birthday drew near, our excitement for these milestones was overshadowed by something unexpected—Mira's milk had suddenly ceased. One late afternoon, when Musa was down for his second nap, Mira came to the living room with Noon, who was contentedly drinking a bottle of mixed breast milk and formula.

"I don't understand why this is happening again," Mira said, her voice tinged with sadness. She looked down at Noon, who drank happily, oblivious. "It's like my body is giving up."

I could see she was just as bewildered and disheartened as she'd been when this happened with Musa. In that moment, an idea came to me. I took her hand and locked eyes with her, as one might when proposing.

"Do you know what this means?" I asked her.

She shook her head no.

"You can get high again!"

She forced a smile. She'd gone from being pregnant to breastfeeding, then pregnant and breastfeeding again, with limited agency over her own body. I wanted to help her see the freedom that came with this new lack of responsibility.

It worked just as I'd hoped. Mira's guard dropped, and she let out a genuine smile. "I just hate that Musa got three more months of breast milk before we switched. I feel awful."

I gave her a mischievous grin. "You know what helps with those feelings?"

She didn't need much more persuasion after that. Mira got up and rummaged through the little stash box we'd kept locked away since she became pregnant with Musa.

"Look at what's still in here!" she exclaimed, finding my little yellow grinder shaped like Pikachu and small baggies of what looked like ancient weed.

"But *this* is what I was looking for," she said, digging out a small plastic package. Inside were four cannabis-infused gummy edibles. "Want one?"

"Let's do it!"

We didn't make a big ceremony out of it. Mira took a bite of the gummy to split it in two, and handed the rest to me. I popped it into my mouth like popcorn. It took a few hours for the effects to kick in, but once they did, it was clear that our small nibbles had done the job.

A grin crept across my face, and when I saw Mira wearing a similar expression, I knew we were on the same wavelength.

I suddenly felt an overwhelming urge to hold my daughter, like I'd missed her after not seeing her for ages. I cradled her in my arms, gazing at her as if for the first time, studying each delicate feature of her face, gently holding her fingers, and letting her press her hands and cheeks against my beard. She had grown so much since I last held her like this. She squealed with delight, her version of a giggle, wriggling in my embrace. It hit me that I'd unintentionally neglected her, focusing more on Musa's needs as a toddler. But in that moment, the sheer sensation of holding her melted away any doubts or worries. The cannabis was in full effect.

I sensed Mira was having a similar experience with Musa. She watched him with wide eyes as he used his spoon to scoop up bean salad, serving himself generous portions, like it was the most amazing thing she'd ever seen. When he reached for his open cup of water and took a careful sip, she let out a gasp.

Neither of us could believe what happened next. Seated comfortably at the kitchen table, Musa let out a tiny fart, the faintest sound, almost like the creak of a wooden chair. He giggled in response.

"Did he just fart?" I exclaimed.

"Oh my God, he thinks farts are funny," Mira said, her smile widening. "That's the first time he laughed at a fart. Look! He's smirking!"

"He's become a boy!" I proclaimed, marking it as a milestone.

Until then, he'd felt like a baby, but now we could peer through a window into his budding personality and sense of humor. It was a turning point—our children would eventually grow into unique individuals with their own quirks, likes, dislikes, and expressions. We'd been in the trenches for so long, we'd apparently forgotten that this transformation was always possible.

AFTER DINNER, INSTEAD OF OUR USUAL RUSH TO GET MUSA READY for bed, we felt a newfound ease. Mira would typically handle the kitchen cleanup while I bathed Musa and got him ready to sleep. But tonight, we could tell he wanted some playtime with his toys first.

Mira picked up a little lion figurine, and Musa responded by grabbing a dinosaur, making the toys "talk" to each other. "Hi," he repeated, still in the early stages of speech.

Mira made the dinosaur exclaim, "Whee! We landed on Musa Island!"

Musa reacted by gleefully tossing the toy across the room, narrowly missing Noon's head. She didn't even notice, too busy trying to fit an entire dinosaur figurine into her mouth.

This was the first time we'd all played together as a family. I couldn't help wondering if the relaxed vibe was the effect of the edibles.

After Mira put Noon to sleep, she gently asked if I wanted to join her for Maghrib, the fourth of the five daily prayers. Her tone was soft, almost hesitant, as if she wasn't sure what I'd say. Since Noon's birth, Mira had been consistent with her prayers, carving out time in the chaos of our new lives as parents, but I had fallen completely out of practice. Whenever I walked in on her praying, I'd quietly retreat, giving her the space I felt I couldn't claim for myself. Now it felt as though she was extending an invitation, not just to join her in prayer but to return to something I had left behind.

She led me to the salon, a room that in Egyptian culture acted as the second living room, a formal space off-limits to kids and reserved for special occasions, with comfortable couches encircling a large wooden coffee table, inviting the kind of unhurried gatherings we hadn't had time for in years.

We also called it the prayer room, for its arabesque aesthetic. Over the years, Mira and I had collected pieces of Islamic art and Arabic calligraphy, and we'd placed them all here, hoping to infuse the space with a sense of intention. Dominating one wall was my favorite piece, a vibrant red, yellow, and black print by eL Seed, the French-Tunisian artist whose fusion of classical Arabic calligraphy with street art felt both rooted and revolutionary. His *calligraffiti* swept across the canvas like waves, embodying a tension between East and West, tradition and modernity. To me, his work symbolized how blending worlds could create something richer and more meaningful, despite purists who argued for preserving sanctity. It was a balance I aspired to achieve in my own identity.

The room's arrangement, though deliberate, had unintentionally become a physical representation of the compartmentalization of faith in my life. Once Musa became mobile, we moved all our fragile treasures—an alabaster vase, crystal keepsakes—into the salon, securing them behind a thigh-high baby gate to protect them from the chaos of toddlerhood. Returning to this room, popping open the gate and stepping through, I couldn't help but smirk at the thought of the gate as a symbol of how parenthood had distanced me from practicing my religion. Yet, in that moment, it felt as though the room had been patiently waiting for us, its purpose incomplete without the presence of prayer.

That night, stepping into the salon felt ceremonious, like an invitation to reclaim something I'd lost. With Noon asleep, the room's silence was amplified by the weight of the moment. Even Musa, normally a whirlwind of energy, seemed unusually subdued as he took in the space with wide eyes. I held Musa in my arms as Mira donned her isdal, the thin, oversized hijab she used to prepare for prayer. She spread out the mat and invited me to lead.

But the edible Mira and I had taken earlier hadn't worn off—I was still high.

I'd never prayed in this state before. It wasn't something I ever intended to do; it felt inherently wrong. The Quran is explicit: *"O believers! Do not approach prayer while intoxicated until you are aware of what you say . . ."* Unlike other aspects of Islam that seemed vague and nuanced, this felt black and white. Yet, as Musa stood beside us, imitating our movements with wide-eyed fascination, I chose to embrace the moment rather than retreat.

"Allahu Akbar," I called out, initiating the prayer. Each verse I recited felt amplified, the cadence resonating as if the air itself vibrated. "Allahu Akbar," I repeated, louder this time. Mira and Musa followed me into sujood, bowing their foreheads to the mat. Musa, still learning, stretched his tiny body flat on the ground, a sight so pure it sent a wave of excitement through me, momentarily eclipsing my doubt.

The effects of the edible heightened everything—the texture of the prayer rug beneath my hands, the steady rhythm of my breathing, the suspension of time. I had expected to feel distracted, weighed down by guilt and shame. Instead, I felt present in a way I hadn't in years.

For so long, I had carried a sense of disconnect from Islam, as though it were a tradition I'd inherited but never fully internalized. That night, the act of prayer wasn't about circumstances or perfection—it was about showing up, imperfections and all, and finding a way to connect.

As my forehead pressed against the prayer mat, I realized my barriers to prayer had never been about the faith itself. They stemmed from my own feelings of inadequacy—a belief that I could never be the kind of Muslim who truly belonged. Yet that night, in my over-analytical and imperfect state, I glimpsed the beauty of surrender—not to my doubts, but to the possibility of grace.

Perhaps this is what my parents had experienced all along: an actual relationship with the prayer mat. One that I hadn't ever established because for me, prayer had always felt like an interruption—a hurried obligation performed under the watchful eyes of my parents. But now, for the first time, I saw the mat as something more. It could be something I could get to intimately know, a space of renewal of the day's intention, and connection with not just God, but my own family.

This was all possible despite the current imperfection of being high, but also my overall feelings of being an imperfect Muslim.

After the prayer ended, my eyes drifted to Musa, who had already wandered off to explore the room, knocking over pillows and climbing onto the couches. I resisted the instinct to chase after him and instead stayed seated beside Mira, who remained deep in her supplications, her hands open in quiet appeal to Allah. Mira had a way of setting aside the demands of parenting to prioritize something greater, something that anchored her. Watching her, I admired that balance and resolved to make these moments of stillness and ritual a permanent part of our lives.

Invigorated by the experience, I wasn't ready to promise it would be the last time I prayed high. But one thing I had come to understand since returning to Islam as an adult was that Allah's mercy far exceeded anything I or any human could ever truly comprehend. Perhaps God, in infinite patience and understanding, would extend more grace to me than I had ever managed to offer myself.

AT OUR NEXT BIG FAMILY GATHERING, MY BROTHER AHMAD AND HIS kids visited from Virginia, which they did only about twice a year. Now that we each had a pair of children, I was thrilled for the chance to watch the little cousins play together.

The sounds of their amusement—and petty arguments—floated through the walls. The sunset call to prayer sounded on Mama's cellphone, but only Baba heeded it. He'd given up on convincing his kids to join him years before.

I retreated to one of the two living rooms on the first floor, where I could hear both Baba's praises to Allah and the rest of the family erupting in laughter down the hall. Mama followed me in, offering some fruit she had cut up and placed in a bowl. She joined me on the couch. She could always tell when something was weighing heavily on my mind. I put my arm around her, rested my head on her shoulder, and confessed what worried me most about becoming a baba—that I would be the chain to break my family's connection to Arabic and

Islamic tradition, kept sturdy by innumerable generations before me, and I'd lose my children to American culture entirely.

In the past, she would have reached for a comforting adage or a lesson rooted in Islam that I should consider, and I had always yearned for her to be vulnerable with me. Now I sensed that Mama saw me differently, maybe as someone who no longer needed to be protected from her emotions, a peer. To my surprise—and for the very first time—Mama told me that, for as long as she'd been in America, she had been afraid of losing her kids in the same way.

"You wanted to celebrate Christmas and all this non-Muslim stuff, habibi," she said in Arabic. "That's why we put you in Islamic school, so you'd learn to read the Quran and learn to put your trust in Allah. That's why I'm talking to you in Arabic now."

As it turns out, my Arabic is not nearly as good as hers. I can get by at a Middle Eastern restaurant and make conversation, but certainly not enough to pass the language on to my children. I miss prayers for months at a stretch, and go to the mosque just a few times a year. And yet it's down to me to ensure that my children feel connected to the faith and culture that birthed me, my wife, my family.

How did Mama manage it? How did she go about trying to raise good Muslim kids in a place with such a strong aversion to Islam as she knew it? With so many seemingly insurmountable obstacles, so many outside influences, and a complete lack of control over our own social and political experiences, in a society that expected me to be anything but what I was . . . Well, it astounds me still.

BUT THAT DAY, OVER A BOWL OF FRUIT, I SAW TEARS WELL UP IN HER eyes. She admitted she had no advice to offer, because she felt that she had failed as a mother.

"If I could do anything differently, I wouldn't have come to America," she replied. "When I had my first kid, I wanted to go back to Egypt and raise him there." I heard the pain in her voice. She continued, unraveling as though she had been keeping this in her entire life, waiting for someone to ask her this very question. "I didn't listen to my heart. I thought we could teach you to love Allah. To fear Allah. To understand that this life is temporary—a test before the next life. But look at you all. You care so much about your jobs, your *stuff,* I don't ever see you pray without someone telling you to. I failed."

Before I could process what she was saying or begin to console her, she abruptly stood up. "Eat, habibi. I'll bring you more fruits," she said before stepping away.

IT HAS TAKEN ME A LONG TIME TO UNDERSTAND WHY SHE FELT SHE'D failed us. I thought of my siblings and myself as successes, college graduates, high achievers, Muslims (admittedly, to varying degrees of religiosity). When I considered the migration story of my mama and baba—what they left behind and what they gained—"failure" struck me as an unduly harsh appraisal.

Until I began to see it myself. I'm a baba now, and my whole world has changed. That I don't feel all that different from Mama about wanting to preserve their cultural and religious connections terrifies me. At every major milestone, from my first job to my wedding, I expected some kind of revelation that would push me to be the kind of man I needed to be to meet those new challenges. When I became a baba, I expected to receive the tools I would need to parent Muslim children. But how could I raise kids if I still felt like a kid myself? The thought that I won't ever become that kind of religious person, and that my kids may not know Islam and Egyptian culture well enough to pass it on to their kids, makes me worry that I've failed even before I've begun.

And I do doubt I'll become a model Muslim Egyptian American man, at least not the kind of parent into whom I would suddenly snap after the birth of my first child. Is it possible to raise kids who feel secure and confident in their ability in an increasingly confusing and isolating time for Muslim Americans? And, if so, can I learn?

THAT NIGHT, AS I CRADLED NOON IN MY ARMS, GIVING MIRA A BREAK before her shift, I reflected on the challenges my parents faced and how different ours were now. Though my mama believes she failed to protect us from losing our cultural and religious identity, and my baba can't look past the fact that I struggle to pray five times a day, they have my love for all the sacrifices they've made and the patience they continue to show.

"You're going to Islamic school," I whispered to Noon.

I laid her on her back in the bassinet next to her mama. In a soft voice, I whispered a du'a in English. It was unfamiliar—every du'a I'd memorized as a child was in Arabic—but speaking in my native language felt intimate, like speaking directly to Allah.

Praying for guidance felt uncharacteristic for me. I'd always been the type to wrestle with problems until I found a way through on my own. But after talking with Mama, something finally clicked. Raising kids with a connection to Islam wasn't something I could entirely control or plan for—it was rooted in something deeper than logic, something I didn't fully understand. I couldn't predict who my kids would become or who I would grow into as a parent.

For the first time, I made a genuine appeal to God—not out of reflex, reciting words I had memorized as a child, but with intention. I wasn't asking for a miracle. Instead, I wanted to define my hopes for my children and make a quiet pact with a greater power. As I watched my baby sleep peacefully in her cradle, I closed my eyes and allowed myself to surrender to my uncertainty. In that moment, I felt like I finally understood what it meant to be a Muslim parent.

I asked God to help make my kids patient so they could strive to be better without punishing themselves for any missteps, as I had punished myself. And I asked Allah to give them the strength to forgive their parents for wanting more from them, as I had learned to. Both Noon and Musa were too young to hold grudges or to see Mira and me as anything but the center of their world, and so I also asked Allah to let me savor these fleeting moments.

I knew there would come a time when Noon and Musa would question why they're different from the non-Muslim or non-Arab kids their age. I told God I'd do my best to prepare them, but to also prepare myself as they experience the cycles of losing, finding, and perhaps losing themselves again. Above all else, I prayed they would never give up seeking answers—in Islam or otherwise.

I also prayed they'd come to understand what I've learned: show love, get love. The love and grace we offer—to ourselves and to others, even in moments of fear or hostility—have a way of coming back to us, opening doors to meaning, connection, and faith.

Finally, I asked Allah to help my kids see being Muslim American as I have come to understand it: as a path of perpetual seeking. Belonging to a community might give the illusion that truth is clear-cut, and I prayed they would embrace their human flaws and the paradoxes of life, inviting faith to take root rather than becoming frustrated with themselves for having doubts at all.

As I finished my du'a, I leaned down, kissing Noon gently on her forehead, and closed my conversation with Allah, whispering, "Ameen."

Chapter 15

Show Love, Get Love

TWO KIDS IN EIGHTEEN MONTHS HAD HIT US LIKE A TSUNAMI. WE'D settled into a divide-and-conquer strategy, finding an odd comfort in our divided tasks—a fragile cease-fire in the battle against exhaustion.

Seven months in, Noon's crib remained empty in Musa's room, still awaiting the day when she could sleep without night feedings. One morning, Mira emerged from the bedroom, serene in her soft white robe, with Noon cocooned in a cream-colored blanket. They both looked rested.

"She did it again!" Mira proclaimed proudly.

"That's three nights in a row, right? Is it time?" I asked cautiously, pushing another spoonful of tepid eggs toward Musa, trying to offload the breakfast he hadn't eaten as his lunch.

"We'll see tonight," Mira replied cheerfully.

THAT NIGHT, WE PUT NOON DOWN ON HER OWN FOR THE FIRST TIME. Mira shut the door gently, not wanting to disturb her as she slept in the office where I'd been camping out since her birth. With Musa asleep in his own room and Noon now settled in the office, Mira and I slipped back into our bedroom and declared victory.

"Do you hear that?" I teased.

"Hear what?" Mira replied.

"Exactly," I said.

But we were wrong to take that peace for granted.

————

Baba seated at the table, arms crossed,
giving a side-eye to the camera, 1980s.

ON AN OTHERWISE UNEVENTFUL OCTOBER WEEKEND MORNING, MUSA was focused on his budding masterpiece—a twelve-piece puzzle of an orange dump truck. I glanced away to check the news on my phone, only to be interrupted by Musa's frustrated shriek. Noon's chubby fingers were inching toward the puzzle, and he wasn't having it. I promised myself that one day they would entertain each other; for now, though, we had to make a constant effort to keep the peace.

Mira emerged from the bedroom earlier than usual, poured herself a cup of coffee, and added the rest of the pot to her cereal for an extra kick. With her up, I was finally free of my morning duty, corralling the kids in their room.

As Mira settled in, I pulled out my phone again—only to see something shocking on Instagram. Men stood atop an Israeli tank, pumping their fists in defiant victory. "The prisoners have escaped," the caption read, referring to Gaza. It was a stark departure from the usual images of Gaza—mothers in headscarves and gaunt men enduring a barrage of Israeli missiles razing their cities.

I continued to scroll in disbelief, seeing Palestinians bulldozing through Israel's fortified border fence, breaking free from the very barrier that had been deadly to approach during the Great March of Return. The face of Rouzan al-Najjar—a young volunteer medic shot and killed by Israeli snipers—was still fresh on my mind. Watching the wall of their prison topple was heart-wrenching.

"Mira, look at this," I said, turning my phone toward her. Each image felt more surreal than the last. Neither of us could comprehend the sight of the improvised flying vehicles or Palestinian incursions into Israeli military outposts. Mira joined me on the couch, holding Noon. With each passing minute, the extent of the havoc on the kibbutzim bordering Gaza became painfully clear.

"Have you seen the clip of the girl in the bloodied pants?" Mira asked softly. I nodded. "What the fuck," she muttered. As I scrolled for updates, a video blared from my phone—a woman's anguished scream as she was abducted on a motorcycle. The sound caught

Musa's attention, and I quickly switched to my photo app, letting him browse old videos of himself to shield him from the horror.

IN THE DAYS THAT FOLLOWED, ISRAEL LAUNCHED ANOTHER BOMBING campaign, and the media constructed a familiar narrative in real time. American journalists abandoned neutrality, throwing around words like "barbaric" and "evil," branding Palestinians as fanatics driven by hate, without regard for the generations-long militarized occupation they exist under.

I knew what was coming, as did any Arab. The pattern was all too familiar. Thousands of defenseless civilians would be horrifically slaughtered by one of the world's most advanced militaries, and their deaths minimized as nameless collateral damage using the grotesque trope of "human shields." Grieving their loss would be misconstrued as tacit support for violence.

I SCROLLED MY PHONE INCESSANTLY, UNABLE TO SLEEP. NIGHT AFTER night for months, I saw images of babies torn to bits, parents who looked like me wailing over the unrecognizable remains of their infants. The feed was endless.

To reach the news from Gaza, I had to scroll past memes and viral dance clips. Life was carrying on as a massacre unfolded. I wondered if my grief was personal, if I cared only because I was Arab. But no—the world had lost its mind.

ONE VIDEO STAYED WITH ME: A FATHER IN THE RUBBLE OF THE JABA-lia refugee camp, frantically digging through debris with his bare hands, searching for his three daughters. Covered in dust, with tears cutting through the dirt on his face, he looked to the sky and thanked God amid his devastation—"Alhamdulilhah." How could he show gratitude in such a state of ruin, I wondered. It sparked a confusion in me, like a heartbreaking testament to all the ways I fall short in both faith and fatherhood. In another video, three young brothers wailed for their father after learning that the grocery store he had entered had been flattened by Israeli airstrikes. Their cries of "Baba" echoed painfully inside me.

President Biden embraced Israel's prime minster, Netanyahu, and cast doubt on Palestinian death tolls, saying he had "no confidence in the number that the Palestinians are using." Hearing that made me sick.

Like Palestinians in Gaza, anti-war protesters were cast as violent extremists, which led to arrests, deportations, and job loss. The message was clear: empathy for Palestinians was criminal.

I felt powerless as an Arab American. Somehow, despite fear of becoming a target simply for empathizing with Palestinians, I managed to write. I interviewed a prominent Jewish critic of Israel, and a Palestinian political leader with Israeli citizenship, and penned an op-ed about American tolerance for the dehumanization of Palestinians.

UNEXPECTEDLY, MY EDITOR, JEFF, CALLED ME IN FOR A ZOOM MEETing. "Are you okay?" he asked gently. I hesitated, uncertain if empathizing with Arab suffering would be misinterpreted as a loss of objectivity.

"I feel really good, actually," I said, keeping my guard up.

Jeff nodded. "I think you've been doing good work, but maybe you should refocus a bit," he suggested.

"Refocus to what?" I replied, defensive.

"I think you should lean into your strengths more."

"I am playing to my strengths," I cautiously countered. "I'm conducting interviews in Arabic so they're more candid. Who else at *Slate* can do that?" The notion of shifting focus just as the conflict was intensifying felt repugnant to me. If I wasn't speaking directly to Palestinians, then who would?

Jeff's feedback was hard to digest, but I reminded myself he was the person I trusted most at *Slate*. He'd been my editor since I joined seven years earlier, backing me through some of my toughest stories. That included my 2021 report titled "I Did Have Some Trouble Reporting the Truth," which delved into the persistent doubts and skewed editing journalists faced when covering Palestine and Israel, often under the guise of an overinflated and elusive concept of impartiality. When he suggested that I wasn't physically there, and that I could only do so much from a distance, I knew he was being genuine.

He paused before suggesting, "What about that story in Chicago? The six-year-old who was killed?"

I remembered it well: a Palestinian American boy stabbed to death by a man he called "Grandpa." It felt personal, relevant. "What if you went to Chicago and investigated that?" he proposed.

"I'd love to do that," I replied, already thinking about how I'd bring this up with Mira. Leaving her alone with our two toddlers wasn't something I took lightly.

THAT NIGHT, AS I LAY IN BED WAITING FOR MIRA, SHE RECOUNTED A conversation she'd had with her best friend, Mais. Though they first met in Saudi Arabia during high school and now lived half a world apart, they'd never been closer.

"How's she doing?" I asked.

"She's overwhelmed. She told me the world thinks Palestinian blood is cheap, but it's not. That Israel's been trying to erase her people, but they'll never succeed."

Hearing those words made my heart ache. Mira's eyes drifted, her thoughts somewhere far away.

She explained Mais's perspective: her determination to raise her son, Malik, to identify with and uphold Palestinian tradition. "Mais said that, as a Palestinian mother, raising her kids is like throwing a stone heavier than any tank against the Israeli military machine. It's up to us to teach kids their language, their history, their culture."

Hearing her words brought me back to my parents and their fierce determination to raise us as Muslims in America. Their insistence on teaching us our faith, history, and traditions suddenly felt less like overbearing rules and more like an act of survival. It wasn't just about religion—it was about protecting a part of us they feared might slip away, pushing back against a world eager to erase us.

Mira's voice carried admiration as she switched to Arabic to repeat Mais's words verbatim: "Amana 'ala ra'abtik"—a duty on your neck.

I nodded. "She's right." I reached out to hold Mira, feeling the weight of the moment. "What do you think about me going to Chicago? To write about the Palestinian boy who was killed?"

Mira didn't hesitate. "Take as much time as you need."

"It'd be for four days," I warned. "Maybe more than one trip."

"Don't worry about us," she said.

WITHIN A WEEK, I FOUND MYSELF SITTING ACROSS FROM ODAI Al-Fayoume, the father of six-year-old Wadee, in Bridgeview, Illinois. I struggled to keep my emotions in check. I hadn't anticipated meeting him directly; I'd only planned on speaking with members of the local Palestinian community.

Before heading over, I stopped at a sweets shop. Even in journalist mode, I couldn't ignore basic Arab hospitality.

Odai greeted me with exhausted olive-green eyes. He showed me photos of his son, including one of him in a sparkling blue birthday hat just days before the attack.

"He loved to pray," Odai said in Arabic, showing me a photo of a little Wadee kneeling on an adult-sized prayer rug that showed just how small he was. His son reminded me of Musa, who also liked to imitate us when we prayed. They shared similar features, too. They might have even passed for siblings.

Odai recounted the horrific story of how he had learned of his son's death—over the phone. The man who killed Wadee had been their neighbor, someone who greeted them with "Assalamualaykum," a blessing of peace. Odai couldn't fathom how this same man could have stabbed his son twenty-six times. The police said his motive was shockingly simple: he wanted to kill Palestinians.

I hadn't prepared any questions. Instead, I sat quietly and listened to Odai speaking for over two hours, sharing memories of his life in Jordan, his move to America, and his dream of having a son he'd name Wadee. "It is killing me, knowing that my dream has come to an end," he said.

I left with tears in my eyes, struck by the way he described his only solace—that his son had died a martyr, destined for heaven. I was in awe of how his commitment to faith played such a pivotal role in what would be the darkest moment of any parent's life. I wondered if I could hold on to my faith in the face of such loss. The thought of anything happening to Musa or Noon rattled me.

Later, I received a message from the family's lawyer, letting me know that Wadee's mother, Hanan Shaheen, was also willing to meet. She hadn't done any interviews since the attack, in which she, too, was stabbed multiple times. She greeted me warmly, bandages and cuts still visible on her face and neck. Over tea and sweets, we found comfort in conversation, mostly laughing together over her memories of Wadee. She called him "a bird in heaven."

I had come to Illinois unsure if I'd find anything and left with more than any other journalist had gathered. Writing the article was difficult but meaningful; it gave me a sense of purpose amid the unrelenting brutality being livestreamed from the ongoing war. I'd never seen so many dead children, or babies with their bodies torn apart. The guilt I felt as a tax-paying American grew heavier by the day.

I also felt more conviction as a parent, and privileged for having a safe environment I could offer my own children. Arab babies felt more precious than ever, like fragile symbols of resilience and peaceful resistance—a living testament to a heritage that others were actively erasing.

AS LATE SUMMER SET IN AND NOON GREW OLDER, I BECAME CAPTIvated by how she and Musa played together.

At the park, surrounded by older Newark kids, their differences became especially entertaining. Noon, her wild curls bouncing as she darted across the grass, was a bundle of contagious energy. She had Mira's spark, doing everything her own way. Opening your arms for her to run in your direction was a surefire invitation for her to sprint the other way. Her determination was evident, especially when she learned she could swipe Musa's toys to get him to chase her around the house. She was always on the move, just like me. I saw myself in her every time she squeezed out of the stroller, her face lighting up with triumph.

Meanwhile, Musa found comfort in order, spending hours lining up all his dinosaurs and trucks meticulously in color-coordinated rows whose arrangement only he seemed to understand. He had Mira's love of stillness, and would often sit quietly in the swing, watching other kids play, his little legs swaying in the breeze. His eyes narrowed in concentration as he turned the pages of his favorite book, absorbed in worlds far away. His methodical nature reminded me of my own need for structure, the part of me that found calm in spreadsheets in a chaotic world.

I had expected things to get more challenging as the kids entered their toddler years, but I found myself having more fun than ever. The so-called terrible twos felt like a myth. With Musa beginning to speak and Noon figuring out her own way of communicating, they were an absolute joy to be around. Sure, they could be defiant and bursting with energy, but their creativity and excitement were infectious. Hearing Musa say "Come play with me," or Noon tugging at my hand to go to the park, brought me a sense of euphoria I hadn't anticipated.

I knew the day would come when they'd grow older and want less to do with me, so I resolved to cherish these fleeting moments. I started shutting my laptop, leaving my phone in another room, and postponing chores to be fully present with them. I wanted to make sure that when I eventually mourn their outgrowing of their toddler years, I could do so knowing I had embraced every moment to the fullest.

It was during these moments with the kids that I felt the pull to invest more time in the local Muslim community. I enjoyed feeling like their sole source of fun, but I wanted them to feel part of something bigger—a network of trusted adults with kids their age, like I had growing up. Deciding to attend Friday prayer was easy; deciding whether to take it further was not. Baba had never missed a Friday prayer.

ONE THURSDAY AFTERNOON, I CALLED HIM. JUST WHEN I THOUGHT it would go to voicemail, he picked up, catching me off guard.

"Assalamualaykum, Baba," I greeted him formally.

"Wa 'Alaykum Assalam," he replied. He sounded distracted. "Do you need something?"

"Where do you usually pray on Friday?"

"Anywhere," he answered vaguely.

After a pause, I suggested we try praying together in Newark. "Like we used to," I said.

His response was swift—"Good idea!"—delivered with more enthusiasm than I'd witnessed from him in ages. "I don't know where I will be, but if I'm close by, I will call you."

"Works for me." As I was about to end the call, Baba asked if I would bring Musa.

"Isn't he too young? He's not even three," I said.

Baba scoffed at my concerns. "This is the age you get him used to it. Do not be lazy with religion, or else your son will be lazy with it, too," he warned.

I'd hoped to avoid a lecture over the phone, but this time I sensed he was right. If I wanted to nurture in Musa a comfort with going to the mosque, I needed to start now.

"I'll bring him. See you tomorrow!" I said.

"Inshallah," Baba replied, and we hung up. I checked to see how long we had spoken: not even a minute.

WITH MAMA, MY RELATIONSHIP HAD STARTED TO FEEL MORE OPEN, like we'd become friends, participating in thoughtful conversations. But with Baba, it was different. He still seemed to see me as an unsolvable puzzle, never quite hearing what I had to say.

I was also beginning to worry about the influences around Musa and Noon. Both were now enrolled in a daycare in the next town over, where the staff spoke Spanish, only a little English. Mira and I had no real idea what was happening inside: our questions were often met with shrugs and apologies for the language barrier.

It did expose them to different languages—Spanish at school, Arabic with their mama and grandparents, and English with everyone else. But when Musa and Noon seemed to get more excited about Christmas and Halloween than anything else, I worried I wasn't doing enough to preserve their connection to their Arab roots.

So, when Baba called me early the next day, to ask if I could pick him up on the way to the mosque, I took it as a sign.

By the time I changed Musa's diaper and packed his bag with spare clothes, diapers, wipes, and snacks, an hour had passed. Baba climbed into the car with a look of disapproval.

"The sermon is part of the prayer. You need to show up on time," he stressed.

"Of course," I muttered, holding back frustration as I reversed out of the parking lot. As I drove, I pointed to my outfit: the galabiya I'd bought in Egypt.

"We're in America. You should dress normally," he scoffed.

"You used to wear galabiyas all the time!" I protested.

"At home," he countered. "Look outside. Do you see anyone wearing a galabiya?"

I remembered plenty of times when he'd worn a galabiya to the mosque. But, for the sake of surviving the rest of the drive in peace, I let it go and continued to the nearest mosque in downtown Newark, which was now relocated in the bottom floor of a charter school. The space, once a basketball court, was far less impressive than the original mosque, which had been sold during the COVID pandemic. Outside, a row of e-bikes lined the curb as Uber Eats delivery drivers slipped inside for prayer between orders. We left behind whatever made us different to stand shoulder to shoulder, equal before God. That was always my favorite part of walking into the mosque. But even though Newark was changing, following Baba inside and watching him withdraw a Quran to read as we waited for prayer felt comfortingly familiar.

About twenty men were seated in the front of the room, and four women in the back—a small congregation compared with the bustling Friday prayers of the old mosque. This community seemed in its infancy, which added to its draw for someone like me, hoping to integrate his family more into our faith.

I'd brought toys for Musa to keep him occupied: six magnet tiles so he could practice making a cube, and a small cat toy to fit inside it. Baba sat a few feet away, his expression unreadable as he bowed his head in quiet reflection. A few minutes later, the call to prayer echoed through the hall. Musa listened, taking in the unadorned space with curiosity.

The imam, dressed in long white robes and a tarboosh, began his sermon on the importance of family, recounting stories of how the Prophet Muhammad encouraged love and gratitude within families. I glanced at Baba, who sat with his head bowed, his expression unchanged, while Musa continued to absorb the atmosphere around him.

When it was time to pray, we stood shoulder to shoulder, toe to toe. But as soon as I lowered my forehead to the carpet, Musa seized the chance to jump onto my back, shouting, "Baba! Horsey!" I continued the prayer, focused on my composure, as Musa wrapped his arms around my neck and dangled like a monkey. His laughter filled the room, bringing smiles to the other worshippers and reminding me of the way I used to play with Baba during his prayers.

After the prayer ended, I lifted Musa from my back and held him close. "I'm so proud of you, habibi," I told him as he hugged me tightly. I glanced at Baba, who surprised me with a rare approving nod.

As the mosque emptied, Baba remained seated, contemplative. He struggled slightly to get up, his age more apparent than ever. The imam, recognizing Baba, approached with a warm smile.

"Assalamualaykum, Mohamed. It's been many years," he said.

He seemed vaguely familiar, though I couldn't quite place him. The imam's eyes then fell on me in disbelief. "This is Aymann? You're kidding!" he said to Baba, unable to believe I was now a baba myself.

"Mashallah," the imam said warmly. "I remember when you were just a baby, coming to the mosque with your father. And now, to see you here with your own son . . . it brings me great joy," he remarked in Arabic. "May Allah preserve them for each other. Three generations of men, Mashallah. It's beautiful to see you pray together." He placed his hand on Musa's head. "May Allah bless your family and keep you strong in your faith," he added.

Baba gave a small nod. "May Allah bless the families of *all* believers," he replied, his voice softer than usual, though he couldn't resist the urge to correct someone, even if it was an imam.

WHEN WE WERE LEAVING THE MOSQUE, BABA LOOKED MORE CONTENT than I'd seen him in years. The imam's words had set my heart ablaze. "This was great, wasn't it, Baba?" I said.

He gave me a faint smile, his eyes softening as he looked at me. "Thank you for inviting me."

"Musa did really, really well," I added. "Should we do this again next week?"

To my delight, Baba nodded. "Great idea."

Baba reached for Musa's hand, and together they began to jog down the street. I trailed behind, quickly pulling out my phone to capture the sight unfolding in front of me. Baba was laughing, his usual reserved demeanor melting away as he matched Musa's energy. My heart was full.

With a broad smile, Baba watched as Musa's little legs struggled to keep up with his. The two of them, hand in hand, their laughter mingling with the city sounds—it was more than I could have hoped for.

ON THE DRIVE BACK, MUSA SAT QUIETLY, AS IF SHARING THE SAME peace that had settled over me. I dropped Baba at his tow truck, and, before parting, we promised to make this a weekly tradition.

As Musa and I made our way home, the events of the day replayed in my mind. It felt like I had managed something new: using religion to bring Baba and me together rather than allowing the subtle differences in our practice to tear us apart. The image of Baba and Musa running hand in hand repeated in my mind. I couldn't wait to show the video to Musa when he was older.

Afterward, Baba seemed to soften as our relationship evolved. He'd sometimes call to check in on his grandchildren, and we were finally having conversations that weren't built entirely on quiet gestures and Islamic expressions of respect. One morning, he even came over for breakfast. I served him eggs with bastarma and fuul—Egyptian-style. He told me he only stayed to make sure I ate, too. I smiled, not buying his excuse. He didn't need to say more. His presence said everything.

It wasn't everything I'd imagined, but it was enough.

Although I was working to deepen my connection with Baba, this didn't overshadow my commitment to build a stronger relationship with Mama. I told her how much I appreciated her for giving herself entirely to our family, instilling Islamic values in us, whether we welcomed them or not. She told me she was proud of my commitment to raising Musa and Noon with Islam in their lives—even if the role I played didn't perfectly mirror her ideals of Muslim men. We'd made strides in communicating openly and honestly, and now we talk almost every day.

But the most meaningful shift was the way she came to genuinely appreciate Mira, finally seeing not only what a devoted mama she was, but how she had been pivotal in reconnecting me with Islam. Mama was beginning to trust the family Mira and I were building together. For the first time, I felt we understood that, despite our differences, we were all walking the same path.

I WONDERED IF MUSA AND NOON WOULD FACE A CRISIS OF FAITH LIKE I had. But I knew I'd approach it differently from my parents. I didn't want to overexplain God to my children. I wanted them to know Islam the way they would come to know the warmth of the sun—constant, unspoken, simply understood. More than doctrine, I wanted them to experience faith through rhythm and habit, through the quiet consistency of gratitude, the instinct to say Alhamdulillah without thinking. I hoped that, in time, they would understand that faith cannot exist without faithfulness, that God would live in their bones—something they could return to not out of obligation, but because it was a part of them, as natural as breathing.

I was certain of the baba I wanted to be. Given the privilege of understanding the culture in which I was raising my children, I knew I could be close to them, deeply connected, without losing any sense of myself.

As I started attending congregational prayers more regularly, I found myself lingering afterward, chatting with other parents as our kids raced across the mosque carpet. What began as polite small talk soon turned into exchanges of parenting tips, shared laughter over toddler antics, and plans for playdates. At the same time, I made friends with parents from the schools my kids attended, slowly building a sense of community that spanned all backgrounds. We talked about everything from bedtime routines to navigating the school system, and I realized how much I had been craving these kinds of connections. For the first time, I felt truly anchored, surrounded by role models and friends who could help me and my children navigate the beauty of parenthood together.

For a moment, I considered calling Baba to thank him for sharing those laughs with Musa that day, for giving me something I had longed for my entire life. But instead, I simply smiled.

"Alhamdulillah," I murmured.

Noon and Musa at the Pyramids, creating
family memories, 2023.

Acknowledgments

This book exists because of all the people in my life who challenged me. *Becoming Baba* started as a messy, tangled attempt to understand my father, my own journey into fatherhood, and the weight of carrying two identities at once. It was written in fits and starts—between work deadlines, bottle feedings, diaper changes, and eventually school drop-offs, and stolen moments of clarity. And at every stage, there were people who pushed me to keep going.

First and foremost, I owe endless gratitude to my wife, Mira. Ya hayati. Without you, so much of this book would've stayed in my head, a scattered mess of ideas I talked about but never sat down to really understand. You took on more than your share so I could write, encouraging me even when I didn't know what I was trying to say. Your patience, your wisdom, your partnership, they're in every page. I owe you more than I can put into words. But I know you prefer the simple kind. Shukran!

To my kids, Musa and Noon. You were always in the back of my mind—or more accurately, in my ear—as I wrote. I didn't start this book until just after you were born. So imagine it: you're both tiny, brand-new to the world, and I'm somewhere in the house with headphones on, trying to focus through your screaming. I cradled you with one arm and typed with the other. I rocked you to sleep, whispering *shhh-shhh-shhh,* and the second your eyes closed, I rushed back to the keyboard, holding on to some fleeting memory that had just bloomed in my head.

The entirety of this book was written while you were babies, and I'm so glad it happened that way. Everything written after your birth is practically time-stamped in our life. This book will forever remind me of who you were back then. Tiny little nuggets with legs, demanding cereal and strawberries. Musa, you used to call them "fuddies"! Noon, you pronounced "snack" like "mat"! And as you learned to walk, talk, and drive me crazy, you taught me to be a baba who can multitask.

Even though you're too young to read this now, as I wrote I imagined you one day picking up this book and searching for yourselves in its pages. I fantasized about someone saying, "Did you know your baba wrote a book?" and you going, "What?" And I'd say, "Check this out," blow the dust off an old copy, and hand it over like some long-lost family heirloom. If you do ever read it, my only real hope is that you don't think it sucks. But if you find something useful—an answer, a connection, or even just the comfort of knowing that the questions you're asking about identity and belonging have been asked before—that would mean everything.

To my parents, Mama and Baba, writing this book made me see you more clearly, or in some ways, for the first time. Baba, so much of this book was written to understand you. I never doubted that you loved me, but it's obvious that I was being raised in a different world than the one you grew up in. It took me writing this entire book to decode the quiet ways you showed love, to make sense of the things you didn't say. I love you, too. Mama, your warmth and strength held everything together, even (or perhaps especially) when I made it difficult. I know I didn't always appreciate the effort you both put into preserving our heritage in us, but I do now. You were right to say, "You'll understand when you're older." *Becoming Baba* is, in many ways, a thank-you for that.

And to the parents who face impossible struggles, especially Palestinian parents. Too often, your struggles are unseen and dismissed. But your strength, your unyielding faith, and your determination to raise children with dignity—even in impossible circumstances—are woven into every word of this book. And still, that will never come close to capturing the depth of what I've learned about life from getting to know you. The world may be against you. But the people are with you.

To my siblings, Mohamed, Ahmad, and Hebah. Consider this book the full history we share—the small moments that shaped our family, and the stories that belong to all of us. Hebah, I would've gotten so much wrong without you. Thank you for spending hours fact-checking my memories, helping me separate rumor from truth, and reminding me of the things I'd forgotten.

I know not everyone will agree on the details—whether something happened the way I said it did, or whether I cried a lot . . . or way too much. Our family is notorious for being on separate pages, sometimes in entirely different books. But now I can say, with full confidence: if you feel so strongly that you remember it better, go write your own book! (ˆ‿ˆ)

I am deeply grateful to my editor, Thomas Gebremedhin, who made this entire process fun from the start. You saw the potential in this book even when it was still a sprawling 350,000-word mess. You generously lent your sharp eye to read all of it, and helped shape it into the book I'm now so proud of. You pushed me to be more honest, to go deeper, to tell the story like it actually mattered. This book is stronger—so much stronger—because of your guidance. I'm grateful for every hard conversation, every tough note, and every moment you reminded me that this story could find its readers.

This book is also for my dear friends at *Slate,* the most talented storytellers in the game. For Julia Turner, who took a chance and hired the kid with the skateboard, for John Swansburg, who encouraged me to tell stories that mattered to me, for Lowen Liu, who gave me the space to take chances, for Hillary Frey, who encourages me endlessly, and for Jeffrey Bloomer, who has championed my voice from the beginning, and continues to be one of my most trusted friends. You all gave me the courage to take on the challenge of writing this book.

To my friends at *ANIMAL New York.* For Bucky Turco, Marina Galperina, and Tom Webster, who first taught me to be critical, even of the things I loved. That instinct—to question everything—shaped much more than just the way I approached this book. It shaped how I see the world, how I write, and how I navigate the blurry line between love and criticism, especially when it comes to the things that made me.

To Andrew Teheran, who saw his high school students as collaborators rather than obstacles for getting through the day. You triggered a cascade of creativity that led to every passion in my life.

To my friends, both old and new, who listened to early drafts, provided feedback, or simply checked in on me during this process—thank you for being my sounding board and for reliably coming out to shout *YERRRR!*

To my best friend, Mike Molina. Your friendship shaped me into someone more deliberate and reflective, helping me to better align my actions with my values. You also taught me to survive in Newark, a place that could have consumed us both. For some reason, God chose for us to outlive so many of our friends. I'm grateful for each time you've encouraged me to be brave.

To the Muslim community worldwide—especially those of us raising kids right now. I know parts of this book might feel daunting. *Sinning? Astaghfirullah!* I get it. I'm pretty sure the only reason my mama hasn't lit up the family WhatsApp about it is because I'm her favorite. (And yes, I have it on good authority.)

Of all readers, this may be the hardest for you. We're carrying the weight of the world's suspicion while trying to carve out identities that feel honest, strong, and enduring. I want that too for myself and for my kids. That's why I chose to write openly about the parts of myself that feel vulnerable as a Muslim. And yeah, that might make you feel vulnerable too.

But I've learned there's no such thing as staying pure or untouched by doubt. And I've experienced how shame can lead people away. This book, if anything, is meant to be a kind of road map—not just for Muslims, but for anyone trying to return to something they once wrote off.

Writing this book, and becoming a baba, taught me that faith doesn't have to be loud or perfect. Sometimes it's just showing up—at the masjid, in the world, or in your kid's room at bedtime. That alone can be a kind of worship. So many of the tensions in this book became clearer because of you. And so did the joy.

To the many mentors, colleagues, and collaborators who have influenced my work over the years, especially during the often chaotic process of time writing this book and beyond. You've all left your fingerprints on these pages. I owe you.

And to you, the reader—thank you for picking up this book with the angry-looking kid on the cover. Thank you for sticking with me through the mess and the meaning. I hope this story sparks something in you. Maybe reflection, maybe connection, maybe just a reminder that all of us are stumbling our way through it, trying to do right by the people we love. We're all works in progress. This is mine.

With gratitude,
Aymann Ismail

Aymann Ismail is a staff writer at *Slate* known for his multimedia journalism exploring identity, religion, and the human stories behind national headlines. His work often blends photography, audio, and video to create intimate, deeply reported pieces. He is the creator of *Who's Afraid of Aymann Ismail?*, a *Slate* video series that confronts stereotypes and offers nuanced portraits of American Muslims and their perceived adversaries. Ismail also hosted the podcast *Man Up*, which examined modern masculinity through conversations about family, relationships, race, and vulnerability. His work has been featured by *The New York Times*, CNN, NPR, *GQ*, *Fox News*, *The New York Post*, *Adweek*, *The Atlantic*, *Columbia Journalism Review*, *Gawker*, and *The Guardian*. His essay "The Store That Called the Cops on George Floyd" was nominated for a National Magazine Award for Reporting and won a Writers Guild Award. He lives in Newark, New Jersey, with his family.